Satan Exposed

Satan Exposed

A Biblical Theology of Spiritual Warfare

WILLIAM P. PAYNE

WIPF & STOCK · Eugene, Oregon

SATAN EXPOSED
A Biblical Theology of Spiritual Warfare

Copyright © 2019 William P. Payne. All rights reserved. Except for brief quotations in critical publications or reviews, no part of this book may be reproduced in any manner without prior written permission from the publisher. Write: Permissions, Wipf and Stock Publishers, 199 W. 8th Ave., Suite 3, Eugene, OR 97401.

Wipf and Stock
An Imprint of Wipf and Stock Publishers
199 W. 8th Ave., Suite 3
Eugene, OR 97401

www.wipfandstock.com

PAPERBACK ISBN: 978-1-5326-5605-7
HARDCOVER ISBN: 978-1-5326-5606-4
EBOOK ISBN: 978-1-5326-5607-1

Manufactured in the U.S.A.   JULY 15, 2019

Unless otherwise stated, Scripture quotations are taken from the Holy Bible, New International Version®, NIV®. Copyright © 1973, 1978, 1984, 2011 by Biblica, Inc.™ Used by permission of Zondervan. All rights reserved worldwide. www.zondervan.com The "NIV" and "New International Version" are trademarks registered in the United States Patent and Trademark Office by Biblica, Inc.™

Scripture quotations from the New Revised Standard Version Bible, copyright © 1989 National Council of the Churches of Christ in the United States of America. Used by permission. All rights reserved worldwide.

Scripture quotations taken from the New American Standard Bible® (NASB), Copyright © 1960, 1962, 1963, 1968, 1971, 1972, 1973, 1975, 1977, 1995 by The Lockman Foundation. Used by permission. www.Lockman.org

For my children, William, Elizabeth, and Mary. They have witnessed the spiritual warfare that surrounds my life. A special thanks to my teaching assistant, William Applebee. He has labored to edit my manuscripts and to give me invaluable feedback.

Contents

Introduction | ix

1. A Biblical Orientation to Spiritual Warfare | 1
2. What about Ghosts and Spirits? | 8
3. Ghost Stories | 14
4. The Disciples Believed in Ghosts | 19
5. Who Believes in the Devil? | 24
6. Gehenna in the New Testament | 33
7. The Gates of Hades Will Not Prevail | 41
8. Hades in Paul's Letters and the Book of Revelation | 48
9. Satan before His Fall | 55
10. The Heavenly Council and the Nation Gods | 63
11. High Gods and Territorial Spirits | 71
12. Introducing Demons | 87
13. The Fall | 107
14. The Serpent in the Garden | 118
15. The Temptation of God | 134
16. Spiritual Warfare in the New Testament | 151
17. Spiritual Warfare Versus Social Justice: Discerning a Kingdom Approach | 166

Bibliography | 177
Subject Index | 185
Scripture Index | 193

Introduction

WHEN Martin Luther challenged the error of the prevailing church by appealing to the authority of Scripture and the example of the New Testament Church, the institutional church and its aligned powers launched a vicious attack against him. During the dark years when he remained sequestered at Wartburg Castle in Saxony, Luther came to realize that the spiritual powers of wickedness were working through the human powers that opposed the reformation he advocated. In his mind, he wasn't fighting against flesh and blood, but against an entrenched spiritual evil that had attached itself to the institutional church.

Since he lacked political power or ecclesiastical standing, Luther avoided a direct counterattack. Instead, he assaulted the spiritual evil in high places (Eph 6:12) by translating the Word of God into the common language. When the common people began to read the Bible, God shone light into their darkness (John 1:5; 2 Cor 4:6) and began to free them from their spiritual bondage. In turn, this enabled the reformation that Luther sought.

In addition to printing Bibles, Luther also wrote songs that popularized aspects of his theology. For example, "A Mighty Fortress Is Our God" illustrates his burgeoning understanding of spiritual warfare. Ponder the following stanzas from that hymn. "For still our ancient foe doth seek to work us woe; his craft and power are great, and armed with cruel hate, on earth is not his equal . . . And though this world, with devils filled, should threaten to undo us, we will not fear, for God hath willed his truth to triumph through us. The Prince of Darkness grim, we tremble not for him; his rage we can endure, for lo, his doom is sure; one little word shall fell him."[1]

Luther believed in a powerful Satan who opposed the saints and stymied reformation. He calls him "the Prince of Darkness grim." The Prince

---

1. Luther, "A Mighty Fortress Is Our God," 110.

of Darkness is aided by multitudes of vile demons who work to destroy the saints. Even though Luther's outward situation seemed bleak when he penned the song in 1529, he believed that his followers would triumph over the deep-rooted darkness because they were aligned with God.

Pay close attention to this verse. "Did we in our own strength confide, our striving would be losing; were not the right man on our side, the man of God's own choosing. Dost ask who that may be? Christ Jesus, it is he; Lord Sabaoth, his name, from age to age the same, and he must win the battle."

Lord Sabaoth is a biblical name for God. The Hebrew Scriptures employ it 261 times. *Sabaoth* is rendered as "hosts" or "armies" in English translations. Lord Sabaoth indicates that God is the Lord over the heavenly armies. He's the Lord of Hosts. Yes, God has an army, and the heavenly army has a commander. The book of Joshua portrays him.

> Now when Joshua was near Jericho, he looked up and saw a man standing in front of him with a drawn sword in his hand. Joshua went up to him and asked, "Are you for us or for our enemies?" "Neither," he replied, "but as commander of the army of the Lord I have now come." Then Joshua fell facedown to the ground in reverence, and asked him, "What message does my Lord have for his servant?" The commander of the Lord's army replied, "Take off your sandals, for the place where you are standing is holy." And Joshua did so. (Josh 5:13–15)

Two clues within this theophanic text identify the Commander of Yahweh's armies. First, Joshua fell on his face and reverenced him. Other translations say that Joshua worshipped him. In the Bible, angels do not let people worship them (Rev 19:10; 22:19). Second, the Commander of Yahweh's armies tells Joshua to take off his shoes because the ground on which he is standing is holy ground. Yahweh said the same thing to Moses when he appeared to him in the burning bush (Exod 3:5). In a similar way, when God descended on Mount Sinai in fire and smoke, he told the Hebrew people that they couldn't approach the mountain because God's presence made it holy (Exod 19).

In "A Mighty Fortress," Luther rightly identifies the "Lord Sabaoth" as Jesus Christ.[2] By standing on his name, the saints will defeat (fell) Satan. In a possible reference to his identity as the Lord of Hosts, Jesus reminds his followers that he could call down twelve legions of angels to protect them (Matt 26:53). He is the Commander of the heavenly armies.

---

2. For a helpful explanation of the phrase, see Heiser, *Angels*, 21–23. After reviewing all the descriptions of the Angel of the Lord and the two Yahweh theory, Fred Dickason concludes that the Angel of Lord is Jesus Christ (*Angels*, 78–84).

In 1983, an old Marine Colonel from the Navy War College in Newport, Rhode Island inspected my Navy Officer Basic Class. While we were standing in formation after having endured a grueling seabag (junk on the bunk) inspection, the reviewing officer declared that God was a warrior God. Not only did God have an army, he also had an enemy. Furthermore, he reminded us that Jesus was the Commanding General of God's heavenly forces.

As a highly decorated officer who had led battletested infantrymen through the jungles of Vietnam, the old colonel spoke warriorese fluently. However, since we were a bunch of chaplain recruits who had not been combat-tested, he condescended to us by connecting his remarks to the uniform inspection that we had just completed. He opined, "God's enemy [Satan] caused a large wrinkle in the fabric of his perfect plans when he rebelled against God's rule and led creation into its fallen state. In this age, God is ironing out that wrinkle. Until the wrinkle is eliminated, God's iron will stay hot and his hand will remain firmly pressed against his enemy."

As the colonel waxed eloquent about a warrior God, a villain Satan, a hot iron, and an evil wrinkle, my eyes fixated on the slightly ruffled uniform of the hapless chaplain standing in front of me! His uniforms were always wrinkled. Silently I prayed, "Lord, spare him from the wrath to come!"

The Bible, Luther, and the old Marine all agree that God has an army and an enemy. Still, that doesn't answer a fundamental question. Why does the Almighty God need an army? Wouldn't it be less messy if God snapped his fingers and imposed his righteous will upon Satan, the fallen angels, and all who have sinned? At a more profound level, the question probes theodicy. Why does evil exist? Does it have a purpose or is it the byproduct of free will?

Many who emphasize the sovereignty of God have argued that God has ordained evil in order to accomplish the ultimate good that he desires. This view assumes that everything is running according to a master plan that God designed. If this is true, God is an accomplice to the evil that God hates, and Satan is an unwitting puppet who was predetermined to rebel and become evil. Moreover, if God decrees evil, he becomes morally responsible for the evil he permits. As such, spiritual warfare is an illusion and the biblical narrative that portrays it is a carefully scripted metaphor.[3]

On the other hand, to be made in God's image requires that sapient beings be able to exercise free will. In order to exert free will, said beings must have the ability to rebel against God. Even though God doesn't purpose rebellion or desire it, he allows it. When it happens, the act of rebellion

---

3. Boyd, *God at War*, 44.

is like a pebble thrown into a placid pond. The impact creates ripples that churn the water. Once a ripple has been generated, it doesn't dissipate until its energy has been spent.

In truth, the Bible presents a tension between the absolute sovereignty of an omniscient God and the free will of the sapient beings that he created in his own image. The Bible doesn't fix the tension by going to an extreme. Instead, it tells the story of a warrior God who battles to correct the devastation that fallen angels and sinful people have fomented through their sins. In the unfolding story, the warrior God is a benevolent Creator who sacrifices himself in order to save a humanity that he loves from an evil that he hates. In fact, before the Fall happened, God foresaw it and determined how he would respond to it. The Bible declares that Jesus is the lamb of God who was slain before the foundation of the world (1 Pet 1:19–20).

This view distinguishes between God's design and God's foreknowledge. Additionally, it makes Satan fully responsible for his evil actions. Finally, when properly understood, spiritual warfare is God's response to Satan's rebellion and the means by which he re-establishes his rule over all of creation.

Through a careful reading of scripture, *Satan Exposed* offers a behind the scenes look at Satan and the deep darkness that characterizes his rule. Each chapter deals with a specific aspect of spiritual warfare. The book will challenge old ideas and offer seminal insights.

Since I write as a missiologist, my encounter with the global church has shaped my reading of Scripture and my understanding of spiritual warfare. Because of that, some of this book's content may sound exotic to American readers. I don't apologize for this. Instead, I remind my American readers that the Gospels would also sound exotic to the western church if we had not domesticated them by means of higher criticism and a theology that minimizes evil supernaturalism.

Fortunately, the rapidly growing churches in Africa, southern Asia, and Latin America are articulating a theology of spiritual warfare that more precisely aligns with the biblical emphases, the practices of the New Testament, and their interpretation of everyday reality. The western church needs to encounter this corrective. When the global church's theology of spiritual warfare finally deflates the anti-supernatural orientation of western theology, the western church will be able to reassess the ontology of evil and its need to prioritize the spiritual warfare hermeneutic when reading the Bible and seeking to understand the mission of the church in the world. I have written this book because I want to influence that outcome.

1

A Biblical Orientation to Spiritual Warfare

On a warm November day, John appeared in my office doorway. I instantly recognized his cool demeanor and infectious enthusiasm. He's the quintessential youth pastor. Since I've seen him in action, I know that he lives the stereotype. Teens flock to his ministry. As he peered in at me, a momentary frown eclipsed his easygoing face. "Perturbed" was deeply etched on his burrowed forehead. After exchanging small talk, he told me his tale.

By way of background, every year he and his youth group go on a mission trip to Brazil. For two full weeks, they teach Vacation Bible School, work on building projects, and do street evangelism. When doing evangelism, the local pastors take the American youth to the *favelas* (slum areas) because their presence attracts a large crowd. The evangelism excursions include a light meal, praise music, open-air preaching, praying for the sick, exorcisms, and dramatic conversions. During these events, the youth work alongside the native pastors.

Every night before going to bed, the youth read a selected Bible passage from Jesus' ministry in Galilee. As they contemplate the various Bible stories, they become increasingly aware that they are doing the same thing that Jesus did. This creates a vision for anointed ministry, and it gives the youth a shot of badly needed confidence.

The youth pastor hopes that the encounter with apostolic Christianity will transform their faith and keep them from falling away from the church when they become adults. He believes that too many Christian youth walk away from Jesus when they leave home because they are not grounded in biblical Christianity. In his words, he's not babysitting kids. He's raising up the next generation of church leaders.

After returning from the most recent mission trip, a visitor to his youth program presented with a demon during the praise time. Those who had ministered in Brazil recognized what was happening and knew how to respond to it. Following a short consultation, they prayed over the boy and cast out the offending demons.

When the teen's mother arrived to pick up her son, she assumed that he had suffered from a seizure and excoriated the youth pastor for not calling an ambulance. When she took her son to the emergency room, the tests didn't find any evidence of a seizure. He was perfectly healthy.

In the wake of the event, the elder board voted that the youth couldn't perform exorcisms in the church. They cited risk management concerns. When the youth pastor asked what they should do if another demon manifested during their worship time, the elders told him to ignore it. The response touched a raw nerve that prompted a straightforward question. "Since the church elders know that we do power ministry in Brazil, why do they disavow deliverance ministry in our home church? Don't they realize that the demons who brazenly obstruct our ministry in Brazil also disrupt our ministry in our home church? Why should we expect evil spirits to remain subtle and unobtrusive when we're in America?"

Evangelicals Prefer to Ignore Demons

The response from the church elders fits an established pattern that has dominated American churches for a hundred years. Expelling a demon doesn't create a theological or cultural problem when done in an outlying Brazilian village. It's mostly expected because the people who live in the *favelas* practice a type of West African shamanism. However, when a demon manifests in an American church, leaders are reluctant to acknowledge that the interloper is a demon. If they conceded the presence of a demon, they would be obligated to do something about it. Since seminary classes in pastoral care don't teach local pastors how to deal with demons, they prefer to ignore demonically induced behavior. For that reason, Satan can hide in broad daylight and remain unchallenged when doing his work in most American congregations.

The above statement stands in stark contrast to what evangelicals say they believe. First, they believe that the Bible is true in all that it affirms. Second, they believe that the Bible is the final authority for matters of faith and right practice. Third, they believe that Jesus and his disciples routinely combatted demons while doing ministry. Fourth, they believe that Jesus gave his disciples authority to cast out demons and told them to do it. Ergo, Bible-believing pastors should presume that demons will interfere with their work in America. Moreover, they should equip themselves and their church members to join in the battle. That is why the biblical authors constantly reminded the New Testament church that the devil and his allies were united against them. In order to advance the kingdom of God, the Bible authors knew that they had to deal with the demonic.

Jesus hinted at this when he told his disciples to pray that God would establish his kingdom on Earth like it is already realized in heaven because God's will can't be fully achieved on Earth until the Evil One and the allied forces of darkness are subdued (Matt 6:10). He also told them to pray, "Deliver us from the Evil One" (Matt 6:13) because "the devil prowls around like a roaring lion looking for someone to devour" (1 Pet 5:8).[1] Later, Jesus reminds Peter that Satan wanted to sift him like wheat (Luke 22:31).

In the epistles, the Apostle Paul tells the believers to put on the armor of God because "We are not fighting against human beings but against the wicked spiritual forces in the heavenly world, the rulers, authorities, and cosmic powers of this dark age" (Eph 6:12). Even though they seem invincible, he reminds the church that the thrones, powers, rulers, and authorities were created by Christ (Col 1:16). Ultimately, the demons and powers won't be able to pull the believers from God's protective embrace (Rom 8:38). In 1 Corinthians 15:24–26, Paul offers an eschatological perspective. "Then the end will come, when [Jesus] hands over the Kingdom to God the Father after he has destroyed all dominion, authority, and power. For he must reign until he has put all his enemies under his feet. The last enemy to be destroyed is death." Dominions, authorities, powers, thrones, the rulers, death,[2] enemies, wicked spiritual forces in the heavenly world, and cosmic powers of this dark age refer to a demonic hierarchy that opposes God and the work of God's church. These evil beings are in league with Satan.[3]

It should be noted that a similar hierarchy of power exists in the heavens. First Peter refers to this when he writes, Jesus "has gone into heaven and is at God's right hand—with angels, authorities and powers in submission to him" (1 Pet 3:22). The word "angels" shows that he is not speaking about

---

1. Most English translations render *apo tou ponerou* as "from evil." Deliver us from "the wicked one" is a better translation.

2. In the Greek New Testament, death is a double-entendre. It can refer to a divine being named Thanatos or physical death. Most likely, Paul intends both meanings. Eventually, Thanatos and Satan will be cast into the Lake of Fire (Rev 20:14).

3. Arnold, *3 Critical Questions*, 38. According to Arnold, instead of calling them demons, Paul uses a series of terms to characterize what type of spiritual rulers they are. From foot soldiers to generals, evil spirits exist in a hierarchy with corresponding jobs.

demonic powers and authorities. In fact, as the Commander of the heavenly hosts, all the powers in heaven bow before King Jesus.

Heavenly Treason

Besides Satan, Psalm 82 also identifies the cadre of high-ranking rulers who have joined forces with Satan. "God presides in the heavenly council; in the assembly of the gods he gives his decision . . . 'How ignorant you are! How stupid! You are completely corrupt, and justice has disappeared from the world. You are gods,' I said; 'all of you are children of the Most High. But you will die like mortals; your life will end like that of any prince.' 'Come, O God, and rule the world; all the nations are yours.'"[4] Psalm 58 picks up on the theme of corrupt gods who pervert justice in the earth. "Do you indeed decree what is right, you gods? Do you judge people fairly? No, in your hearts you devise wrongs; your hands deal out violence on earth" (Ps 58:1–2, NRSV).

In Psalm 82, Yahweh contends with the dominions, authorities, and powers of which Paul spoke. Because they are "the children of the Most High," he calls them princes. These divine beings are the nation gods who have rebelled. In New Testament parlance, they are demonic forces. They have threatened, sabotaged, corrupted, and despoiled God's good creation. They have supplanted God's will and have done evil.

The rebel gods seek to undermine Yahweh's rule and to establish their own rule by ascending the mountain of God and setting their thrones over his (Isa 14:13; Ezek 28:2; Dan 8:10). They want to be worshipped and to be treated like the God who created them.[5] Some are incarcerated in Tartarus (2 Pet 2:4). Ultimately, all the rebel gods will be cast into the Lake of Fire (Rev 20:10–14). There is only one true God. The pretenders can't win. Until God's reign is fully restored and all his enemies are subdued, God will remain at war.

In addition to Satan and the rebel children of God, the Bible mentions numerous premortal entities who have contended with God. Leviathan, Rahab, Behemoth, Sheol, Abaddon, Yamm, Mot, and Resheph are some of the names by which the ancient beings are identified. Many of the names don't

---

4. "So too, since Christ has in principle defeated the fallen 'gods' (principalities and powers) who have for ages inspired injustice, cruelty and apathy toward the weak, the poor, the oppressed and the needy (Ps. 82), the church can hardly carry out its role in manifesting, on earth and in heaven, Christ's victory over these gods without taking up as a central part of its missions" the call to rectify the evils that they have caused (Boyd, *God at War*, 254).

5. Boyd, "Ground-Level Deliverance Model," 130–37.

appear in the English Bible because they have been translated as a common noun. For example, Mot is death, Abaddon is destruction, and Sheol is hell. In the New Testament, Mot becomes Thanatos, Abaddon becomes Apollyon, Sheol becomes Hades, and Satan is called the devil.[6]

Kingdom Conflict

The notion that the kingdom of God battles against the kingdom of Satan goes to the core of spiritual warfare theology. The phrase, "kingdom of God" indicates the place where God rules.[7] As long as Satan is the god of this world (2 Cor 4:4), the Almighty will fight against him and his vast empire. That is why John the Baptist declared that the kingdom of God was at hand at the inauguration of Jesus' ministry (Matt 3:2; 4:17). Jesus manifested the kingdom, the church grows it, and God will fully establish it at the second coming of Christ.

In the Gospels, Satan and his hosts fight against God's plans by trying to neutralize Jesus. First, the Evil One tries to destroy Jesus by murdering all the baby boys (Matt 2:16). Second, Satan tries to make Jesus his slave during the wilderness temptation (Matt 4:1–11). Third, a maniacal demon tries to kill Jesus by fomenting a great squall while Jesus and his disciples were on the Sea of Galilee (Mark 4:35–41). Finally, Satan tries to win the war by killing Jesus on the cross. That ploy backfired on him.[8]

In the Gospels, Jesus is not a passive victim of Satan's egregious malice. Instead, he takes the battle to Satan. Jesus is the strongman who binds Satan and sets his captives free. Every healing, exorcism, cleansing, and recovery of lost people is a direct strike at Satan and his evil empire. When a sinner repents and turns to Jesus, Satan loses.

Greg Boyd captures this point when he writes, "Understood in its original apocalyptic context, every aspect of Jesus' life can be understood as part of his battle against, and a victory over, the powers of darkness. Every

---

6. For a detailed understanding of the premortal monsters, see Keel, *Gods, Goddesses, and Images* and Day, *Yahweh and the Gods*. You may also look up each monster by name in the *Dictionary of Demons*. Wink counters the above analysis by calling it the myth of redemptive violence. He traces the pattern back to the Babylonia creation myth. He believes that references to the premortal gods (chaos monsters) may be borrowed from that story (Wink, "Facing the Myth").

7. Ladd, *Gospel of the Kingdom*, 13–23.

8. Based on a conflation of messianic texts, the Jews believed that the Messiah would remain forever (John 12:34). Satan may have shared their opinion.

one of Jesus' healings and deliverances, for example, should be viewed as an act of war that advances God's kingdom and diminishes Satan's kingdom."[9]

To enable people to enter the impending kingdom, Jesus invites them to flee from their slavery to Satan by siding with God. People are manumitted when they reject Satan, repent of their sin, believe the gospel, put their faith in Jesus, and become a Christ-disciple in the context of a community of faith that gives evidence to God's reign in tangible ways (Matt 21:32; 28:18–20; Mark 1:14–15; 6:12; Luke 13:1–5; 15; 24:47; Acts 2:28; 3:19; 8:22; 17:30; 19:4; 20:21; Rev 2:5; 16–22). Baptism is a new believer's enlistment into God's army. Jesus is the head of the body (Rom 12:5; 1 Cor 12:12–27; Eph 3:6; 5:23; Col 1:18; 24), the captain of our salvation (Heb 2:10), and the commander of the heavenly forces who are arrayed against the enemy (Jos 5:13–15; Ps 46:7; Rev 19:11–16). In short, when one becomes a disciple, one becomes a foot soldier in the ongoing conflict against the kingdom of Satan.

Paul uses the soldier metaphor often (1 Cor 9:7; Phil 2:25; 2 Tim 2:3–4; Phlm 1:2). He also employs the "fight on behalf of God" metaphor (1 Cor 9:29; 2 Cor 10:4; 2 Tim 4:7). For example, he urges Timothy, to "fight the good fight of faith" (1 Tim 1:18). In Ephesians 6:10–17, Paul combines the soldier and the fight metaphors. Similarly, a disciple should endure suffering as a good soldier perseveres in the struggle. Like a long-distance runner persists in a grueling marathon, a disciple must agonize to win in his battle against Satan and sin (Heb 12:1). Winning the race requires training and discipline (Acts 20:24; 1 Cor 9:24; Gal 2:2; 5:7; 2 Tim 4:7). In the conflict against Satan, God's children must not conspire with the enemy. Sin is rebellion against God. For that reason, disciples must submit to God's rule (1 Cor 6:18; 10:14; 1 Tim 6:11; 2 Tim 2:22; Jas 4:7).

According to the Bible, Satan's kingdom is the dominion of darkness (Col 1:13). Sinful actions are referred to as the deeds of darkness because they accomplish the work of the dark lord (Rom 13:12; Eph 5:11). Since God's light exposes evil deeds, people who do evil love the darkness and hate the light (John 3:19). Darkness reigned during the time of Jesus' suffering because it was Satan's hour (Luke 22:53). To symbolize the dark hour, literal darkness covered the land while Jesus made atonement for humankind on the cross (Luke 23:44).

Biblical revelation exposes the deep darkness (*skotia*). Since darkness is the lack of light, the brilliance of God destroys the darkness when it shines on it (John 1:4–5). In like manner, when Jesus went down into the depths of darkness (Hades) after his crucifixion, he destroyed the darkness and broke

---

9. Boyd, "Ground-Level Deliverance Model," 137.

down the Gates of Hell. The powers of darkness couldn't prevail against him (Matt 16:18).

Consider this: a single candle in a black cavern will reveal the deep contours and hidden crannies that trip unenlightened people who must traverse the cave. In the same way, the Bible is a spotlight that reveals God's truth (Job 29:3; Ps 18:28; 43:3; 119:105; Prov 6:23; 2 Pet 1:19). When you read what it says about spiritual warfare, the light of God's revelation will shine on your path so that you will be able to see the snare of the devil (Ps 91:3; 124:7; 2 Tim 2:26). In truth, the light of God's word pulls back the curtains and exposes the sinister beings who lurk in the darkness. One can't combat an enemy that one doesn't see. That's why God gives us the light of his word.[10]

In summary, Jesus is the light of the world. He came to drive out the Prince of this World (John 12:31), to destroy the works of the devil (1 John 3:8), and to annihilate the one who has power over death in order to free those who live in slavery to Satan and the fear of death (Heb 2:14). Paul affirms that Jesus disarmed the spiritual rulers and authorities when he triumphed over them (Col 2:15). Jesus continues to destroy the rule of Satan by enlarging his kingdom on Earth. The endgame of the ongoing war is the realization of "thy kingdom come, thy will be done, on earth as it is in heaven" (Matt 6:10). When that happens, Eden will be restored. In the meantime, those who name the name of Jesus live on the battleground. As we war against Satan and those who have joined forces with him, we are commanded by Jesus and assisted by his holy angels. We cannot win the battle until we know our enemy and engage him.

---

10. The New Testament uses the light metaphor to describe believers. Because Jesus is the light of the world, his disciples don't walk in darkness (John 8:12; 1 John 1:7). In order to enter God's kingdom of light, a would-be follower must abandon the domain of darkness (1 Pet 2:9). Darkness is the default condition of those who don't follow Jesus. Thankfully, when a person turns from the darkness, the light of God embraces him (Acts 26:18). Jesus tells his followers to let their light shine before others because they are "light bearers" (Matt 5:16). When the light of God's truth illuminates their witness, their preaching reveals the darkness and enables those in bondage to Satan to turn to the light.

2

What about Ghosts and Spirits?

Unlike people from other parts of the world, Americans are evenly divided on whether ghosts and spirits are real. During the last thirty years, belief in ghosts is on the rise. In 1990, 25 percent believed in ghosts and spirits. In 1996, 30 percent believed. In 2005, 32 percent believed.[1] By 2017, 57 percent of Americans believed in ghosts and spirits. Surprisingly, according to a 2017 survey, 35 percent said that they had personally experienced a ghost or a spirit.[2] Similarly, a 2015 Pew report indicated that 29 percent of Americans have connected with the dead and 18 percent have seen a ghost. Practicing Christians are less likely to have seen a ghost (11 percent).[3] However, Christians are more likely than non-Christians to have angel visitations. Incredibly, 77 to 81 percent of Americans believe in angels.[4] One wonders if the average American can distinguish between a ghost, angel, demon, the Virgin Mary, or ancestor when seeing an apparition.

Do you believe in ghosts and spirits? If you do, what do you believe about them? Personal experience, ethnicity, the media, educational attainment, and stories from your personal acquaintances affect what you believe about the supernatural. If you are a Christian, the Bible should be a primary source of information. The next two chapters show how culture strongly influences what a person believes about ghosts and spirits. The third chapter

---

1. Moore, "Three in Four Americans Believe in the Paranormal."
2. "Majority of Americans," paras. 2, 3.
3. Lipka, "18% Say They've Seen a Ghost," Table 1, para. 6.
4. "Nearly 8 in 10 Americans," para. 1.

explores the New Testament teaching on the topic. The outcome may surprise you.

A Spiritual Orientation Predisposes Traditional Societies to Believe in Ghosts and Spirits

As I compose this sentence, I am teaching at a seminary in Nigeria. Having lived in Asia, Latin America, the Middle East, and Europe, I have observed how cultural identity strongly influences the way a person conceives of the supernatural. For instance, while working with Spanish speaking people in several countries over many years, I discovered that a native spirituality permeates their culture. Navajos and other indigenous tribal groups share a similar spiritual orientation. Such people allow their spiritual awareness to influence everyday issues of life. Additionally, most Latinos have had some personal experience with ghosts, ancestors, or Mary apparitions. Almost everyone from Latin America believes in them and will tell you stories about them once they have gotten to know you.

To understand the spiritual orientation of the Latino soul, one must realize that a large proportion of traditional Latino society holds to beliefs and practices that are commonly associated with folk religion; that is, seeking help from folk healers with special powers (*curanderos, herbalistas, brujas,* or *espiritistas*), participating in spiritual cleansing services that use incense or herbs, and making offerings to spiritual beings other than God. Additional practices include pilgrimages to sacred sites, use of empowered rituals, prayers to spiritual intermediaries, participation in religious processionals, use of blessed objects, and wearing special clothing that symbolizes devotion to specific saints. These external markers point to a worldview that takes the spirit world seriously and a felt need to have some control over it.[5]

Typically, evangelical or Pentecostal Latinos refrain from the above practices. However, I have argued that they have indigenized their faith so that is compatible with the prevailing worldview. I refer to it as "folk Christianity."[6] Bluntly stated, Western Protestantism doesn't excite the Hispanic soul because it doesn't deal with the people's holistic understanding of

---

5. Payne, "Folk Religion." Gailyn Van Rheenen describes and contrasts the worldviews of animism, secularism, and theism (*Communicating Christ in Animistic Contexts*, 169–71). From my experience, I would contend that most Latinos operate under a worldview that blends elements of animism, secularism, and theism. In fact, one could graph Latino worldview orientations in terms of the emphases each gives to the three main categories. Indigenous peoples would be closer to animism. People from the southern cone region (Argentina, Uruguay, and Chile) would be closer to secularism.

6. Payne, "Folk Religion," 145, 163–64.

the supernatural in the same way as traditional shamanism or syncretistic aspects of folk Catholicism do. For one thing, Western Protestants tend to separate the spiritual from the mundane. When something happens, Western Protestants automatically look for natural answers and natural causation. On the other hand, Latinos have a both/and approach to life. For them, spirituality is sewn into the fabric of the routine.

In short, Latino Pentecostalism has become an explosive faith in forty-five years because it has taken the Hispanic understanding of everyday supernaturalism seriously. For that reason, it has largely displaced native shamanism in the areas where it has become established. Additionally, it helped to jumpstart the burgeoning Roman Catholic charismatic movement in Latin America.

A similar phenomenon has occurred in Africa, India, and in other parts of the global church. Today, over 500 million Christians follow some sort of charismatic faith that takes the supernatural seriously. Furthermore, there is a relationship between the movement toward a charismatic faith that addresses the supernatural in practical ways and the growth of worldwide Christianity. The rapid expansion of the church in Sub-Saharan Africa illustrates this.

Even though Christianity has existed in Africa since the time of the New Testament church, it didn't cover the continent. When Western missionaries planted the seeds for the current membership explosion, they came with colonial expansion, mixed faith with ideas of Western civilization, and exported their Western denominations with their ministry practices and low understanding of practical supernaturalism. This led to a type of split-level Christianity in which everyday spirituality was separated from formal religiosity.

Because the religion of the missionaries didn't deal with demons, ancestors, evil spirits, the evil eye, curses, and routine rituals to ensure blessings and good health, shamanism continued to meet the spiritual needs of the people. The Sub-Saharan church didn't expand rapidly until the advent of massive Holy Spirit revivals and native preachers. These gave rise to the African Independent churches. The African movements Africanized Christianity by adapting it to their worldview.

This point became clear to me in 2016 while teaching a theology of mission class in Nigeria. When the topic of power ministry came up, a group of Anglican students began to talk about healing the sick, casting out devils, and receiving revelations from God. I told them that they did not sound like normal Anglicans. They retorted that they were "African" Anglicans. Point made.

What You Believe Determines What You See?

A few years ago, I taught a cultural anthropology class that included students from Africa, Latin America, Ireland, Ukraine, and America. When the topic of folk religion was discussed, the African students told about shamans, witches, and their encounters with tribal ancestors. The Irish student spoke about a ghost who routinely made its presence known at her childhood home. A Latina student recounted her experience with a Virgin Mary apparition that comforted the family of a dying mother. An African American student "testified" about his encounter with three angels during a night vision. The Anglo-American students didn't relate any personal stories about the supernatural. Rather, they contended that ancestor spirits, ghosts, Virgin Mary apparitions, and saint visitations are disguised demons. However, they did say amen when the African American student told about his angelic encounter.

An Atheist student may have argued that the supernatural encounters that my international students reported represent a type of cultural phenomena in which people read their beliefs back onto the things they experience. One person's ghost is another person's ancestor and one person's ancestor is another person's saint. As such, even though paranormal stories make great movies, anecdotal reports about supernatural encounters don't prove that ghosts and spirits really exist. In this case, the comments by the atheistic student would most closely align with the majority opinion of academicians who teach in the physical sciences.

Due to an emphasis on the Enlightenment values of science, reason, and materialism, aspects of Western culture condition people to doubt the existence of ghosts and spirits in the same way that people from other cultures are conditioned to believe in them. Many Westerners associate these words with fairytales, make-believe, sci-fi movies, or superstition. Even though these categories still exist in entertainment (the X-Files, Black Panther, Harry Potter, Scooby-Doo, or Ghostbusters) and folk culture, they no longer represent real beings.

At the same time, many atheists, agnostics, and scientists who don't believe in ghosts or spirits do believe in UFOs. I refer to this as the "Ancient Aliens effect." The theory of evolution teaches that life on Earth created itself and subsequently humans evolved into sapient creatures with no divine assistance. Since two billion other Earth-like planets exist, a similar process must have happened on other worlds.[7] Furthermore, because of the law of probability and the purported age of the universe, they affirm that a percent-

---

7. See Institute of Physics, "How Many Planets Are There Like Earth?"

age of life on other planets must be more evolved than life on Earth. As such, they expect that humans will be contacted by aliens.[8] In fact, researchers at the Massachusetts Institute of Technology are so confident that aliens are traveling the universe, they have proposed shooting a massively powerful laser into space in order to guide them to our planet.[9]

Curiously, the late Stephen Hawking, a noted astrophysicist who was called the smartest man on Earth, warned that the world should stop all efforts to contact aliens because they might destroy humankind.[10] Kevin Knuth agrees with Hawking. "As a NASA research scientist and now a professor of physics, I attended the 2002 NASA Contact Conference, which focused on serious speculation about extraterrestrials. During the meeting a concerned participant said loudly in a sinister tone, 'You have absolutely no idea what is out there!' The silence was palpable as the truth of this statement sunk in."[11]

For some who reject the existence of the supernatural, UFO tracking and alien hunting have become scientifically sanctioned alternatives to ghost chasing and paranormal investigations. In "Don't Believe in God? Maybe You'll Try U.F.O.s," Clay Routledge argues that many non-religious scientists believe in UFOs in the same way that superstitious people believe in the paranormal because they are searching for significance and transcendence. "I am not suggesting that if you reject traditional religious belief, you will necessarily find yourself believing in alien visitors. But because beliefs about UFOs and aliens don't explicitly invoke the supernatural and are couched in scientific and technological jargon, they may be more palatable to those who object to the metaphysics of more traditional religious systems."[12]

Of course, some of the same people who reject the possibility of the supernatural also refuse to ponder the troves of evidence about UFOs. Even though they must accept the plausibility of UFOs because their scientifically informed worldview requires it, they staunchly reject the notion that people have been contacted by extraterrestrials or that UFOs are real.

---

8. "Many scientists believe we are not alone in the universe. It's probable, they say, that life could have arisen on at least some of the billions of planets thought to exist in our galaxy alone—just as it did here on planet Earth. This basic question about our place in the Universe is one that may be answered by scientific investigations. What are the next steps to finding life elsewhere?" (Dunbar, "Finding Life beyond Earth." Also, see Lewis, "Do Aliens Exist?").

9. Molina, "Lasers Could Help Us Attract Aliens."

10. Wall, "Stephen Hawking Is Still Afraid."

11. Knuth, "Are We Alone?," para. 2.

12. Routledge, "Don't Believe in God?," para. 11.

A person who holds to a biblical worldview doesn't need to reject the notion of UFOs or refuse to consider the evidence.[13] For example, if I would have asked the evangelical Anglo-American students from my previously mentioned anthropology class to say what UFOs were, most would say that they relate to Nephilim, angelic transportation devices, Watchers, or demons. Many evangelicals who have studied UFOs and alien abduction stories have determined that they can be halted by invoking the name of Jesus. For them, this evidence reinforces their belief that all such things are demonic in origin.[14]

In the end, we must admit that UFOs, ghosts, ancestors, and spirits exist. Such things are labeled as social facts. They exist because people of all ages and locations have said they exist. Both science and theology attempt to say what they are based on their own theoretical commitments.

In summary, because of the influence of natural philosophy, many scientists in the West expect that aliens exist but dismiss the tangible encounters that non-Western people have with the supernatural (ghosts and spirits). However, when I probe this topic with people in Africa and Latin America, almost everyone admits to having an intimate awareness of the supernatural. Many describe interactions with ancestors, ghosts, and late members of their immediate family. In fact, the vast preponderance affirms having personal contact with deceased humans or supernatural beings. In some places, the contact is routine and ongoing.

---

13. Michael Heiser, a noted biblical scholar who has written extensively on the sons of God and the supernatural, has written two novels that portray a historical UFO deception and an end times in which demons disguised as extraterrestrials align with a particular reading of prophecy. See *The Façade* and *The Portent*.

14. For a good example, see Sling and Stone, "Alien Abductions."

3

Ghost Stories

Over the years, I have collected "ghost stories" from people that I have interviewed all over the world. Mediums and shamans who allow themselves to host (be possessed by) departed spirits offer some of the most interesting stories. Students from my spiritual warfare classes have also collected and submitted scores of ghost stories. Finally, while doing inner healing sessions, people have shared ghost stories with me.

For the purposes of this book, a ghost story includes any account in which a person claims to have had a personal encounter with a spiritual being. I do not impose my categories on the ghost stories that I receive. Instead, I affirm that each flows from a particular cultural context and reflects the worldview orientation of the person giving it. The following stories are a sampling of the hundreds that I have collected.

A white couple from Zimbabwe told me about a ghost apparition that often stood at the foot of their bed when they slept. At first, the female in a flowing white dress scared them. Soon, they made peace with her. They decided that the apparition was a young mother who died in their bedroom while giving birth in 1952. They didn't feel threatened by it and it never communicated with them.

A Marine father reported that his family suffered from a series of disturbances. The problem started when an eerie figure kept tapping on their windows. Later, they smelled cigarette smoke in the house and heard the voice of an older man. After that, the smoke alarms started to go off. They wouldn't stop blaring even though the father disconnected the wires and removed the batteries. About that time, they received a text picture from an old phone that they no longer used. It showed the ghostly image of the man who had been tapping on their windows.

An African American woman recounted that she saw a figure when she woke from sleep. The being sounded like her recently departed sister. It asked her to give a message to her other sister. She said, "Let Valerie know that I didn't want to leave her but I had to go. Tell her I am ok and not to worry about me." At first, the woman didn't deliver the message. After the messenger returned, she finally gave the message to her living sister. Once delivered, the message greatly assuaged the sister's profound grief.

An African man told me that his family kept a special room for their ancestors. The elders placed food and libations in the chamber every morning in case the ancestors visited. One day when this man was young, he became sick and rested on the sickbed in the ancestors' room. While hiding under the covers, he watched some ancestors come into the room and eat the food. When he described the people that he saw, his parents identified each of them by name. After that, he always respected the ancestors.

A naval officer reported that he encountered his deceased father on a military base.

> When I was stationed at NAS Meridian, I once saw a master chief who looked exactly like my late dad. His gray hair was combed straight back and he was wearing wash khakis. In every way, the man was the spitting likeness of my dad when he retired from the Navy before he died from war complications. Plus, I'm certain that the master chief that I saw didn't work on the base because I knew all the senior enlisted personnel. Since the base was in the middle of nowhere, it rarely received visitors. I couldn't talk to him because I was driving in traffic. When I turned around, I couldn't find the red pickup truck that he was driving. I never saw him again.

A police officer reported a similar incident. Soon after his father died, his mom sold the family Peugeot. It was a one-of-a-kind white car with a beige roof and a lot of bumper stickers. One day, the policeman came upon the old Peugeot. Since he wanted to see who had purchased it, he pulled up next to it when it was stopped at a red light. When he looked over, he saw his late father in the driver's seat. His father looked at him with a twinkle in his eyes, smiled in his old way, and drove off.

A Nigerian man became very ill with the Ebola virus. While suspended between life and death, he left his body. When this happened, he could see himself and everyone around him. Since he couldn't return to his body, he decided to explore. On the edge of the village, he met seven recently departed people from the community. He knew and recognized each of them. They sat in a circle and talked with one another. When he tried to join the circle, they told him to return to the village because he was too young to die.

A woman from the Yoruba tribe told me that a spirit husband claimed her. He wouldn't let her have a child. Every time she became pregnant, he came to her, had intercourse with her, and killed the baby. Besides the aborted babies, she also had physical evidence in her body. Finally, she went to a Christian pastor for help. He anointed her with oil, declared the name of Jesus over her, and rebuked the ancestor spirit. The next week the spirit husband returned intending to rape her. This time he couldn't come close to her because God had protected her. After that, she became a Christian.

An African American evangelist completed a successful meeting on a Sunday and was driving back to his town late at night when his car malfunctioned on a deserted country road. The preacher had to get home in time to go to work or he would be fired. As he prayed, a white man sprinted across a recently harvested field. The man asked the evangelist if he needed help. The man was barefooted, but his feet weren't dirty. The white man fixed the car and sprinted away. The preacher didn't know his name and never saw him again. He says that the man was an angel that God sent to help him.

While serving in Iraq, a soldier heard knocking on his chu door at night. When he answered it, no one was there. After the second occurrence, the chaplain told the soldier to ask whatever was knocking what it wanted. On the third visit, the knocker told the soldier to pray. He and his chaplain prayed together until the burden was lifted. Afterward, the soldier went to the tactical operations center and looked at the battle tracker. At the moment that they started to pray, a platoon of his friends had been ambushed. Somehow, they all survived with no injuries.

A woman worried that her nephew might die while she babysat him. So, she sat up through the first night to watch him. She tried to sit up the second night, but just couldn't stay awake. As she was falling asleep, she prayed for divine help. Suddenly, as though someone had slit a black curtain in the night, a silver wing protruded through the darkness and hovered over the crib. Then a voice said, "You can sleep; I'll watch the baby."

A young wife was struggling with a difficult pregnancy. She and her husband thought the child would be a boy, but hadn't agreed upon a name because they didn't think that the baby would survive. One night, as the wife went to sleep, she prayed for God to protect the baby. During the night, an angel came to her and told her, "Do not worry about this baby. God is protecting it, but the baby is a girl and her name is Jeanelle."

One woman reported that something used to touch her feet and legs almost every night when she went to bed. After enduring this annoyance for several weeks, she prayed that God would protect her. Later in the evening, while she read her Bible, a brightness appeared at the foot of her bed. When she peered through the glow, she saw a figure of a man dressed in white. He looked at her with kindness. Peace flooded her soul. The figure then vanished. She claims that the figure was an angel sent to protect her.

God gave an African American minister a burden to pray every morning at a certain time. The sacrifice of getting up early to pray would add to the efficacy of his prayers. His spirit was willing, but his body was weak. Every time that he tried to get up and pray, he fell back to sleep. The problem infuriated him.

One night he asked God to wake him up at the appointed time and not let him fall back to sleep until he prayed. When the time came, he heard the doorbell ring. When he got up to answer the door, his body remained asleep on the bed. In his spirit, he went to the door. When he arrived, he discovered three figures with swords drawn. The angels informed him that God sent them to help him pray. He invited them in. Afterward, he awoke and prayed with power and diligence.

Several of the people that I interviewed in Costa Rica questioned why I didn't talk with my deceased parents. When a loved one dies, many expect to be visited by that person in a dream or in some other way. One highly articulate teacher calmly exhorted me to take the time to connect with my dead parents because she communes with hers several times each week when she gets home from work. In fact, she was a bit shocked that I didn't talk to my late parents.

A good friend recounted the best story about conversing with a passed loved one. After a lifetime of love and marriage, Dr. Robert Crick's wife developed Alzheimer's dementia. When she finally died, Dr. Crick felt disconsolate because he was unable to connect with her emotionally as she was dying. She thought that he was her father. His pain and grief consumed him. While crying out to God, God sent his beloved wife back for a visit. During the forty-minute encounter, Jeanette spoke to him about their life together, their children, and about heaven. The meeting forever changed Dr. Crick.[1]

Communicating with the dead is more common than many Westerners believe. Recently, an influence-peddling scandal embroiled South Korean politics. President Park Geun-Hye did not survive the uproar. The media claimed that she used her influence as president to help a close friend become rich. The close friend is Choi Soon-Sil. She is the daughter of a famous cult leader named Choi Tae-min. In 1990, her father helped President Park Geun-Hye communicate with her murdered mother. Interestingly, the current controversy isn't about the president using a medium to

---

1. To read the full story, see Crick and Miller, *Journeying with Jeanette*, 239–47.

communicate with her dead mother. Communicating with the dead barely raises an eyebrow in Korea.[2]

On two occasions, Jesus spoke to the dead. First, he commanded dead Lazarus to return to his body (John 11:43). Wherever Lazarus was, he heard Jesus and obeyed his command. Second, when Jesus went up the tall mountain and was transfigured, Moses and Elijah came and spoke to him about his imminent death. Seeing the glorified Jesus talking to two departed prophets caused the bewildered disciples to go into sensory overload (Matt 17:1–13).

Some have suggested that Moses and Elijah weren't dead because they went to heaven before they died. While that applies to Elijah, it is not true of Moses. The Bible teaches that Moses died because it says that the Archangel Michael disputed with Satan over his body (Jude 1:9). The fact that Moses had a conscious existence after he died brings the doctrine of soul sleep into question. As such, one should allow for the possibility of ancestor spirits or ghostly apparitions because the Bible doesn't teach that they do not exist, and a significant percentage of the world's population has had personal contact with one.

---

2. "South Korea's Park in Trouble."

4

The Disciples Believed in Ghosts

Most have heard about the Witch of Endor (1 Sam 28). When King Saul desperately desired a word from God and couldn't get one, he went to a medium in order to communicate with the prophet Samuel. When the prophet returned from Sheol, he gave Saul a grim message.

The New Testament also makes explicit references to ghosts. After Jesus fed 5,000 hungry people with two fish and five loaves of bread, he sent the apostles across the Sea of Galilee while he dismissed the vast crowds (Matt 14:22–33). When the apostles made it to the middle of the lake, a great storm beat upon them. It was déjà vu of when a fierce storm tried to drown them in the same lake (Matt 8:23–27). In the previous encounter, Jesus woke up, cast the demon out of the storm, and calmed the waters. This time, Jesus wasn't with them.

Sometime after 3 am, Jesus came to the disciples by walking on the raging waters. Symbolically, walking on the water showed that Jesus has conquered the chaos and has authority over the demonic. He can tread on the angry waves and not be pulled down by them. The light has shown in the darkness and the darkness cannot overcome it (John 1:5). While separated from Jesus, the disciples remained vulnerable.

When the disciples saw Jesus walking on the waters in the furious storm, fear gripped them. Instinct told them that the figure was a ghost (*phantasma*). After all, what walks on top of the splashing waters in a terrible storm? Experience and reason taught them that people sink in stormy waters. However, their folk knowledge as experienced fishermen told them that storm spirits and ghosts could glide across the water's surface because they lacked material substance. Since they believed in the traditions or had firsthand experience with the folktales, they assumed that Jesus was a ghost.

They were so committed to their folk beliefs that they weren't mollified when Jesus told them not to fear. To prove that he wasn't a specter, Jesus bid Peter to walk on the water. After Jesus had rescued Peter, he quieted the waters. At that point, they fell before him in worship.

A similar thing occurred when Jesus materialized before the hiding disciples after his crucifixion (Luke 24:36–43). Immediately before this story, Jesus had appeared to two disciples who traveled the road to Emmaus. They didn't recognize him until he went through his bread-breaking ritual with them. When they recognized him, he vanished into thin air.

Later, Jesus reappeared in the Upper Room. When he did, the disciples felt great fear because they thought that he was a spirit (*pneuma*). Evidently, they recognized him but didn't believe that he was a real person. In other words, the disciples knew that dead people could be brought back to life because they saw Jesus raise the dead. However, whenever Jesus raised people from the dead, the people remained fully human. They couldn't pass through walls or materialize in the middle of a room. Jesus' behavior wasn't typical of a brought-back-to-life person. Since humans can't do what Jesus did, those in the Upper Room believed that he was a ghost or a spirit that came back from the dead.

Jesus fully understood their problem. In order to accommodate their incredulity, he told them to see and touch his crucifixion wounds. Then he took some food and ate it in front of them. Since they could touch his corpuscular body and see that the food stayed concealed in it when he ate it, they finally believed that Jesus wasn't a ghost. Of course, this raised other questions. How did a material Jesus go through the solid walls? What would have happened to the food that he ate if he had passed through the wall when he left them?

Jesus also met Thomas at the point of his unbelief. When he appeared to him, he said, "Put your finger here; see my hands. Reach out your hand and put it into my side. Stop doubting and believe" (John 20:27). At that point, Thomas released his doubt and believed in the resurrected Jesus.

Interestingly, when Martha met the resurrected Jesus in the early morning light, she didn't assume that he was a ghost (John 20:11–18). Rather, she thought he was the gardener. She asked a very practical question. Where have you moved the body? Since the body was missing, she supposed a natural cause. In this case, she had no reason to default to supernatural categories. The gardener explanation worked fine. Typically, people only suggest supernatural explanations when natural ones don't work.

In summary, when Jesus walked on the water and when he appeared to the disciples in the Upper Room, the disciples assumed that he was a ghost because he acted like one. Language restrictions require that people use a clearly defined word when they must interpret sensory data. Because the disciples didn't have a normal word for a human being walking on the violent water or passing through walls, they automatically assumed that the specter was a spirit or a ghost. In both cases, Jesus designed tests to prove that he was human. Because of the tests, the disciples believed that Jesus wasn't a ghost.

When people believe in ghosts, they interpret sensory phenomena in terms of that operating category. When people who don't believe in ghosts encounter the supernatural, they interpret it in terms of their existing worldview categories. Clearly, these texts teach that the disciples believed in ghosts.

Folk Beliefs of Jews in Palestine

Without exaggerating, the entire world of Jesus' day believed in ghosts. For example, Roman lares (ancestor ghosts) served as home guardians. They also protected neighborhoods, sea lanes, and important passes. People throughout the Roman world constructed shrines to them. In the Roman world, ghost only referred to one type of spirit being. Other types included ancestors, nature spirits, angry souls, demons, angels, and gods.[1]

The extent to which the folk beliefs of the Roman world influenced the thinking of Galilean Jews in Palestine cannot be fully determined. Because the Greco-Roman culture (Hellenism) firmly planted itself throughout that area, archeology offers hints. For example, researchers have discovered striking examples of religious blending in Jewish funerary practices. Artifacts include food for the dead, coins, religious objects, and items to help with the afterlife journey. Some ossuaries from the time of Jesus show that Jews placed a coin (Charon's obol) in the mouth of the dead person.[2] This practice was widely popular in ancient Greece and was given so that the deceased would get safe passage into the netherworld.

Certainly, the ancient Jews were familiar with the Canaanite pantheon of gods and spirits. The pagan practices and beliefs of the surrounding peoples always intermingled with the Jews. The Hebrew prophets waged an ongoing war against them. This fact is indicated by the prohibitions listed

---

1. Guerber, *Classical Mythology*, 199–200, and the entry on "Lares" in Dixon-Kennedy, *Encyclopedia of Greco-Roman Mythology*, 188.
2. Evans, *Jesus and the Remains*, 329.

in Deuteronomy 18:9–12: "When you enter the land the Lord your God is giving you, do not learn to imitate the detestable ways of the nations there. Let no one be found among you who sacrifices their son or daughter in the fire, who practices divination or sorcery, interprets omens, engages in witchcraft, or casts spells, or who is a medium or spiritist or who consults the dead. Anyone who does these things is detestable to the Lord; because of these same detestable practices the Lord your God will drive out those nations before you." This prohibition is repeated twenty-five times in the Old Testament. The penalty for consulting the dead is death (Exod 22:18).

The Old Testament uses many words to describe those associated with necromancy. They are called diviners of the dead, women who consult ghosts, knowing ones, seekers of the dead, and magicians. Also, the Jews had specific words to describe ghosts and familiar spirits because specialists dealt with them and common people feared them. Isaiah 8:19 speaks to the practice of consulting the dead. "When someone tells you to consult mediums and spiritists [familiar spirits and wizards], who whisper and mutter, should not a people inquire of their God? Why consult the dead on behalf of the living?" Those who sat on graves and spent the night inquiring from the dead (Isa 65:4) are also guilty of necromancy.

In short, Judaism doesn't deny that ghosts, spirits, and ancestors exist. Rather, God forbids his covenant people from interacting with them. God wouldn't outlaw communicating with the dead if one couldn't consult with the dead. Clearly, the Jews believed departed spirits can interact with the living through mediums and that the spiritual realm can be manipulated through magic.[3]

Strangely, the teaching of standard Judaism is somewhat silent on the issue of the paranormal. It doesn't tell the Jews what the spirits are or how to vanquish them when they interfere in life. Yet, common belief saw a connection between bad things and the spirit realm. Whenever a high (official) religion doesn't deal with the problem of everyday spirituality, folk religion will evolve in order to fill in the gaps that the high religion ignores. This fact is clearly visible in ancient Judaism. For example, the Dead Sea Scrolls offer incantations for casting out disease-causing spirits and freeing people from spells.[4]

---

3. Bloch-Smith, *Judahite Burial Practices*, 121–26.

4. For examples, see "The Song of the Sage for Protection against Evil Spirits" (4Q510–11) and "An Exorcism" (4Q506), in Wise et al., *Dead Sea Scrolls*, 526–30 and 566–67.

Did Jesus Believe in Ghosts?

Based on Jesus' reaction to the disciples when they thought he was a ghost, one could say that Jesus endorsed belief in ghosts. However, one should proceed with caution at this point. Even though the New Testament shows that the disciples believed in ghosts, it doesn't say that Jesus believed in ghosts. Additionally, in the New Testament, Jesus never combated one. In fact, apart from his "ghostly" encounters with the disciples, he never taught on the topic. For that matter, the rest of the New Testament is silent on the subject. Furthermore, even though all the religions of the ancient world included references to ghosts in their sacred literature, with the exception of the Witch at Endor, the Hebrew Scriptures say very little about ghosts, ancestor spirits, or nature spirits. Instead, the Bible talks about the gods (*elohim*), demons, and angels. If the ancient folktales about ghosts were real, one would expect that the Bible would have a lot to say about the topic.

Because of this, many Westerners who do spiritual warfare assume that ghosts, ancestors, and nature spirits don't exist. People who operate with this mindset use demon language when they or a person with whom they are doing ministry encounter one. This approach works well in the West because the West largely ignores ghosts, ancestors, and nature spirits. However, this method may cause significant problems in parts of the world where people believe in ghosts. Plus, it doesn't model Jesus' approach to the issue.

In short, the New Testament doesn't teach that ghosts are real; rather, the gospels show that Jesus met the disciples in terms of their cultural categories. In other words, he accommodated their folk beliefs without endorsing them. If Jesus didn't want his disciples to believe in ghosts or if belief in ghosts caused problems, he would have chastised the disciples when they thought that he was a ghost. Instead, he only demonstrated that he wasn't one by allowing a culturally appropriate proof. At the end of the day, even though Jesus never endorsed the idea that ghosts, ancestors, and nature spirits exist, Christ followers are free to believe in them or reject them.

If they choose to believe in them, they must not worship them, communicate with them, placate them, or seek power from them. Unfortunately, demons are masters at disguise. I have worked with people who thought that they were communicating with a deceased family member or some other benevolent spirit. Instead, the demons played on their grief to bring them into bondage. Since Satan can appear as an angel of light (2 Cor 11:14), one must assume that demons can appear as ghosts, ancestors, or nature spirits. For that reason, Christians must remain vigilant and never let their guard down when dealing with this class of spirit.[5]

5. For an interesting read that deals with this topic, see Aardweg, *Hungry Souls*.

5

Who Believes in the Devil?

PER a 2013 survey, 57 percent of Americans believe in the devil.[1] African Americans, women, and born-again Christians are the most likely groups to believe in a real Satan. The percentage diminishes with increased education and income. People in the Northeast are the least likely to believe in Satan.

A 2016 poll found that 61 percent of Americans believe in Satan, 27 percent didn't believe in Satan, and 12 percent didn't have an opinion.[2] Ninety percent of Americans believe in God or a higher power and 84 percent of them believe in angels. Curiously, despite the push of secularism and evolutionary theory in public schools, only 3 percent of Americans self-identified as an atheist.

Not everyone who believes in personified evil believes in a real Satan. A 2008 survey discovered that 60 percent of Christians don't believe in a literal Satan. Specifically, 40 percent of Christians believe that Satan isn't a living being but a symbol of evil. Another 19 percent of them "somewhat agreed" with that statement. An additional 8 percent weren't sure what they believed about Satan's existence. Only 35 percent of American Christians believe in the biblical Satan.[3] Ironically, Christians are less likely to believe in a living Satan than people from the general population.

1. "Poll Results: Exorcism," 1.
2. See Newport, "Most Americans Still Believe in God," para. 7.
3. Barna Group, "Most American Christians Do Not Believe," para. 4. The survey questions may have influenced the differences in the outcomes of the studies. For example, the first survey asked, "Do you personally believe in the existence of the Devil or not?" The second asked, "Do you believe in Satan?" The third asked, "Do you believe

Of course, differing surveys get different results because of the way they pose questions. For example, "Do you believe in Satan" forces a yes or no response. However, when one is given the ability to pick from a list of responses that include, "I believe in evil supernaturalism but don't believe in a literal Satan," the results are more nuanced. Also, some respondents are reluctant to tell a surveyor that they believe in a real Satan. During the 2016 presidential election season, pollsters referred to the "Trump" effect. That is, a percentage of people will tell the pollster what they think the pollster wants to hear.

Interestingly, a longitudinal survey shows that belief in Satan incrementally increased from 1991 to 2007 by 18 percentage points. During the same time, belief in God declined. In 2007, only 21 percent of Americans didn't believe in Satan.[4] Since polling trends during that timeframe show a steady decline in religiosity indicators and a gradual rise in the "not religious" category, one would have expected a decrease in the percentage of people who affirmed belief in a real Satan.[5] In short, the decline in organized religion hasn't signaled a decline in the belief in Satan.

Recently, I spoke to a young college student who works at a local video rental store. She said that half of the store videos dealt with spiritual evil and/or included supernatural themes. Moreover, she stated that the supernatural genre is more popular than the sex category. Who would have guessed that? According to her, young people live in a rationalistic world that denies the demonic. Yet, in their hearts, they know that spiritual evil is out there. As such, many rent B-rated sci-fi or horror movies to help them escape from rationalism by naming the evil that they sense and see in the world around them.

When I queried her on the issue, she said that young people are hungry for authentic encounters with the supernatural and might respond well to a church that dealt with the mystical in concrete ways. Perhaps this is the reason that belief in Satan has increased while participation in church has decreased.

Some have referred to these young people as the "spiritual but not religious" generation. They reject institutional church and dogmatic creeds but haven't rejected the supernatural or a desire to transcend the rational. A previous generation of Americans turned to drugs, rock music, and the New Age Movement to satisfy that longing. The Jesus Freak and Charismatic

---

that Satan is not a living being but a symbol of evil?" Some people who answered positively in the first two surveys may have answered negatively in the third if given the chance to clarify their response.

4. Newport, "Americans More Likely to Believe," Tables 4–5.
5. See Wormald, "America's Changing Religious Landscape."

Movements that emerged at the same time were God's response to the alternative religions of the 1960s. How will God respond to the current crisis in American Christianity?

Know God by His Names

In the ancient world, gods, spirit beings, and humans had names that captured some attribute of their being. For example, Dagon (Judg 16:23–30) was a Philistine god whose name relates to fish because he had fish characteristics. Mithra was a Zoroastrian god of covenants and oaths. His name means, "that which causes to bind." Leviathan (Ps 104:24) was a primordial sea monster. His name means twisted or coiled. Zeus (Acts 13:13–14) was the high god of the Greeks. His name is derived from sky. Thor was the Norse god of strength and storms. His name means thunder. Odin, was the powerful king of the Norse gods. His name means rage and fury.

Adam means earthling because he is made from the ground. He called his wife Eve because she gave life. Abraham means father of many. Jacob means "holder of the heel" or usurper. The Prophet Elijah lived during a time when the king and most of the people served false gods. His name means "My God is Yahweh." Every time that King Ahab or wicked Jezebel spoke his name in wrath or with contempt, they had to proclaim that Yahweh was their God.

In the Quran, the God of the Muslims doesn't have a personal name. Allah is an Arab word that refers to the High God. Arab speaking Jews and Christians also referred to God as Allah before the time of Islam. The Allah of Islam is utterly transcendent, inaccessible, and unknowable. However, his character can be determined by his ninety-nine glorious names. Examples are the Merciful, the Compassionate, the Pure, the Revenger, the Killer, and the King.[6] People cannot have a personal relationship with Allah.

The God of the Jews names himself Yahweh (Exod 3:14). He is the uncreated Creator who fills all things. Creation flows from him, points to him, is energized by him, and is dependent upon him. If creation and everything in it dissolved tomorrow, he would still exist.

The Jews called Yahweh by many names. He is *Elohim*, *Adonai*, the God who heals, the Lord our righteousness, the Lord who provides, the God who sees, and the Most High God. When the angels bow before him, they sing "Holy, holy, holy is the Lord of Hosts" (Isa 6:3). Even though his absolute holiness separates him from sinners and requires that he judge sin,

---

6. See Syed, "Asma al-Husna."

he is a relational God who abounds with lovingkindness. Many messianic prophesies point to his love and long-term purposes for humanity.

When Jesus became human, God entered the creation and attached himself to it. His name means, Yahweh saves. Jesus is God with us, the Man-God, Messiah, King of Kings, Savior, Lion of the Tribe of Judah, Captain of our salvation, and the Alpha and Omega. John's Gospel calls him the Word who became flesh, the Great I Am, the Lamb of God, the Bread of Life, the Light, the Way, the Truth, the Resurrection, the Door, the True Vine, and the Good Shepherd.[7] In Jesus, God is called Love (John 3:16; 1 John 4:8). Unlike Allah, he is accessible and very personable.

Names for the Evil One

Evil also has a name, a face, and a story. The Bible employs a multitude of appellations to personify Satan. Each says something about the Evil One, points to his character, and shows his work of malice. The sheer magnitude of the names indicates the central importance of Satan in the Bible. To understand him, one should study his names and the titles that are associated with him.[8]

The below list only references one biblical usage for each name or title.[9] Even though all of the below-listed names are associated with Satan, some may also refer to other supernatural beings in league with Satan.

Abaddon/Apollyon (destroying angel) Revelation 9:11;

Accuser of our brethren Revelation 12:10;

Adversary (opponent) 1 Peter 5:8;

Angel of light (messenger of light) 2 Corinthians 11:14;

---

7. For a devotional guide on the names by which the New Testament authors refer to God, see Loeks, *Glorious Names of God*.

8. When Michael Green, a New Testament scholar from Oxford, examines the names for Satan, he includes Son of God because the Evil One was numbered among them when he fell. Other names that he discusses are Satan, Tempter, Dragon/Serpent, Destroyer, Prince of the Power of the Air, Beliar/Beelzebub, Ruler of this World, and the Evil One. Based on these, he assesses the characteristics of Satan (*I Believe in Satan's Downfall*, 42–57). Fred Dickason, the former Chair of the Theology Department at Moody Bible Institute, identifies twenty names for Satan (*Angels*, 120–40). Based on the names, Dickason analyzes Satan's character, power, position, purposes, and activities.

9. I use the term "Satan" as a collective name for the fallen being who tempted Eve, Adam, and Jesus. He is the one who was hurled down to the earth. Even though Satan is used as a proper noun in the Bible and refers to an individual being, it may also refer to a type of being who accuses God's people. In the latter case, there may be many satans.

Angel of the bottomless pit Revelation 9:11;

Azazel (Satanic Goat-Demon who had a legal right to be propitiated on the Day of Atonement) Leviticus 16:8–10;

Beelzebub (Lord of flies) 2 Kings 1:2;

Beelzebul (Ruler of the demons) Luke 11:15;

Belial (Lawless, worthlessness) 2 Corinthians 6:15;

Devil (the accuser, one who hurls accusations, used 33 times in the New Testament) John 8:44;

Dragon, Great Dragon, Ancient Serpent Revelation 12:7–9;

Enemy (the hateful one, hostile one, wicked one) Matthew 13:38–39;

Evil One (a favorite term in Matthew and 1 John) Matthew 5:37;

Father of Lies John 8:44;

God of this world (god of this age) 2 Corinthians 4:3–4;

Great fiery red dragon (serpent) Revelation 12:3;

Guardian cherub Ezekiel 28:14–16;

Lucifer (shining one) Isaiah 14:12;

Morning Star (a leading member of God's heavenly council) Isaiah 14:12;

Murderer John 8:44;

Power of darkness Colossians 1:13;

Prince of the power of the air Ephesians 2:2;

Roaring Lion 1 Peter 5:8;

Ruler of this world (head of this world, prince of this world) John 12:31; 14:30; 16:11;

Satan (accuser, enemy, adversary, and slanderer) 1 Chronicles 21:1;

Serpent (snake) Genesis 3:1; 2 Corinthians 11:3;

Son of the Dawn Isaiah 14:12;

Spirit that currently works in the children of disobedience Ephesians 2:2;

Strong man Mark 3:26–27;

Tempter (the tester, one who entices) 1 Thessalonians 3:5; and

Thief John 10:9–10.

In Talmudic Judaism, Samael is a proper name for Satan.[10] He is a tempter, the Angel of Death, and a member of the Heavenly Council. He commands

---

10. For more information, see Davidson, "Samael," 255.

millions of angels. Three Enoch 14:2 calls him the Head of the Accusers (satans) who is greater than all the princes of the kingdoms on high. This attests to celestial power and may show that he was the highest-ranking heavenly being next to God. His name means poison of God. In his original form, he is covered in eyes like one of the living beings in Revelation 4:8. When he deceived Eve, he took the form of a serpent with a lion's head. That image aligns him with the god Mithra. In Hebrew folk literature, he is the father of Cain and he spawned other demons.[11] He has access to the seventh heaven but rules over the fifth heaven.[12]

Biblical references to the Evil One are voluminous. For clarity, his names can be organized into thematic categories. Each corresponds to a function and/or some aspect of his character. 1. Causing harm: Abaddon, Apollyon, Enemy, Evil One, Murderer, Roaring Lion, and Thief. 2. Deceitful: One who can appear as an Angel of Light, Father of Lies, Tempter, and Spirit that Works in the Children of Disobedience. 3. Accuser: Accuser of the Brethren, Adversary, devil, and Satan. 4. Ruler: Angel of the Bottomless Pit (king), Azazel, Beelzebub, God of this World, Power of Darkness, Prince of the Power of the Air, and Ruler of this World. 5. Dragon Images: Ancient Serpent, Dragon, Great Dragon, Great Fiery Dragon, and Serpent. 6. Previous State before Fall: Guardian Cherub, Lucifer, Morning Star, and Son of the Dawn.

Obviously, corruption and wickedness flow from the list. Malice and hatred toward all that is right or loved by God also emerge from the list. One should never forget that the Evil One is a powerful being who can do harm when God doesn't restrain him. He is a roaring lion and a destroyer. He is described figuratively as a great and powerful dragon.

He accuses the saints before God like a prosecuting attorney. In Revelation 12:10, Satan is styled the accuser of the saints who accuses them before God day and night. In Zachariah 3:1, Satan stands beside the Angel

---

11. Dennis, "Cain," 74.

12. Ancient Near East literature refers to heavens instead of heaven. The number of heavens ranges from three to ten. Paul went to the third heaven when he was "caught up to paradise" (2 Cor 12:2–4). See chapter 13. Using this as a point of reference, John Hagee says that the earthly sky is the first heaven, the realm where Satan reigns is the second heaven, and the place of God is the third heaven (Hagee, *The Three Heavens*). See chapter 8. In Hebrew, the word for heaven is the masculine plural *shamayim*. In the Tulmud, the various heavens are called *Vilon* (Isa 40:22), *Arafel*, *Raki'a* (Genesis 1:17), *Shehaqim* (Ps 78:23), *Zebul* (Isa 63:15; 1 Kgs 8:13), *Ma'on* (Deut 26:15; Psalm 42:9), *Machon* (1 Kgs 7:30; Deut 28:12), and *Araboth*. *Araboth* is the seventh Heaven where the *ofanim*, the *seraphim*, the *hayyoth*, and the throne of the Lord are located (Morton, "Seventh Heaven"). Third Enoch has much to say about this. Consult Mullen's "Heaven, Heavens, Heavenlies" (332–35) for a scholarly article on this topic.

of the Lord to accuse the high priest Joshua. Job also portrays him in that role (Job 1–2). When the angels present themselves to God, Satan also appears. In the ensuing conversation, he receives permission to test Job by inflicting him with many calamities. In the end, God vindicates Job because he refuses to sin. In a similar way, Jesus told Peter that Satan asked to sift him like wheat. Jesus interceded on his behalf so that he wouldn't fall from the faith (Luke 22:31).

Jubilees 17:15–16 contains a parallel to the Job story.[13] In it, Mastema, a powerful prince from the heavenly council, convinces God to test Abraham's faithfulness by causing him to sacrifice Isaac.[14] His name means hatred, hostility, enmity, or persecution. In Jubilees 10:7, he is identified as Satan. He is the enemy of God. He rules over the spirits of the Nephilim (evil spirits) who remain free (Jub. 7:8–9) and directs them to cause people to do evil (Jub. 11:5–6). In Jubilees 48, he tried to kill Moses before he returned to Egypt. He is identified as the wicked power behind the Egyptian captivity of Israel. He gives the Egyptian magicians their ability to counterfeit the signs of Moses. He is called an accuser.

In the Bible, Satan hurls accusations as he seeks opportunities to provoke the saints into sin. However, since Jesus' resurrection, the saints are represented by an excellent defense attorney. Jesus Christ is their advocate! Because his blood washes them from their sin, they are declared guiltless before the tribunal of God when Satan brings accusations against them. Still, Satan tempts, tests, and tries the saints. That is why Jesus taught the disciples to pray, lead us not into temptation and deliver us from the Evil One (Matt 6:13).

In John 17:15, Jesus asks the Father to keep his disciples from the power of the Evil One. First John 5:18 declares that the Father protects those who do not sin from the Evil One. Paul teaches that God will guard his people from the Evil One (2 Thess 3:3). Still, the child of God must do his part by abiding in Christ, bearing the fruit of the Spirit, doing good works, resisting the devil, and putting on the armor of God. By properly utilizing the shield of faith, one can extinguish the flaming arrows of the Evil One (Eph 6:16).

---

13. "And it came to pass in the seventh week, in the first year thereof, in the first month in this jubilee, on the twelfth of this month, there were voices in heaven regarding Abraham, that he was faithful in all that He told him, and that he loved the Lord, and that in every affliction he was faithful. And the prince Mastema came and said before God, 'Behold, Abraham loves Isaac his son, and he delights in him above all things else; bid him offer him as a burnt-offering on the altar, and Thou wilt see if he will do this command, and Thou wilt know if he is faithful in everything wherein Thou dost try him" (Jub. 17:15–16, Charlesworth).

14. The Hebrew root for Mastema is STM. It is a conflation of the Hebrew root for Satan STN (van Henten, "Mastemah," 553).

Satan's authority names should cause concern. God of this World (Age), Power of Darkness, Prince of the Power of the Air, Strong Man, and Ruler of this World describe Satan's current rulership over aspects of this world. First John 5:19 declares that the whole world lies under the power of the Evil One.

Jesus' epic battle with Satan in the wilderness amplifies this idea. During the contest, "the devil led him up to a high place and showed him in an instant all the kingdoms of the world. And he said to him, 'I will give you all their authority and splendor; it has been given to me, and I can give it to anyone I want to. If you worship me, it will all be yours'" (Luke 4:5–7).

Was Satan lying? As the Father of lies, one would expect him to mix lies with truth in order to deceive Jesus so he could gain a tactical advantage. Still, he was talking to Emmanuel (God with Us). Unlike Eve, Jesus knew the difference between truth and lie.

Notice that Jesus didn't argue with Satan's assessment. The temptation struck a raw nerve because it offered to give Jesus authority over the world systems without him having to die on the cross. In some way, it would have accomplished what Jesus wanted. However, it would have bypassed what the Father had ordained. Plus, the shortcut would have left Satan as the shadow ruler of the world. If Jesus would have bowed down to him, he would have been subject to him in the same way that Adam was subject to him when he disobeyed God.

Even though Satan is a light bearer, Acts 26:17–18 and Colossians 1:13 call him the Power of Darkness. Satan has authority over the deep darkness. Darkness is personified in John. John says that Jesus shines in the deep darkness and it doesn't overcome him (John 1:5). In contradistinction to Satan, Jesus is the light of the world. Whoever follows him will not walk in the darkness but will live in the light (John 8:12). The light cancels out the darkness when it shines on it. Jesus is "anti-darkness."

The phrase "Angel of the Bottomless Pit" refers to the king over the demons who torments wicked humankind in the end times. Contrary to what many gleefully affirm, Satan isn't a toothless tiger or a powerless Stay Puft Marshmallow Man (think Ghostbusters). If the above descriptors are correct, Satan still has power and authority on the earth and in the afterlife.

Beelzebul is another authority name. In 2 Kings 1:2, it is a chief god of the Philistines. Originally it referred to the Lord of the High House. He was the head of the Canaanite pantheon of gods or the lord of the gods.[15] In the time of Jesus, it was a synonym for Satan. It meant Lord of the Demons (see Matt 9:34; 10:25; Mark 3:22; Luke 11:18–19; 40:15).

Certain people claimed that Jesus cast out demons by Beelzebul (Luke 11:14–23). Jesus argues that he can't be Satan because Satan isn't divided

---

15. Herrmann, "Baal Zebub," 155.

against himself. Rather, Jesus is the strong man who plunders Satan's kingdom. He is the finger of God.

In the Bible, Beelzebul (the high god) and Beelzebub (the lord of the flies) are used as synonyms even though they have different roots. Literally, Beelzebub was the Lord of Gehenna, the place of the swarming flies. Gehenna was the valley outside the ancient city of Jerusalem. Because the valley of Gehenna was a smoldering trash dump from which rancid smoke wafted and flies buzzed, Beelzebub becomes the Lord of the incessantly burning garbage pit where the refuse of humanity (those not worthy of burial) was thrown at the time of death. The imagery is poignant and very symbolic. It is easy to see why Gehenna is used as the name for the burning hell in biblical and extra-biblical literature.[16]

In sum, Beelzebub and Beelzebul refer to a wicked ruler of demons who is associated with the lordship of a place called Gehenna. It is a cursed pit where burning refuse constantly smoldered. Bodies of detestable people were often thrown into the pit. Some have argued that Jewish kings practiced child sacrifice by throwing living babies into the pit. In common parlance, Gehenna is hell and the Lord of Gehenna is Satan.

A lieutenant of Satan is called Molek. He is a Canaanite god that is often associated with Baal Hammon, an Ammonite god. This high-ranking demon caused much evil in Israel because he seduced the people to throw their babies into the fire as sacrifices to him. The practice empowered the evil demon and sealed a covenant with him. The custom was so vile that God issued six warnings against it in Leviticus. Modern archeology has discovered physical evidence of child sacrifices to MLK (Molek).[17]

Today, child sacrifice has been associated with paganism and satanic ritual abuse. Sadly, around the world, infanticide is also related to gender selection and the deselection of humans with deformities. Some have argued that the abortion epidemic proves that the spirit of Molek is strong in America.

---

16. Dickason, *Angels*, 121–22.

17. Archeological evidence shows that the place where the Jews sacrificed their children (made them pass through the fire) was called Tophet. The primary place of child sacrifice was in the valley of Hinnom (Gehenna) outside the southwest walls of Jerusalem. Before the Jews "rediscovered" the Book of the Law (2 Kgs 23:10), the practice may have been widespread among the covenant people. The law requiring that Jews give their firstborn sons to Yahweh may have played into this practice (Exod 22:29). Jeremiah 32:35 attributes Tophet sacrifices to Baal (Bloch-Smith, *Judahite Burial Practices*, 112–13).

6

Gehenna in the New Testament

A FEW years ago, I evangelized a young woman who had lived a hard life far from God. In her words, she was a serial adulteress, viewed pornography every day, had sex with other women, went to psychics, read palms, did seances, used mind-altering drugs, tried to commit suicide, mistreated her kids, disliked Christians, and felt miserable most of the time. She came to me because she died from a drug overdose. Technically, she had a near-death experience. Before she came back, she experienced hell.

Her journey to hell began with piercing darkness. She felt disoriented, afraid, and paranoid. Even though her senses worked, she was lost in the darkness. She said that the darkness clung to her. In some way, it sucked the life out of her. Soon, she sensed the presence of other beings. She called them demons. Searing pain gripped her as the vile creatures tore at her body and violated her in every imaginable way. In the distance, she saw a burning fire and could hear the groaning of the damned.

With wide eyes and a pleading voice, she said that she would do anything to avoid that place. In the most vehement tone, she declared that she didn't want to return to hell. Thankfully, after forty-five minutes of intense gospel sharing, she accepted Jesus. Before coming to me, she had convinced herself that Jesus couldn't love her and that she deserved to go to hell because she had rejected him and lived an untoward life.[1]

---

1. The phenomenon of near-death experiences (NDE) has received a lot of publicity. In the burgeoning literature, most people describe good experiences. Some of the stories that don't fit the established NDE pattern may be demonic counterfeits. Regardless, 28 percent of people who have had an NDE describe hellish encounters. Researchers believe that the number of hellish NDEs is underreported because people

Gehenna

The English New Testament translates Gehenna as hell. Matthew describes the place of judgment as a furnace of fire where the damned will weep and gnash their teeth (13:42; 50) and a place of deep darkness (8:12; 23:13; 25:30). It is the destination of evildoers who bear bad fruit, of people who cause sin, and of those who reject Jesus. All who are not ready for Jesus when he returns will suffer judgment in the same way that the wicked in the antediluvian world died when the flood came upon them (24:38–39). In lieu of this, Jesus commands the disciples to watch, endure persecution, and do his work (7:15; 24:4; 42–43; 25:13; 26:41).

The call to flee from the wrath to come (judgment) looms large in Matthew's Gospel (3:7). An ax is laid at the root of the tree that doesn't bear good fruit. The bad tree is chopped down and thrown into the unquenchable fire (3:10; 7:20). The disciples are admonished to fear God because he can destroy both the soul and body in Gehenna (10:28). Jesus warns the disciples that it is better to lose a hand, foot, or eye that causes you to sin than to go to Gehenna with a complete body (5:29–30). Destruction (Apollyon) awaits the masses who travel down the broad way (7:13). The wicked disciples are cast away on the Day of Judgment (7:23).

The Greek verb to judge (*krino*) implies separating. In Matthew's gospel, Jesus' winnowing fork is in his hand. He separates the wheat from the chaff (3:12). The chaff is thrown into the fire. The man not wearing the wedding garment is separated from the other guests when he is forcefully removed from the wedding celebration and thrown into the deep darkness where there will be weeping and gnashing of teeth (22:13). When judgment comes, two men will be in the field. One will be taken and the other left. Two women will be grinding at the mill. One will be taken and the other left (24:41–42). The unfaithful servant who was not doing the master's work when he returns is cut in pieces and thrown out with the unbelievers (24:51). The Pharisees are called a brood of vipers. They won't escape being judged and dispatched to Gehenna (3:7; 23:33). Jesus separates the wheat from the tares (13:30), the good fish from the bad fish (13:48), the wise virgins from the foolish virgins (25:10), the faithful servant from the wicked servant (25:30), and the sheep from the goats (25:41). In each case, fire, darkness, gnashing of teeth, weeping, and destruction await those who are sent to hell.

Those who oppose Jesus are called the children of Satan (John 8:44). Like the weeds sowed among the wheat (Matt 13:38–39), they are the seed

---

are ashamed to talk about them. For a good overview of this topic, see Burke, *Imagine Heaven*, 215–36, and Long and Perry, *God and the Afterlife*, 157–72.

of the Serpent and will share his fate on the Day of Judgment. In John 15, the vine branches that don't bear fruit are cut off and thrown into the fire because they didn't abide in the vine (Jesus). The barren fig tree in the vineyard suffers the same fate (Luke 13:7). To illustrate the point, Jesus cursed a fig tree that had no fruit. Afterward, it withered to the roots (Mark 11:14; 20). Only those who are accounted worthy will enter into the age that is to come (Luke 20:35).

In the Gospels, bearing bad fruit is a primary reason why people are thrown into hell. In contrast, a person who bears good fruit is a disciple who walks in the kingdom of God, has a relationship with Jesus, and is being transformed into the image of Christ.

Michael Green, an eminent biblical scholar, observes that judgment awaits those who practice sin and reject God's gift. Like the Gospels, Green portrays this ultimate reality in terms of a series of binary oppositions. There are two realms, light and darkness; two rulers, God and Satan; two ways, the broad and the narrow; two destinations, life and destruction; two choices, for Him or against Him; two foundations, the shifting sand and the solid rock; and two groups, the evil and the righteous.[2] Per the Gospels, there is no escaping the truth of judgment and damnation. If the words of Jesus are true, wicked people will be cast into hell on the Day of Judgment.

Is Satan the Lord of Hell?

Before moving on, I need to probe some questions. If Satan is Beelzebub or the Lord of Gehenna, could he be the master of the wicked or the caretaker of the damned who are thrown into Gehenna (Matt 13:42)? If people die in his service, do they remain in bondage to him after they die since those who serve God in this life continue to live with God when they die? Would a loving God let wicked people who reject him and choose to serve Satan live in the devil's domain as a form of judgment in the afterlife? In other words, are the dead who lived wicked lives Satan's booty? What is the domain of the damned and who has the proximate rulership over it? The next chapters will address these questions.

Following the conquests of Alexander the Great (323 BC), Greek culture (language, customs, values, laws, and religion) firmly planted itself in Palestine and around the Mediterranean basin. Not only did Greek become the *lingua franca*, it also lessened national parochialisms and unified that world.[3] Jews who lived in diaspora soon became assimilated into the Greek

---

2. Green, *Evangelism through the Local Church*, 23.
3. For a detailed explanation of Hellenism and its influences (*praeparatio evangelica*),

way. Because Greek became their primary language, many Jews stopped reading Hebrew. To accommodate the Hellenistic Jews, seventy-two rabbinical scholars translated the Hebrew Old Testament into Greek around 200 BC. This translation (Septuagint) became the primary Bible for most of the Jews. Also, it was widely quoted by New Testament writers and the early church fathers.

When the Jewish scholars translated the Old Testament into Greek, they didn't transliterate Sheol. Instead, they rendered it as Hades. In the thought of the Greek-speaking world, Hades was a defined word that included a Lord of Hades and an underworld that was sectioned off into different places where the dead resided depending on their final disposition. Bad people suffered in the Fields of Punishment. Indifferent people meandered in the Asphodel Meadows. Good people enjoyed a paradise existence in the Elysian Fields. The Isles of the Bliss resided in Elysian. Tartarus was a deep jail-like pit that lay under Hades. The defeated Titans, monsters, and other gods were banished to Tartarus.[4]

Slowly, the Greek meaning of Hades encroached upon the Old Testament meaning of Sheol and changed how Jews conceived of the afterlife. To put it bluntly, a cultural overhang created a syncretistic outcome in which the resultant Jewish Hades wasn't the same as the Hebrew Sheol or the Greek Hades.

The Old Testament doesn't present a cogent theology of heaven. Sheol is the place for the departed dead. It's described as a place of sleep and shadows. It is the resting place for the righteous and the unrighteous. When people die, they go down to Sheol. It is below (Isa 14:9). The cords of Sheol embrace the dead (2 Sam 22:6; Ps 116:3). There is no life, joy, wisdom, or remembering in the grave (Eccl 9:10). In contrast to the colorful and highly developed afterlife scenarios in Egypt, Persia, Greece, and the Mesopotamian cultures, the Jewish afterworld was insipid and unimaginative.

People were not annihilated when they went down to the grave. When Jonah cried out to God, he was rescued from Sheol by being brought back to life (Jonah 2:2). Job confesses that he would see God with his own eyes after his flesh had been destroyed because his Redeemer lives (19:25–27). David declares that he cannot escape the presence of God even if he makes his bed in Sheol (Ps 139:8).

Hebrew synonyms for Sheol are the grave, death, the depths, and the pit (see Ps 88:4–6; Ezek 31:14). In some instances, the pit refers to a separate place in Sheol. For example, in Psalm 88:6 one is sent to the lowest pit in the darkest depths.

---

see Harnack, *Mission and Expansion of Christianity*, 10–60.

4. Dixon-Kennedy, *Encyclopedia of Greco-Roman Mythology*, 143–44.

Sheol Morphs into Hades

In the New Testament, Sheol is no longer viewed as a sleepy hollow where the dead quietly rest as they await their final fate. Jesus' Parable of the Poor Beggar and the Rich Man illustrates how Sheol became a hybrid Hades (Luke 16:19–31). In the story, Hades contains a place of torment (Gehenna), a paradise (Abraham's bosom), and a great chasm (the pit). The chasm separates the place of torment from the paradise section. Each of these places corresponds to an aspect of the Greek underworld (Fields of Punishment, Elysium, and Tartarus). Interestingly, even though the Hebrew Sheol is similar to Greek Asphodel, it isn't mentioned in Jesus' parable. Gerard van den Aardweg would argue that Purgatory is the equivalency of Asphodel.[5]

When employing parables, Jesus uses common imagery that everyone readily understood. He talks about sowing seeds, fishing, weddings, lost coins, sheep, pigs, harvesting, vinedressers, wayward children, and unjust judges. The original audience could identify with his parables because they related to everyday life. This enabled Jesus to use parables as a delivery mechanism to communicate spiritual truths. A spiritual truth is embedded in each parable. One will not understand the spiritual truths that are conveyed in parables if one doesn't understand the imagery of the stories.

Even though the parable genre doesn't require one to interpret the context in a literal way, one can assume that the people who heard the Parable of the Rich Man and the Poor Beggar already bought into the language of Hades and were familiar with the concept as Jesus employed it.[6] Otherwise, the Hades language would have occluded the main point. In other words, the people who heard the parable about the poor beggar already understood the concept and accepted Jesus' use of Hades and Paradise.

The parable isn't about Hades. Rather, the story illustrates the future plight of the Pharisees who don't keep the Torah and refuse to follow Jesus. In this case, the place called Hades is like a movie set in which a drama is played out. In the drama, a poor beggar (Lazarus) died and went to Paradise and the greedy rich man (Pharisee) died and went to Gehenna where he

---

5. Aardweg, *Hungry Souls*, 20–22.

6. According to Blomberg, *Interpreting the Parables*, 203–4, and Jeremias, *Parables of Jesus*, 183–86, the Parable of the Rich Man and the Poor Beggar borrows material from the story of the Poor Scholar and the Rich Publican. In that story, a dream reveals that the poor scholar will live in paradise and the rich publican will suffer on the banks of a stream trying to reach the water to get a drink. The punishment of the rich publican is similar to that of Tantalus in Greek mythology. He stands in clear cool water. Whenever he tries to drink, the water moves away from him. In the Parable of Rich Man and the Poor Beggar, the rich man asks Abraham to send the poor beggar to him with a glass of water because he suffers from thirst.

agonized in fire because he didn't love his neighbor or care for the poor as God required. Even though he voiced deep regret, the rich man couldn't escape from the flames. Sadly, a great chasm prevented kindly Abraham from sending Lazarus to help him. While being consumed by his suffering, the rich man begs Abraham to send Lazarus to tell his brothers to repent so they won't share his fate. Abraham replies that even if a dead man returned from the grave to warn his brothers, they wouldn't repent.

In the larger context of Luke, Jesus is the man who came back from the dead. When his disciples preached the gospel and warned about the wrath to come, the religious leaders rejected them just like they rejected Jesus. The story gives hope to the righteous poor and motivates the wicked rich to repent.

The fact that Jesus used a common understanding of Hades to tell a parable about the need to repent and avoid the horrors of divine judgment doesn't mean that Jesus endorsed the Hades imagery that he used. Still, he built every other parable around something that really existed. It's hard to find anything in the text to indicate that Jesus didn't expect the hearers to accept the Hades he described as a real place.

If Jesus intended the story to illustrate a literal place, Hades is a catchall for the dead who are in limbo while they await the final judgment. Furthermore, a great chasm separates the damned from the blessed in a singular place. The torment section could be termed Gehenna and the heavenly section could be termed Paradise. The chasm could refer to the pit (Ps 88:6).[7]

In the Old Testament, the pit was a deep spot associated with death and Sheol. If the chasm is the pit, it could refer to Tartarus. It is where the Watchers who defiled women in Genesis 6 are reserved in chains of darkness as they await the coming judgment (2 Pet 2:4).[8] In Revelation, it is termed the "bottomless pit." The pit is styled an abyss or a deep well that is locked from the outside. Like a jail, Satan and evil spirits are held prisoner in the deep pit (Rev 9:1). In the Bible, Tartarus, the abyss, and the pit have a parallel meaning.

Interestingly, Paul says that he was caught up to the third heaven and snatched up to Paradise (2 Cor 12:2; 4). Most likely, this vision occurred after he was stoned and left for dead in Lystra. He revived when the believers surrounded him (Acts 14:19–20). I would argue that Paul had a near-death

---

7. First Enoch 22:8–13 refers to a place where the dead are partitioned into three sections. Some have suggested that this text influenced how Jesus told the Parable of Lazarus in Hades. See Lumpkin, *Book of Giants*, 42.

8. In 1 Enoch 21, Enoch views the place where fallen Watchers are bound until the Day of Judgment. He describes it as a chaotic place with no heaven above or earth below. The fallen angels burned in fire.

experience with a vision of heaven and that the believers called him back from the dead when they prayed over him. Others who have come back from the dead have recorded similar visions.[9]

Cancer doctor, Jeffrey Long, has collected and reviewed thousands of detailed testimonies of people who have died and been revived.[10] Each entry includes answers to an extensive questionnaire and narrative summaries. Even though variation exists between individual accounts, a clear pattern emerges when all the accounts are viewed together. For example, approaching a bright light is one of the most common features of those who have good afterlife experiences. When people claim to see God, they describe him as a brilliant light that is brighter than a million suns. Paul uses similar language to describe God in 1 Timothy 6:16 when he says that God dwells in unapproachable light.

Additionally, Paul's autobiographical commentary in 2 Corinthians 12 matches what people who have heavenward NDEs state. Paul was out of the body, was caught up to Paradise, received great revelations, and saw things that cannot be explained or easily recounted. In 1 Corinthians 2:9, Paul says that God has revealed to him that which no eye has seen, no ear has heard, and no human mind has conceived. These are the things that God has prepared for those that love him. One will see an obvious parallel when these comments are compared to the collective comments of those who have had heavenly NDEs.

More to the point, in the Pauline passage, Paradise and third heaven are used interchangeably. Paul went up to the third heaven. Obviously, the Paradise to which Paul is referring isn't the same Paradise to which Jesus' story refers since the third heaven is the abode of God and isn't juxtaposed to hell. In popular thought, the second heaven was the abode of Satan because he is the ruler of the kingdom of the air (Eph 2:2). Ruler implies a kingdom and kingdom assumes a place. Still, the paradise to which the parable refers isn't located in the third heaven.

Furthermore, unless Jesus resides in the paradise section of Hades, Hades isn't the location of his departed saints in this era. Scripture makes it clear that Jesus ascended to the highest heaven. Second Corinthians 5 says that the saints are separated from God while they are in their mortal bodies. However, after they are released from them by death, they will be present with the Lord. "For we know that if the earthly tent we live in is destroyed, we have a building from God, an eternal house in heaven, not

---

9. For an excellent discussion on this episode, see Burke, *Imagine Heaven*, 55–57.
10. Long and Perry, *God and the Afterlife*, 16, 82–87.

built by human hands" (2 Cor 5:1). Jesus' followers will be with him in the Father's house (John 14:3).

If Paradise was a blissful place in Hades before Jesus' resurrection, Jesus may have passed through it on the day he was crucified since he went down to Hades. That would explain why he told the thief on the cross that he would be with him in Paradise on that very day (Luke 23:43). On that day, Jesus descended to Hades. As such, the Paradise to which Jesus referred wasn't the high heavens. Obviously, Jesus didn't remain in Hades (the abode of the dead) after his resurrection. Perhaps the entire death process changed following Jesus' monumental death, descent into Hades, resurrection from the dead, and ascension to the highest heaven.

Regardless, in this post-resurrection age, believers no longer rest in the grave or go to Hades when they die. Rather, they go to Jesus and live very active lives. When one accounts for this change, there is no built-in contradiction between the Old Testament use of Sheol and the New Testament use of Hades.

7

The Gates of Hades Will Not Prevail

In Matthew 16:18a, Jesus says, "You are Peter, and on this rock I will build my church." When commenting on this passage, most people focus on the identification of "the rock." Based on linguistic pointers in the original text, I argue that the rock is not Peter, but the affirmation that Peter made about Jesus when he said, "You are the Christ, the Son of the living God" (Matt 16:16).[1] When people utter Peter's confession, place their trust in Jesus, and reject Satan, God transports them from the kingdom of darkness into the kingdom of light. That affirmation is the foundation on which God has built his church in this world.

Right after declaring that he would build his church on the confession that Peter made, Jesus asserts, "And the gates of Hades will not overcome it" (Matt 16:18b). To what did Jesus refer when he declared that the Gates of Hades would not prevail?[2] There are four main approaches to answering this question. First, many argue that the phrase is a euphemism for "the power of death." They interpret it to mean that physical death won't steal people from God. The New Testament upholds this truth. For example, when Jesus avows that he is the resurrection and the life, he also asserts that believers who die a physical death will continue to live in him. They will never die (John 11:17–34). In other words, the eternal life that believers obtain when they receive Christ continues after physical death.

---

1. Literally, the text says, "You are *Petros* (Peter) and on this *petra* (rock) I will build my church." *Petros* is masculine singular and *petra* is feminine singular.

2. The Gates of Sheol (Hades) are mentioned four times in the Old Testament (see Job 38:10; Ps 9:13; 107:18; Isa 38:10).

Moreover, the Apostle Paul proclaims that physical death can't separate believers from God. Romans 8:37–39 gives this foundational truth a spiritual warfare twist. "No, in all these things we are more than conquerors through him who loved us. For I am convinced that neither death nor life, neither angels nor demons, neither the present nor the future, nor any powers, neither height nor depth, nor anything else in all creation, will be able to separate us from the love of God that is in Christ Jesus our Lord."

The powers to which Paul refers are the spiritual forces of evil in heavenly places. They are the cosmic powers that seek to defeat and destroy the church. In truth, the saints fight against the devil himself when they align with God and do his will in this life (Eph 6:11–13). That is why Paul extols his readers to put on the full armor of God.

Even when the devil wins a tactical victory and the saints die at the hands of Satan's servants, the believers share in Christ's victory. When speaking to those who faced persecution, Jesus exhorted the disciples not to fear those who kill the body but cannot kill the soul (Matt 10:28). Satan can inflict physical harm, but he cannot destroy the soul. Those who die for Christ win the battle and obtain an eternal reward that will never be taken from them.

Likewise, Revelation 2:10 encourages those who are being attacked by Satan. "Do not be afraid of what you are about to suffer. I tell you, the devil will put some of you in prison to test you, and you will suffer persecution for ten days. Be faithful, even to the point of death, and I will give you life as your victor's crown." The victor's crown is called the Crown of Life (*zoe*). Zoe refers to the eternal life that God gives to believers when they believe. It transcends the flesh and can't be taken away by physical death.[3]

In the New Testament, those who suffer for the faith are called martyrs. In the original language, the term means witness. In Revelation 2:13, Jesus calls Antipas his faithful witness (martyr) because he died for him. When faithful Christians bear up under extreme persecution and death, they give a clear witness to Christ. When this happens, God works through their suffering to further his cause.

Because of this, killing the saints is a tactic of last resort. Satan would prefer to corrupt the church and cause the saints to recant when persecuted.

---

3. John contrasts physical life (*bios*) with eternal life (*zoe*). The physical life is passing. However, the spiritual life that God gives to believers is eternal. It is a present reality that will never be taken away. Speaking of his disciples, Jesus says, "I give them eternal life, and they shall never perish; no one will snatch them out of my hand. My Father, who has given them to me, is greater than all; no one can snatch them out of my Father's hand. I and the Father are one" (John 10:28–30). The one who attempts to snatch the believers is Satan.

That is why Jesus sternly warns the disciples not to deny him before men when persecuted and threatened with death (Matt 10:33). God won't abandon his children to death, hell, or Satan. In the end, the saints cannot be defeated by death or Satan when they stay faithful to God. Rather, death is the gateway to victory and eternal life.

This point is wonderfully illustrated in Acts 7. While being stoned to death, Stephen peered into heaven and caught a glimpse of God's majesty. As he gazed, he saw Jesus. At that moment, nothing else mattered. He had won the battle. Death was his liberation from suffering and his passport to ultimate victory.

The same wherewithal enabled Peter, John, James, Paul, and Barnabas to stand firm when they were flogged, chained in the inner prison, beaten, stoned, shipwrecked in the cold sea, boiled in oil, crucified upside down, and beheaded. In Hebrews 12:1, they are among the great cloud of witnesses that encourages saints of all ages to stand firm in their sufferings.

In sum, when "Gates of Hades" is understood as a euphemism, it can refer to physical death. When the death of the saints is linked to persecution, death can be viewed as a means by which Satan attempts to destroy the church. In response, Jesus asserts that the intentional killing of the saints won't destroy the church. When one considers the tremendous suffering that the saints of the early church endured for their testimony that Jesus was Lord, this interpretation is appealing. However, the larger context in which Jesus spoke about the Gates of Hades does not support this euphemistic interpretation.

Other Possible Interpretations for Gates of Hades

A second interpretation renders Gates of Hades as Satan's kingdom. In this light, the text could be translated as "the kingdom of Satan won't prevail against it." His kingdom includes cosmic powers and supernatural authorities that have aligned themselves against Christ. Like the above interpretation, Scripture also supports this interpretation. Furthermore, it is central to the spiritual warfare theme that is illuminated throughout the Bible.

Immediately following Matthew 16:18, Jesus tells the disciples that he must go to Jerusalem and die on the cross. Upon hearing this, Peter became indignant. Emphatically, he told Jesus that this would not happen to him. Like the others, Peter believed that Jesus would restore Israel, reign in Jerusalem, and "remain forever" (John 12:34). When Peter tells Jesus not to die on the cross, Jesus hears the voice of Satan. It is the same temptation that confronted him in the wilderness at the start of his ministry.[4]

Jesus responds with an immediate rebuke. "Get behind me, Satan! You are a stumbling block to me; you do not have in mind the concerns of God, but merely human concerns" (Matt 16:23). In plain English, the kingdom of Satan won't prevail against the kingdom of God. When Satan attempts to interfere, Jesus rebukes him. The rebuke is a reminder that God has final authority and that Satan won't triumph.

A third interpretation is similar to the last interpretation. It looks at the Gates of Hades in terms of a symbolic entryway. In the biblical world, the gateway into a city was a guarded place where announcements were made and decisions were rendered. The elders met at the gates. Court could be convened at the gates. It was a place of power and plans. In this case, the Gates of Hades symbolizes Satan's rule, authority, and dominion. Simply stated, Jesus declares that Satan's rule and his scheming won't prevail against God's plan for salvation.

This interpretation sounds inviting. Still, when Jesus talked about the Gates of Hades, was he using figurative language in accordance with one of the above interpretations? If he referred to an actual place in the spiritual realm, none of the above interpretations capture the deeper meaning of the phrase. Could a literal Gates of Hades be the entrance into Satan's abode?

Four, before you dismiss the thought, think about this. There is a real heaven in which God, holy angels, and saints dwell. That heaven has an entrance. In common parlance, it is called the pearly gates (Rev 21:21). The patriarch Jacob claimed to have seen it in a dream. Angels came forth from it. When he awoke, he called the place the Gate of Heaven (Gen 28:17). Many people who have had a heavenward NDE also talked about the gateway into the celestial city.[5] When Jesus speaks of Gehenna, he is also referring to a real place. Wherever that place is, it must have an entrance. Could that entrance be called the Gates of Hades?

Is Hell a Real Place?

It is difficult for the natural mind to grasp this thought because Western people identify "real" with physical reality, things that they can perceive

---

4. "Again, the devil took him to a very high mountain and showed him all the kingdoms of the world and their splendor. 'All this I will give you,' he said, 'if you will bow down and worship me.' Jesus said to him, 'Away from me, Satan! For it is written: "Worship the Lord your God, and serve him only"'" (Matt 4:8–9).

5. Burke, *Imagine Heaven*, 298–316.

by sensory perception. For example, it was famously reported that Russian cosmonaut Yuri Gagarin stated, "I have been to heaven and I didn't see God." Even though the quote has been disputed, it resonated with many atheists and was used by Nikita Khrushchev to poke fun at the idea of a literal heaven.

Also, even when we do not see them, we affirm that spiritual beings are real. In the same way, spiritual topography is real. In fact, historical Christianity affirms that Jesus descended into Hades when he died just as it affirms that he rose from the dead and ascended into heaven.[6] The Bible ratifies this idea when it declares that God didn't abandon Jesus in Sheol (Ps 16:10; Acts 2:27; 13:35). Orthodoxy affirms that a human Jesus died a real death and descended to a real place called Hades before he was raised. In the New Testament and ancient Christian creeds, Hades isn't a mere code word for physical death.

The geographic context of Matthew 16 can help at this point. When Jesus spoke to the disciples about the Gates of Hades, he was in Caesarea Philippi. The Jews called that area Bashan. Purportedly, it is the place where the Watchers came down to Earth (Gen 6). It is also a gateway to the realm of the dead. In other words, it was ground zero for spiritual warfare.[7]

The ancient Roman world had many reputed entrances to the underworld. In fact, recent archeology has uncovered one of them. In Hierapolis, a temple to Pluto (Hades) hides a deep cave. When one ventures into the cave, one will discover a gilded entrance to the underworld with mosaics. In ancient times, any living creature who came near the doorway died because poisonous gases come out of the cave entrance. Only the eunuch priests of Pluto could enter the cave and survive. Some have speculated that they held their breath or that they walked between hidden pockets of fresh air.[8] Regardless of the portal through which a person, hero, or god entered the underworld, when they arrived, all had to go to through the Gates of Hades.[9]

---

6. The Apostles' Creed states, "I believe in Jesus Christ, his only Son, our Lord, who was conceived by the Holy Spirit, born of the Virgin Mary, suffered under Pontius Pilate, was crucified, died, and buried; he descended to hell. The third day he rose from the dead. He ascended into heaven and is seated at the right hand of God the Father Almighty from there he will come to judge the living and the dead."

7. Heiser, *Supernatural*, 112. In *Reversing Hermon*, 96–102, Heiser explores the relationship between the Watchers and the Mount Hermon area by analyzing Gospel texts.

8. Snodgrass, "Archaeologists Find a Classic Entrance."

9. Many ancient peoples had underworld gods who resided in guarded places with pathways to the surface. Recently, the news was widely reported that explorers discovered a Mayan door to hell. Xibalba is the Mayan underworld, or what the Mayans called "a place of fright." The Mayans believed that hell and its entrance were real. The underworld gods were able to go out through a tunnel, cause mayhem, and then retreat to

In Greek mythology, the Gates of Hades were guarded by a great monster named Cerberus. The fearsome three-headed behemoth was the grandson of the primordial gods Gaia and Tartarus. No god or mortal could enter or leave Hades without his permission. The legendary hybrid giant protected the Gates of Hades. In the same way, if Satan had a stronghold, one would expect that its gates would be well protected.

Chapter 5 showed that many of Satan's names refer to him as a ruler. If Satan is a ruler, he reigns over a kingdom. If that kingdom is a real place in the spiritual realm, it has an entrance. The entrance keeps some people out and others in. In the same way that heaven isn't physically accessible in this world, one doesn't have to assume that Hades isn't real because it's not accessible in this world. Likewise, in the same way that one affirms that heaven is real even though one can't see it or go to it; a Bible-believing Christian should affirm that Hades is real.

Furthermore, when speaking about casting out Satan, Jesus refers to overpowering the strong man so he can enter his house and plunder it. He says, "In fact, no one can enter a strong man's house without first tying him up. Then he can plunder the strong man's house" (Mark 3:27). Luke's version is more emphatic. "When a strong man [Satan], fully armed, guards his own house, his possessions are safe. But when someone stronger [Jesus] attacks and overpowers him, he takes away the armor in which the man trusted and divides up his plunder" (11:21–22).

To enter the strong man's house, one must pass through his door. Simply stated, Matthew 16:18 means that the Gates of Hades won't prevent Jesus from gaining access to Satan's stronghold or to those who are in his bondage.

In the Gospels, casting out demons points to the binding of Satan. Yet, in a fuller way, Satan wasn't completely bound until Jesus entered Hades after his crucifixion. At that time, he "plundered" his house (Hades).

Colossians 2:15 gives more details on this event. It declares that Jesus disarmed the demonic rulers and made a public example of them when he triumphed over them. The language comes from a military triumphal procession in which the defeated are paraded in humiliation.

Truly, the Gates of Hades didn't prevail against Jesus when he died. Revelation 1:18 says that Jesus holds the keys to Death and Hades (the Gates of Hell). I have a hunch that he took them from the previous owner.

---

their stronghold. To placate the gods so they wouldn't destroy everything, the Mayans sacrificed humans. Researchers have discovered many Mayan pathways to hell. Each is covered with human skulls.

Setting the Captives Free

To add intrigue to this scenario, some believe that Jesus preached to those who perished before the time of Noah when he descended to Hades. Afterward, he liberated the prisoners who received him (1 Pet 3:19). That is, when Jesus descended into Hades, he defeated Satan and emancipated the confined souls that chose to follow Christ by freeing them from death's (Thanatos') domain. That's why the Bible says that he led captivity captive when he ascended (Eph 4:8–10). This is another example of how Jesus plundered the strong man's house.

The Great Catechism puts it this way.

> The frequent New Testament affirmations that Jesus was "raised from the dead" presuppose that the crucified one sojourned in the realm of the dead prior to his resurrection. This was the first meaning given in the apostolic preaching to Christ's descent into hell: that Jesus, like all men, experienced death and in his soul joined the others in the realm of the dead. But he descended there as Savior, proclaiming the Good News to the spirits imprisoned there . . . Jesus did not descend into hell to deliver the damned, nor to destroy the hell of damnation, but to free the just who had gone before him . . . Christ went down into the depths of death so that "the dead will hear the voice of the Son of God, and those who hear will live." Jesus, "the Author of life," by dying destroyed "him who has the power of death, that is, the devil, and delivered all those who through fear of death were subject to lifelong bondage."[10]

One thing is certain, Jesus didn't sneak out of Hades. The power of God raised him from that place (Heb 13:20). Acts 2:24 says, "God raised Him up again, putting an end to the agony of death, since it was impossible for Him to be held in its power." In the original Greek, when speaking of death, it says that it was impossible for Jesus to be held under him. In truth, the personified Thanatos couldn't hold Jesus. He broke free from his grip.

In sum, I have argued that Hades was the epicenter of Satan's kingdom and his rule. In Matthew 16, Jesus is anticipating his death and descent into hell when he tells the disciples that the Gates of Hades wouldn't prevail. Jesus' response to Peter's words of temptation shows this. When Jesus entered Hades after his crucifixion, he bound Satan and set the captives free in accordance with his teaching on binding the strong man.

---

10. Vatican, *Catechism of the Catholic Church*, paras. 631–35.

8

Hades in Paul's Letters and the Book of Revelation

In the Old Testament, the terms hell, death, and destruction have a parallel meaning. Not only do they relate to the underworld, they also represent various underworld gods who are called Sheol (hell), Mot (death), and Abaddon (destruction). As was noted in chapter 1, the Septuagint and Greek New Testament refer to them as Hades, Thanatos, and Apollyon. The Hebrew Bible imported the names from other Near Eastern languages. When incorporated into the Bible, a dual meaning combines the god with what he represents. The beings are portrayed as powerful demons or monsters who have power over those who dwell in the underworld.[1]

The conflating of underworld gods with places is not unique to the Bible. As a case in point, in Greek mythology, Hades is a powerful god and the place of the dead. Likewise, the Greek god Tartarus is a premortal being and a place where rejected gods are imprisoned. The Bible refers to Tartarus as the pit, abyss, or great chasm.

The coupling of two or more words with similar meanings is common in Hebrew poetry. For example, Isaiah 38:18 says, "For the grave cannot praise you, death cannot sing your praise; those who go down to the pit cannot hope for your faithfulness." In this Scripture, "grave," "death," and "pit" are in parallel. So are "praise you," "sing your praise," and "hope for your faithfulness."

---

1. Barstad, "Sheol," 768–70. For a scholarly explanation, see Kosior, "Underworld or Its Ruler?"

Many Old Testament texts place Sheol and destruction (Abaddon) together (see Job 26:6; Prov 15:11; 27:20). Others place Sheol and death (Mot) together. For example, 2 Samuel 22:6: says, "The cords of Sheol surrounded me; the snares of death confronted me" (NASB). Proverbs 5:5 says, "Her feet go down to death, her steps take hold of Sheol" (NASB). Hosea 13:14 says, "From the power of Sheol I will ransom them, from death I will redeem them" (NASB).[2]

However, when Paul quotes Hosea 13:14, "Where, O death, are your plagues? Where, O grave (Sheol), is your destruction?," he doesn't follow the parallel construction. Instead, he drops the reference to Hades and substitutes death. He writes, "Where, O death, is your victory? Where, O death, is your sting?" (1 Cor 15:54–55).[3] Since Paul knew the original Hebrew and Greek translation of it, why did he change the Sheol/death coupling to death/death when he quoted it? In fact, the Pauline corpus doesn't make a single reference to Hades or Sheol. Yet, it makes fifty-seven references to death and thirty-three references to heaven.

Paul says that the saints are seated with Christ in the heavenlies (Eph 1:20; 2:6), their citizenship is in heaven (Phil 3:20), their hope is in heaven (Col 1:5), and God will bring them to his heavenly kingdom (2 Tim 4:18). Paul believes that death doesn't lead to the grave (Hades). Rather, it leads to heaven. This builds on the idea that Jesus liberated the saints from death and that Hades has no power over them. Simply stated, since the resurrection of Jesus, Paul believes that the saints don't go to a resting place called Sheol (Hades) when they die. They go to heaven. As such, he no longer refers to the place.

Unlike Paul, Revelation 6:8 couples Death and Hades in the same Scripture. Death and Hades "were given power over a fourth of the earth to kill by sword, famine and plague, and by the wild beasts of the earth" (Rev 6:9). Death rides forth and Hades follows behind him. As they go, Death kills the masses and Hades swallows them up.

Even though war, plagues, natural disasters, famine, and acts of God are the means by which people die, there is a force or a will behind the events. The force is called death. He is riding a pale horse. Hades gobbles up

---

2. In an Ugaritic text, the god Mot (death) sits enthroned with the Helel (Shining One) from Isaiah 14:12. Typically, Mot is paired with Sheol. Both are underworld gods. The Shining One (Lucifer) of Isaiah 14:12 is cast down to the underworld. Here he sits enthroned as the lord of hell. It appears that the gods of the underworld have an assembly that parallels the heavenly council (Mullen, *Assembly of the Gods*, 239–40).

3. There is a variant Greek reading of 1 Corinthians 15:15 in which a scribe corrected *Codex Sinaiticus* (AD 330) to align it with the Septuagint. A scholarly consensus agrees that Hades is not the preferred reading in 1 Corinthians 15:55 and that Paul never uses the word in his writings. See Metzger, *Textual Commentary*, 570.

those who are killed. Afterward, he is engorged on the innumerable multitude of sinners that falls into his deep belly.

The Old Testament uses similar language to describe death and hell. In Isaiah 5:14, hell is a monster that swallows those who are dying of famine and thirst. He expands his jaws and opens his mouth wide and engorges himself on those who fall into him. When Korah led the people in rebellion against Moses, the earth opened its mouth and devoured him and his followers. They all went down into the realms of the dead (Sheol). Afterward, the earth shut its mouth (closed over them). Hell was engorged (Num 16).

In the Greek world, Thanatos is like the Death Angel that killed the firstborn of Egypt (Exod 12:23). Many English speakers call him the "grim reaper." He is the collector of souls or the one who takes the dead to Hades. Most societies have stories about him.

In Revelation 20:13–14, Death and Hades regurgitate the dead that are in them so they may be judged. Afterward, both Death and Hades are thrown into the Lake of Fire. How does one throw an inanimate state of being (death) or a place (Hades) into the Lake of Fire? The graphic personification of these terms shows the growing influence of Greek culture on early Christian writers. By the time that Revelation was written, Christianity had become a largely Greco-Roman affair with Jewish roots.

In the Greek world, Tartarus was often considered a part of Hades. Technically, it is below Hades and Hades is below the earth. It is a holding place for the god Chronos, the defeated titans, and other ancient deities. As was previously stated, Tartarus is very similar to the bottomless pit in Revelation in that it is a holding cell for evil supernatural beings (Rev 9:2; 20:1). For example, the "sons of God" who left their first estate and mated with women (Gen 6:2–4) are held chained in Tartarus (2 Pet 2:4; Jude 1:6).[4]

In Revelation 11:7, the beast who comes up from the abyss to attack the two witnesses is Satan. He is called Apollyon. It corresponds to the Hebrew Abaddon (Rev 9:11). He is the destroyer. In Revelation 20:1–3, a great angel from heaven captures Satan and throws him back into the bottomless pit. The entrance is sealed and locked so that he can't return from the abyss. In Revelation 20:7, Satan is released from his "prison" a second time. After a

---

4. "Sons of *Elohim* [God]" refers to a class of angels in the heavenly council. Daniel calls them the Watchers, (4:13; 17; 23). The term is also used in Job 1:6; 2:1; 38:7; Psalm 29:1; and 89:6. The Bible often translates the phrase as heavenly beings. Deuteronomy 32:8 uses the phrase in the Septuagint and the oldest Hebrew manuscripts. Later versions sanitized the phrase. They replace it with sons of Adam or sons of Israel. Neither of the redacted readings makes sense. New Testament believers are called the sons of God. They will judge the world and the angels (cf. Rom 8:14; 1 Cor 6:2–3; Gal 3:26). See Heiser, "Deuteronomy 32:8 and the Sons of God."

time of deception and inciting evil, he is cast into the Lake of Fire. The Lake of Fire is his final disposition. There is no escaping from it.

Who Is the Lord of Gehenna?

This brings us back to the original question. Is Satan Beelzebub, the Lord of Gehenna (the smoldering garbage pit that collected the refuse of humanity)? The names of Satan show that he can rule over a physical location where people give themselves to his service and practice his deeds. In Revelation 2:13, Pergamum is called the throne of Satan. It was a wicked place where people worshipped Zeus and the Emperor, and persecuted God's people. Some were killed. All over the world, spiritual intercessors have discovered satanic strongholds that have a grip over certain areas and populations of people.[5] These strongholds may be like the "throne of Satan" in Pergamum. When the gospel goes forward in those areas, it must confront and neutralize the Satanic linchpin to liberate the people and bring them under the reign of God.[6]

Still, does Satan rule over an actual place in the spiritual realm? One cannot be dogmatic about the answer. However, I have tried to show that one can make a biblical case for this. If God has an abode, Satan has an abode. Even though Jesus destroyed the Gates of Hades and set the captives free, New Testament names for Satan indicate that, with the approval of God, he still rules over some domain.

John Hagee argues that Satan reigns in the second heaven and that God resides in the third heaven. The natural sky is the first heaven.[7] Philippians 2:10; Revelation 5:3; and 5:13 refer to all who are in heaven, on the earth, and under the earth three times. If this corresponds to the three-heaven concept, heaven refers to a place. The use of first, second, and third to describe the various heavens doesn't require one to assume a spatial orientation like a three-dimensional chessboard. They aren't stacked on top of each other. "Up and down" and "high and low" only have meaning when seen from a human point of reference. The second and third heavens refer to places in the spiritual realm. Trying to locate them in the material world

---

5. For New Testament references, see Simon the Sorcerer over Samaria in Acts 8, and Elymas the Sorcerer over Cyprus in Acts 13. Elymas and others are called the son of the devil (see Matt 13:38; John 6:70; 8:44; Acts 10:38; 13:10; 1 John 3:8–10).Also, based on Revelation 2:13 and other related scriptures, Derek Gilbert argues that Zeus and Baal are other names for Satan (The Great Inception, 220).

6. See Silvoso, *Prayer Evangelism,* and Smith and Hennen, *Strategic Prayer.*

7. Hagee, *Three Heavens.*

is futile. The Old Testament uses a Hebrew superlative to refer to the heaven of heavens or the highest heaven (Gen 28:12; Deut 10:14; 1 Kgs 8:27).[8]

Whatever you call it, I believe that Satan rules over a place where the wicked dead reside while waiting for the day of God's final judgment. The Beelzebub name implies this. Also, Revelation distinguishes between the first death and the second death. The first death is the physical death of a person. Afterward, the dead person goes to Gehenna or Heaven. The Paradise that is called Abraham's Bosom no longer exists in Hades. Those who have given themselves to Satan in this life will go into his domain after death while they await their final judgment at the end of time.

The Great White Throne Judgment is the second death (Rev 20:11–15). It is the final judgment for people, demons, and the devil. The wicked are thrown into the Lake of Fire. The Lake of Fire isn't Gehenna. Those who love God and live righteous lives are saved from that judgment. If Satan has proximate rulership over the wicked during this age in a place called Hades or Gehenna, he won't have it in the age to come when he is thrown into the Lake of Fire.

An Inclusivistic Option

Others have modified this perspective by adding an inclusivistic option that tries to reconcile the notion of a loving God with the reality of eternal damnation. Since Scripture doesn't show that God presides over hell, they assert that God allows Satan to manage hell because a holy God would not want to associate himself with it. Afterward, they ask a vexing question. What happens to those who have never heard the gospel and have lived according to the light that they had when they die?

Those who believe in Jesus and serve him in this life go to be with him at death. Absent from the body, present with the Lord (2 Cor 5:8). They have a consciousness after death. They rejoice as they wait for the day of resurrection when they will be given immortal bodies. On the other hand, the wicked dead who reject Christ and do evil in this life go into their master's domain (Satan) when they die. They will remain in that state until the Day of Judgment when all will stand before God.

A third group is composed of those who have never heard the gospel or rejected Jesus. They are people who lived good lives in accordance with the light that they had. They sleep when they die. During that time, they are like the shades who rest in Sheol. If Jesus would have included a place like the Fields of Asphodel in the Parable of the Rich Man and the Poor Beggar,

---

8. For more on this, refer to footnote 12 on page 29.

it would be the place where these people would be held. Possibly, Roman Catholic scholars would place this group of people in a Purgatory-like place.

On the Day of Judgment, like the wicked in Hades, the righteous who have never heard the Gospel will also appear before God's tribunal. On that day, they will be judged according to their works. Those who lived moral lives will be saved because their names will be found in the book of life (Rev 20:12–13). However, they won't be saved because they lived moral lives. Instead, they will be saved because the atonement of Jesus extends to them. Without the grace of God, no one can be saved. Technically, this position is called "inclusivism."

Even though the Bible never explicitly teaches this possibility, some Scriptures hint at it. For example, the fact that some of the people before the Great White Throne Judgment are saved based on their good works seems to affirm this option because the believing saints are excluded from the final judgment (see Rev 20:6).[9]

The possibility of a third option shouldn't influence how the church prioritizes evangelism and disciple-making. Additionally, no one can make a dogmatic assertion that the third option exists since it contradicts many exclusivistic teachings of Jesus and the early church.

In a Thumbnail

At this point, I can affirm several truths. First, those who love Jesus and serve him faithfully in this life will go to heaven when they die. When Jesus returns to Earth, they will be resurrected and given an immortal body (1 Cor 15:35–57). They skip the final judgment because they have passed from judgment unto life. Jesus has paid the penalty for their sins and they live in covenant with him.

Second, the wicked go to hell. Judgment is real. Everyone won't be saved. Sometimes hell is referred to as Hades. Hades is variously seen as a place of rest, torment, and paradise. At other times, the New Testament refers to Gehenna. It is a place of desperate torment. The ultimate hell is the Lake of Fire. Hades and Gehenna seem to have overlapping usages. Biblical hell language isn't precise.

Third, at the end of time, Satan and his demons will be thrown into the Lake of Fire. Their judgment looms. They cannot escape this fate. Satan rages now because he knows that his time is short (Rev 12:12). In 1

---

9. According to Nickelsburg, the text refers to a group of sinners who are in hell but are not being tormented. Their fate will be determined at the final judgment. See Nickelsburg, *1 Enoch*, 306–8.

Corinthians 15:24, Paul refers to this event when he says that Jesus must reign until he has put all enemies under his feet. His enemies are listed as all dominion, authority, and power. In Ephesians 6:12, he calls the enemies the rulers, the powers, the world forces of this darkness, and the spiritual forces of wickedness in the heavenly places. Death (Thanatos) is the last enemy to be destroyed. After Jesus has destroyed all enemies, he will hand the kingdom over to the Father (1 Cor 15:24–26).

Finally, this chapter considers the likelihood of the following points. One, Satan is the Lord of Gehenna and he rules over it during this age. Two, the wicked who die while in Satan's service will remain in his service after death. Three, some will rest at the time of their death. They go to a Sheol-like place. Their final fate will be determined on the Day of Judgment when God judges them according to what is written in the books. At that time, some will be saved. Others will be damned. Four, Jesus passed through Hades after his death before he was resurrected and ascended to heaven. At that time, he disarmed the rulers of hell and triumphed over them. Five, the personification of Hades and Thanatos in Revelation allows people to view Satan as a type of Hades based on the Greco-Roman mythology that dominated the Roman Empire at the time that Revelation was composed.

9

Satan before His Fall

CHAPTER 5 listed the names of Satan and reviewed the Scriptures that describe his fall. Those passages indicate that Satan wanted to become like the Most High. Pride entered his heart. His great beauty and constant access to the presence of God made him arrogant. Familiarity breeds contempt. Eventually, being the most powerful creature in the creation no longer satisfied him. He wanted to be like God. This chapter takes a step backward in time. It explores the origins of Satan.

Guardian Cherub

Ezekiel 28:1–19 speaks to the governor of Tyre. He was a wise, powerful, and crafty man who was judged by God for his sin. In the text, the prophet uses the language of an ancient myth to communicate the downfall of the king. In that way, the text has a dual referent. It also describes the downfall of Satan in that it sees a similarity in the downfall of the two.[1]

In the prophecy, the two stories are intertwined. When Ezekiel 28 is read in light of Isaiah 14, it becomes clear that the language of the prophecy refers to Satan. For example, when telling the story, Ezekiel employs language that cannot refer to a human king or a human being. In fact, Michael

---

1. Some have suggested that the second referent is to Adam and not Satan. Even though both were created perfect, lived close to God, and fell, Adam was not a guardian cherub. Plus, the language doesn't fit him as well as it does Satan. A divine rebellion undergirds the story. Adam fell when he gave into the serpent's temptation. He was a casualty of the rebellion, not the cause of it.

Heiser skillfully argues that the text refers to the serpent from Genesis 3, that the serpent was Satan, and that Satan was a member of God's heavenly council when he tempted Eve.[2]

The following phrases are used to describe the spiritual being in Ezekiel 28. He says, I am God (*El*, the term for the chief God).[3] I sit on the seat of God (*Elohim*, a Hebrew term for God and gods). He was in Eden, the garden of God. He was covered in brilliant stones that radiate light.[4] He was beautiful, wise, and shining. He was the anointed cherub. He was on the holy mountain of God, the place of the heavenly council and the throne of God. He walked among the fiery stones, a reference to other divine beings. He was corrupted by sin and was cast down to Earth.

According to Ezekiel 28, before his fall, Satan occupied a place close to the throne of God. He is called the guardian cherub.[5] This is a term of power, majesty, and special trust. Throughout the Hebrew Scriptures, God is enthroned between the two cherubim who are on both sides of his throne. This image is depicted on the ark of the covenant, the Tabernacle, and in the temple. For example, the inner sanctuary of the temple displayed two large cherubim carved from olive wood and covered in pure gold. They were seventeen feet tall and had a wingspan of seventeen feet (1 Kgs 6).[6] Cherubim were also carved on the walls of the temple and sewn into the large tapestries. One couldn't go into the temple without seeing massive images of the cherubim. Suffice it to say, the cherubim didn't resemble the cute baby cherubs that adorn gardens or the Valentine cupid who shoots love arrows. In real life, their awe evoking sight would fill any mortal with terror.

---

2. Heiser, *Unseen Realm*, 73–82.

3. In the Hebrew Bible, *El* only refers to God. *El* is combined with many other terms that refer to aspects of God or his attributes, (e.g., Eloah [God], El Olam [everlasting God], El Rophe [healing God], and Elyon [highest God]). The term *El* was borrowed from the Ugaritic pantheon. Not only was El strong, he was also wise. He is the *ab adam* or the father of humankind. When the Jews used the term, they applied it to Yahweh and didn't incorporate pagan notions about God. The Hebrew Bible employs the name 230 times (See Herrmann, "El," 274–80).

4. Compare Ezekiel 28:13 to Revelation 21:11 and 19–21. The gems associated with the New Jerusalem (the dwelling place of God) are also associated with the guardian cherub who lived in the presence of God in Ezekiel.

5. For an introduction to cherubim in the Bible, see Dickason, *Angels*, 61–65.

6. Second Chronicles 3:10–14 says that the carved cherubim in the Holy of Holies had a wingspan of twenty cubits. That equals thirty to thirty-four feet, depending on the length of a cubit. A common cubit was eighteen inches. A sacred one was twenty-one inches. If the wingspan was proportional to the body, the carved figures would have been over thirty feet tall. Assigning a natural height to the cherubim is futile since they aren't mortal beings with material bodies. Large indicates powerful.

Since God specifically commanded the Hebrew people not to make graven images that portrayed anything in heaven (Exod 20:4; Deut 5:8), one wonders why God instructed the Jews to put images of the guardian cherubim in all the sacred places. In fact, their images look like idols and could have provoked false worship.

The New Testament prohibited the worship of angels because some began to invoke them and sought to use them as mediators from whom they received divine help and revelation (Col 2:18).[7] Some Old Testament Scriptures portray heavenly beings as those who advocate for the saints. First Enoch 9:3–4, says, "Holy Ones of heaven, the souls of people are putting their case before you pleading, 'Bring our judgment before the Most High'" (Charlesworth). However, that role is not emphasized in the New Testament. Jesus is the great mediator. Christians do not pray to angels.

One can deduce that the emblazoned cherubim had symbolic meaning. They were associated with God's power, his heavenly court, and his worship. Additionally, one can presume that God wasn't averse to being associated with them. They are a permanent fixture in every throne room scene in the Bible. A being with that level of intimate access to God should be revered and respected.

In a veiled reference to the Exodus from Egypt or the descent of God on the mountain (Exod 19), David sees the Lord arriving on the backs of the guardian cherubim. God remains enthroned above the guardian cherubim even when he goes into battle (Ps 18:10). All the elements of nature (e.g., earthquakes, fire, rising smoke, wind, thick clouds, lightning, thunder, and the seas) do his bidding and attend to him. He is the God over nature (see Jonah 1:4–9). The thick darkness that surrounds him hides his glory. The image resembles the arrival of Zeus when he and the gods of Olympus battled with the giants. Four immortal wind gods in the form of horses pulled Zeus's chariot into battle. Yahweh is a warrior God and the cherubim carry him into battle (2 Sam 22:8–16; Ps 18:10).

Second Samuel 22:8-15 paints a vivid picture of God coming down from the heavens to fight. When he does, the Lord is mounted on the cherubim as he flies into battle. Thick smoke, fire, and blazing coals are around him. When God parts the heavens to descend, he soars on the wings of the wind. This is a euphemism that refers to the cherubim who carry him or to

---

7. Veneration and devotion to angels crept into New Testament Christianity. This threatened the monotheistic tone of the faith. As such, Revelation 5 and 22:3–4 portray Jesus as being worshipped in a superior way. Other tests point to the angel veneration problem in the church. See Galatians 1:18; 4:14; Hebrews 1:5–14; and 2:5–18. For more information, read Stuckenbruck, *Angel Veneration and Christology*, and Dickason, *Angels*, 109–11.

angels in general.[8] Dark clouds are under his feet. The darkness is a canopy around him. Yet, it cannot contain his brilliance. Out of the storm, he shoots bolts of lightning like an archer shoots arrows. The lightning routes the enemy.

The same imagery is depicted when God descended on Mount Sinai (Exod 19–20). God descends in fire. Smoke rises from the mountain. Thunder and lightning blast from the mountain. A think cloud envelops the mountain. From the midst of the chaos, a loud trumpet sounds. As it does, the mountain shakes.

Ezekiel 1 continues this imagery. It describes the arrival of four cherubim. They can move in any direction without turning. In some way, they are tied together and work in unison. They have eyes all around them. They move like a blaze of intense light. Fire, flashing light, thunder, splendor, roaring, and rainbow colors accompany their arrival. A dome is over their heads. When a voice speaks from the domed canopy that the cherubim are carrying, they stop moving and lower their wings. When they do, the throne of God is revealed. It is not the "real throne." Rather, it is a portable throne.

In a similar way, the priests carried the ark of the covenant into battle on poles (Josh 6:6–7; 1 Sam 4:3–8). It was the visible presence of the living God who was seated above the cherubim that adorned the top of the ark. When God speaks to Moses, his voice comes from between the cherubim (Num 7:89).

Also, in Isaiah 40:3–5, the image of the people carrying the potentate on their shoulders is associated with the arrival of the Messiah. Those who go before the carried king fill up holes, level knolls, and straighten out turns. When the Messiah comes, the glory of the Lord will be revealed and all people will see it. The Gospels apply the prophecy to John the Baptist when he prepared the people to receive Jesus (Matt 3:3; Mark 1:2–3; Luke 3:4–6). In the Gospels, Isaiah 40:3–5 has a symbolic fulfillment.

According to Ezekiel 10, there are many cherubim. They are in the temple and are close to the glory of God. The thundering of their wings sounds like the voice of God. In Genesis 3:24, God stationed cherubim to guard the way to the Tree of Life. They wield a flaming sword to fight off those who would try to gain unauthorized access. If Satan was the guardian cherub, he was a super-powerful creature who ruled over the order of cherubim.[9]

---

8. See Psalm 104:3–4. God "rides on the wings of the wind. He makes winds his messengers, flames of fire his servants." Wings of the wind refers to cherubim. Wind and spirit are the same. Some divine beings are God's messengers. He calls them, "flames of fire."

9. According to 1 Enoch 19:7, Gabriel is over the cherubim in this era. However, he

Ezekiel 28:12 may refer to another aspect of Satan's power when he was the guardian cherub. It refers to him as the sealing one. Most translations call him the "seal of perfection." However, the Hebrew word is a participle. Possibly, this refers to the one who holds the signet of God. He can seal on behalf of God. For example, in Revelation 5, an angelic being holds a divine scroll on which someone placed seven seals. Only Jesus is able to break the seals. In the ancient world, a trusted advisor to the king could use his signet ring to stamp a seal so that the content carried the authority of the king. To have the signet ring was to share the king's rulership. That duty would be consistent with a guardian cherub who desired to sit on God's throne.

Shining One or Morning Star

Isaiah 14:4–20 is similar to Ezekiel 28. The fall stories of the King of Babylon and Satan are intertwined. Like Ezekiel 28, Isaiah 14 describes a coup attempt in heaven. The Shining One who is called "Son of the Dawn" wanted to set his throne above God's throne and the thrones of the other members of the heavenly council (the stars of God). He wanted to become like God. For his crime, he was cast from heaven and sent to the underworld.[10]

The great ones of the underworld rise to greet him when he comes. They include the giant warrior kings (*rephaim*) who died in the flood. Ezekiel gets to the same point when he says that Satan was flung down to the ground (*eretz* or earth). Earth is a metaphorical rendering of lower realms.[11] Satan's abode was the netherworld, not the land above. In the same way that the serpent was cursed to crawl on its belly and eat dirt (the lowest of all the animals),[12] Satan is cursed to the lowest level. Since he tried to ascend to the highest level when he rebelled, the irony of this outcome is acute.

It should be noted that Jesus confirms what Ezekiel and Isaiah say about Satan being flung to the earth and cast out of heaven. While talking about the disciples' authority to cast out demons, tread on serpents (a veiled referenced to Satan), and overcome the power of the enemy, he reminds

---

is not called a cherub.

10. See Day, *Yahweh and the Gods*, 151–84 for a detailed analysis of this text.

11. There are "two locations of the gods: on high in heaven, and down below beneath the earth. Since the latter realm is included in the word for 'earth,' the standard reference to the pantheon as 'the gods of the heaven and earth' should be understood to mean 'the gods of heaven and the nether world" (Toorn, "God," 356).

12. While commenting on Genesis 3:14, Walton says that the serpent's curse to eat dust does not refer to its diet. Instead, it refers to its location. "The serpent is a creature of the netherworld, and denizens of the netherworld were typically portrayed as eating dust" (*Lost World*, 130).

them that he saw Satan falling out of heaven like lightning (Luke 10:17-18). Lightning doesn't fall like a leaf drops from a tree and gently floats to the ground. The Evil One was shot down to Earth like a lightning bolt. In modern language, we could say that he fell like a ballistic missile or a shooting star. The simile would not have been lost on the disciples. The pagans believed that Zeus (aka, Jupiter), the high god of the Greek pantheon, hurled adversaries down to Tartarus. The lightning bolt was his special weapon.

Lucifer is the Latin rendering of the Hebrew word *helel* (Isa 14:12). It means the Shining One. Lucifer was like the morning star (Venus) because he was the brightest star in the sky (heavens). Similarly, Job calls a group of shining heavenly beings "the Morning Stars" (Job 38:7). They also shine, but not as brightly as Lucifer. They rejoiced with God at the creation. Satan was the head of this group. The star in Matthew's nativity story was also a heavenly being. At one point, it guided the Magi to the small Jesus (Matt 2:2; 9-11).

Even though Satan is a light bearer, God is light and in him there is no darkness (1 John 1:5). He is the father of heavenly lights (Jas 1:17). God dwells in unapproachable light (1 Tim 6:16). When Jesus morphed into his divine self on the Mount of Transfiguration, his face shone like the sun and his garments became as white as light (Matt 17:2). The suffocating darkness cannot extinguish the shining light of God or overcome him (John 1:5). God's brilliance shines so radiantly that it cancels out darkness and makes other things gleam.

When Moses climbed Mount Sinai to receive the commandments from God's hand, he had a direct encounter with God. Afterward, his face shone so brightly that the Hebrew people stood at a distance from him. Out of fear, they veiled his face (Exod 24:29-35). The radiance of God's light emanated from Moses.

Since Lucifer lived in the presence of God for eons, one would expect that he would reflect the light of God. He is called an angel of light. Today, he disguises himself as an angel of light in order to deceive the believers and introduce heresy into the church (2 Cor 11:14; Gal 1:8).

First Enoch 86-88 (the Animal Apocalypse) sheds light on Isaiah 14.[13] It uses the word "star" metaphorically to refer to fallen angels. Like a

---

13. First Enoch 85-89 tells the Genesis 6 story by means of metaphor. The people are cows, the Watchers are stars, and the giants are large animals (elephants, camels and donkeys). After the stars came to the earth, they became bulls and began to mate with the cows. After the cows gave birth to the large animals, the offspring began to eat the cows. When the cows began to cry to heaven, four snow-white humanoid beings descended from heaven. They induced the large animals to kill each other. Afterward, they corralled the stars which had fallen from heaven and threw them into the abyss.

star shines in the sky, angels are luminous beings who shine. "As I looked, behold, a star fell from heaven [Satan] . . . Once again I saw a vision, and I observed the sky and behold, I saw many stars descending and casting themselves down from the sky upon the first star [Watchers]" (1 En. 86:1, 3, Charlesworth). The first star managed to rise when it fell and pastured with the cows (humans). The other stars who fell also pastured with the cows. When they did, they mated with them (women). In 1 Enoch 88:3, the fallen stars are bound by four holy angels and cast into the abyss.

Revelation 20:1–3, uses a similar image when it says "And I saw an angel coming down out of heaven, having the key to the Abyss and holding in his hand a great chain. He seized the dragon, that ancient serpent, who is the devil, or Satan, and bound him for a thousand years. He threw him into the Abyss, and locked and sealed it over him."

Second Enoch 29:3–4 also addresses the same topic as Isaiah 14 when it says, "But one from the order of the archangels [Satan] deviated, together with the division that was under his authority. He thought up the impossible idea, that he might place his throne higher than the clouds which are above the earth, that he might become equal to my power. And I hurled him out from the heights, together with his angels. And he was flying around in the air, ceaselessly, above the Bottomless [pit]" (Charlesworth).

Even though 1 and 2 Enoch aren't canonical books, they were read by the early church and referenced in the New Testament. For example, Jude 14 quotes from 1 Enoch 1:9. As such, one can assume that the New Testament writer of Revelation was familiar with 1 and 2 Enoch when he selected his language about Satan being thrown into the abyss.

Scholarly Concerns

Many Bible scholars contend that Isaiah 14 and Ezekiel 28 don't refer to Lucifer. Rather, they argue that the immediate context refers to great kings who have been thrown down.[14] For certain, both Ezekiel 28 and Isaiah 14 refer to human kings who were thrown down. However, Hebrew prophecy doesn't limit itself to a single meaning or a single referent. Often it has layers of meaning and communities of interpretation. One or more of the meanings may point beyond the immediate context. I have argued that the above-referenced prophecies do that.

---

14. In "Original State and Fall of Satan," Dickason carefully works through the scholarly issues related to the interpretation of Ezekiel 28 and Isaiah 14. He concludes that the texts have a dual reference and that they refer to Satan (*Angels*, 127–37).

Besides these, other Old Testament prophecies have a dual meaning. For example, Isaiah 7:14 says, "Therefore the Lord himself will give you a sign: The virgin will conceive and give birth to a son and will call him Immanuel." The original context clearly referred to King Ahaz's struggle with Aram and Israel. In that case, the NRSV correctly translates the passage "A young woman is with child and shall bear a son." However, the Septuagint writers understood this passage to be a prophetic promise about the coming Messiah (Matt 1:23). For that reason, they used virgin instead of young woman when they translated Isaiah 7:14. The grammatical construction in Hebrew allows for either young woman or virgin. Matthew 1:23 follows the Septuagint and shows that Isaiah 7:14 had a dual meaning. Mary was a virgin when she conceived Jesus.

10

The Heavenly Council and the Nation Gods

As a biblical scholar, Michael Heiser was trained to read the Bible through the lens of his Western, academic worldview. That predisposition caused him to miss what the Bible taught about the heavenly council. Everything changed when a friend challenged him to reread Psalm 82.[1] "God presides in the great assembly; he renders judgment among the 'gods.' . . . I said, You are 'gods'; you are all sons of the Most High" (Ps 82:1; 6). More precisely, great assembly should be translated heavenly council. In chapter 1, I associated the "sons of the Most High" with the powers and authorities that Paul mentions in his writings.

According to Heiser, the gods in the heavenly council weren't wicked demons or territorial spirits who usurped God's authority. Nor were they competing gods with whom the Most High had to fight. Rather, they were God's heavenly family. That is what the term "sons" implies. They were created by God and they served God. He loves them.

In addition to Psalm 82, twelve other Psalms talk about the same gods (*elohim*). "Do you indeed decree what is right, you gods? Do you judge people fairly?" (58:1, NRSV). "Ascribe to the Lord, you heavenly beings [lit. sons of God], ascribe to the Lord glory and strength" (29:1). "Among the gods there is none like you, Lord; no deeds can compare with yours" (86:8). "For the Lord is the great God, the great King above all gods" (95:3). "All

---

1. Heiser, *Unseen Realm*, 11–13. In *Reversing Hermon*, Heiser shows how the apocryphal and pseudepigraphal writings on this topic influenced the authors of the New Testament.

who worship images are put to shame, those who boast in idols—worship [the Lord], all you gods!" (97:7). "For you, Lord, are the Most High over all the earth; you are exalted far above all gods" (97:9). "I know that the Lord is great, that our Lord is greater than all gods" (135:5). "I will praise you, Lord, with all my heart; before the "gods" I will sing your praise" (138:1).

The Hebrew Bible refers to the members of the heavenly council by the following terms: *bene elim*—son of God (Pss 29:1; 89:7), *bene elohim*—sons of God (Deut 32:8), *bene ha elohim*—sons of God (Gen 6:2; 4; Job 1:6; 2:1), *bene elyon*—son of the Most High (Ps 82:6), *kol-elohim*—all you gods (Ps 97:7), and *qedosim*—holy ones (Job 5:1; Deut 33:2–3).

The Hebrew Bible refers to the heavenly council by the following terms: *edat el*—great assembly (Ps 82:1), *dor*—assembly (Amos 8:14), *har-moed*—mount of assembly (Isa 14:13), *qahal qedosim*—assembly of holy ones (Ps 89:6), *sod qedosim*—great council (Ps 89:8), *sod Yahweh*—council of the Lord (Jer 23:18), *sodi*—my council (Jer 23:22), and *sod eloah*—council of God (Job 15:8). The above lists are not inclusive of all scriptural references to the specific terms.[2]

The divine council terminology is similar to the terminology used by the Canaanite counterparts. However, the Hebrew usage is distinctively monotheistic. Yahweh is the only true God. He created the gods who serve him. Often, they are referred to as divine beings, holy ones, or angels.

The idea of a heavenly council or divine assembly seems strange to radical monotheists who equate such an idea with polytheism. The mere mention of the term causes some to envision Zeus presiding over the Greek gods on Mount Olympus. However, the concept is clearly established in the Bible. Even Jesus makes a reference to it in John 10:34. The following Scriptures speak about the heavenly council.

"The heavens praise your wonders, Lord, your faithfulness too, in the assembly of the holy ones. For who in the skies above can compare with the Lord? Who is like the Lord among the heavenly beings? In the council of the holy ones God is greatly feared; he is more awesome than all who surround him. Who is like you, Lord God Almighty? You, Lord, are mighty, and your faithfulness surrounds you" (Ps 89:5–8). "Holy ones" is a synonym for Watchers. They are members of the heavenly council.

Daniel 7:9–10 says, "Thrones were set in place, and the Ancient of Days took his seat . . . The court was seated, and the books were opened." That is, the holy ones sat on their thrones when God presided over the heavenly court. Daniel 4:17 declares, "The decision is announced by messengers, the holy ones [Watchers] declare the verdict, so that the living may know

---

2. Mullen, *Assembly of the Gods*, 117–18.

that the Most High is sovereign over all kingdoms on earth and gives them to anyone he wishes and sets over them the lowliest of people." In this case, the angel that came to Daniel delivered a message to him from the heavenly council.

In 1 Kings 22, God convenes the heavenly council and decrees that he wants to kill King Ahab. The members discuss the matter and agree upon a plan. They dispatch a spirit to entice Ahab into attacking Ramoth Gilead. That will cause his death. Apparently, God consults with the heavenly council, decrees what should be done, and gives the members leeway in how they carry-out his purposes. God doesn't need the council to tell him what to do. However, God wants the council because God is a relational being. In a similar way, God partners with humans to carry out his work in this age.

The book of Revelation is full of references to the heavenly council. For example, Revelation 20:4 says, "I saw thrones on which were seated those who had been given authority to judge." The twenty-four heavenly elders sit on their thrones (Rev 4:4; 11:16). They seem to be the divine counterpart to the Jewish Sanhedrin. The four living creatures (seraphim) are intermingled with them. The same group of ruling elders is referenced in Isaiah 24:23. Revelation 4; 5:5–14; 7:11–13; 14:3; and 19:4 describes the ruling elders and the heavenly throne room. In Revelation, God interacts with the world through the agency of his angels. Angels of all sorts are dispatched to accomplish his tasks. If this is a true depiction of what actually happens, we should assume that angels are very active at this time.

In his vision, Isaiah also saw the seraphim and the throne of God (Isa 6:1–10). After a seraph touched him and made him pure, Yahweh asked the heavenly council who he should send and who should go for us? Isaiah said that he would go. Even though God consults his heavenly council and works through it to accomplish his work, he also enlists the help of humans. Like the angels, they participate in his divine rule when they work to accomplish his purposes.[3] God's interactions with Moses show this.

The *Elohim*

The members of the council are referred to as the *elohim*. It is a masculine plural word that means gods. It can also refer to angels, demons, messengers, spirits, or judges. When the term refers to God, it uses a singular

---

3. First Enoch 14 recounts a similar vision when Enoch entered God's throne room. He was surrounded by the holy ones and cherubim. God's glory shone with pure white. Verse 23 says that God doesn't need his Council, but the holy ones never depart from his presence.

verb. In Genesis, Deuteronomy, Job, and Psalms, the *elohim* of the council are called the sons of *Elohim*.[4] Other Canaanite nations referred to their pantheon of gods as *elohim*. One shouldn't assume that Israel borrowed the name from them.

In Genesis 6:1–7, the sons of God mated with the daughters of Adam. This created the Nephilim or half-breeds. They were the mighty men of renown. They were the demigods of old. They did exploits. Some were giants. Regardless of their pedigree, they were evil. Worse, they corrupted the human bloodline of Adam. God sent the flood to destroy them and the evil that they caused. Before destroying the ancient world, God selected Noah and his sons in order to repopulate the world with a righteous remnant.[5]

Why were the sons of God living among the people? Genesis and the other books of the Bible don't answer this question. However, the Book of Jubilees and 1 Enoch state that two hundred were sent by God to teach people to do justice and live righteously on Earth (1 En. 6:6). They also imparted knowledge by instructing humankind regarding all things (Jub. 4:15; 1 En. 7–10). Since the Watchers and the humans were both part of God's family, it makes sense that God would have dispatched the Watchers to teach the humans how to live properly. It is doubtful that an all-knowing God would have allowed powerful Watchers to secretly go to Earth. I assume that they went with divine approbation.

At some point, the Watchers departed from their original mission and defiled themselves by laying with women. Possibly they wanted to improve the fallen nature of humans by comingling their heavenly DNA with the DNA of fallen humankind. Maybe they became jealous of humans and decided to have their own children. Perhaps, they were overwhelmed by lust and gave in to it. If they had good intentions, they went beyond the permissive will of God. For that, they were put in chains and thrown into the abyss. These powerful beings are no longer allowed to do the work of the council (2 Pet 2:4). They live in darkness as they await the judgment.

If the sons of God who interbred with humans were allied with Satan and came to Earth without God's permission, they mated with humans to corrupt the seed of the woman so that the plans of God couldn't go forward.

---

4. *Elohim* is a masculine plural. It relates to *Eloah* and *El*. Both mean God. *Elohim* takes a singular verb when it refers to God, a divine being, or a spirit.

5. Witzel shows the true universality of the flood myth in the section "The Flood Myth: Worldwide Perspective" (*Origins of the World's Myths*, 348–55). He states, "There is a flood myth, which is indeed universal" (368). Chance, by itself, can't account for this worldwide myth. All the collective flood myths from every part of the world must related to a shared memory or to a universal event. In addition to a universal flood myth, the cultures of the world also have heroes who survive and repopulation the Earth.

God told Satan at the time of Adam's fall that the seed of the woman would crush the head of his offspring (Gen 3:15). Throughout Scripture, there is an interplay between Satan's seed and the woman's seed. Cain, the Nephilim, Judas, and all who do the work of Satan are the seed of Satan. They are the sons of darkness who war against God and the seed of the woman (Matt 5:37; 8:12; 13:38; John 8:44; Acts 13:10; 1 John 3:8–10).

Since the sons of God who transgressed their place were thrown into Tartarus and are held in chains, one must assume that they rebelled against God. Otherwise, God would not have punished them. If this is the case, Satan was aided by other members of the heavenly council after the time of his original rebellion. This is a devastating idea because it means that heavenly beings fell at more than one time and may turn from God at any time.

When the sons of *Elohim* presented themselves to God in the council in Job 1 and 2, An accuser (Satan) also appeared before God. He was a member of the council before his fall and still had the right to appear before it in Job.[6] One wonders why God didn't bind him and throw him into Tartarus when he deceived Eve in the same way that he bound the Watchers who left their first estate? It has already been noted that God cursed him to live in the underworld.

Job 38:7 refers to the sons of *Elohim* as the "Morning Stars." It is a designation for those who are members of the heavenly council. They were with God when he created the physical world. God also consulted them when he created Adam. The "let us" of Genesis 1:26 isn't a royal plural or the Godhead talking to itself. Rather, it is God conferring with his heavenly council. In the Book of Jubilees, Yahweh said to the *elohim*, it is not good that the man should be alone, let us make a helpmate for him (3:4). They were invited to participate in the creation of Eve. Evidently, members of the heavenly council had access to the garden. Afterward, the Watchers brought Adam and Eve to Eden (3:90) and taught them how to till the ground and care for nature (3:15).

Jesus, the Bright Morning Star

Jesus calls himself, the Bright Morning Star (Rev 22:16). He is the chief of the heavenly council. His throne is higher than all the others and he shines brighter than they. In both Hebrews 1:9 and Psalm 45:7, Jesus is viewed as superior to the other members of the heavenly council. God has anointed

---

6. When reviewing the sons of God references in Job, Dickason contends that the satan figure that appears eleven times in Job 1–2 doesn't refer to a nameless adversary. Instead, it manifests the Evil One who was one of the sons of God (*Angels*, 60–61).

him God and set him above the sons of God. His throne will last forever. Technically, this is referred to as the Two Yahweh theory.[7]

Is Jesus just another one of the *elohim* (gods) who sit on the council? Mormonism greatly errs at this point because it sees Jesus and Satan as being of the same order. According to LDS teaching, in premortal times, they were souls without bodies. Satan was cast down to Earth because he didn't think that Jesus was worthy to be the Savior. He was jealous and led a revolt.

If Jesus and Satan were both equal members of the heavenly council, one could arrive at the LDS error by creating a scenario that is similar to the council scenes of other religions. In the false scenario, God would tell the council of his desire to save humanity from their sin. Then he would tell the members that he needed a holy one from the council to go to Earth, show the people how to live righteously, and be a sin sacrifice. The council would consider the need. After due deliberations, they would pick Jesus, the greatest member of the council. One could continue to argue that the New Testament calls Jesus Son of God because he is one of the *elohim* who are called the sons of God.

Instead, the Bible teaches the doctrine of the Trinity. Jesus is true God of true God. He is God with us. When you have seen him, you have seen the Father (John 14:9). He is in the Father and the Father is in him (John 14:10–11). When the guards came to arrest Jesus, Jesus told them, "I, am he." When he said this, the guards drew back and fell on the ground (John 18:4–6). In the original text, Jesus says *ego eimi* (I, I am). It's an intensifier in which the "I" is emphasized. When using it, Jesus identified with Yahweh, the great I Am. It is the same name that God gave to Moses (Exod 3:14).[8]

Jesus is the one through whom all things were created. He shares an eternal oneness with God the Father and the Holy Spirit. He is the expressed image of the invisible God. John 1 says, no one has seen God. However, he has revealed his son. He is the theophany of God in the Hebrew Scriptures when he is called the Angel of the Lord. In the Old Testament, the Angel of the Lord is called God, given God's attributes, worshipped, and speaks with the voice of God. He also displays the majesty and power of God. Zechariah

---

7. In *Two Powers in Heaven*, Alan Segal shows that the Jews of the Second Temple period accepted the notion that Yahweh had two forms. One was invisible to humans. The other was visible to humans when there was a theophany. Often, the second Yahweh figure appears as the Angel of the Lord or the Captain of the Host. Whenever he appears in the Hebrew Bible, he is worshiped and given God-status. He leads the Heavenly Council. In the New Testament, the second Yahweh is identified as Jesus. In addition to Segal, Michael Heiser affirms the "two Yahweh" theory in *Angels*, 121.

8. In John, Jesus identifies as the I Am (Yahweh) in the following verses: 6:35; 41; 51; 8:12; 24; 28; 58; 10:7; 9; 11; 14; 11:25; 13:19; 14:16; and 15:1; 16.

12:8 equates the Angel of the Lord with God when he uses it in parallel with the name of God.

While being tempted by Satan, Jesus reminded the devil that he was God when he said, "Do not put the Lord your God to the test" (Matt 4:7) and "Away from me, Satan! For it is written: 'Worship the Lord your God, and serve him only'" (Matt 4:10). Satan didn't dispute the claim.

Simply stated, when God takes on visible form, it is Jesus in both the Old and New Testaments. The Son isn't a son of God like the other members of the council. Rather, he is Yahweh in flesh. As the embodiment of God, he is also the head of the heavenly council and the Lord of Hosts. He is the general of the heavenly armies.

Furthermore, when the Bible affirms that Jesus created all things, it doesn't limit itself to the material world. Jesus also created the invisible thrones, rulers, and powers of the heavenly realm. That includes the angelic hosts and the members of the heavenly council. He gave them their authority.

Colossians 1:15–17 says, "The Son is the image of the invisible God, the firstborn over all creation. For in him all things were created: things in heaven and on earth, visible and invisible, whether thrones or powers or rulers or authorities; all things have been created through him and for him. He is before all things, and in him all things hold together." The term firstborn doesn't mean that Jesus was created. Rather, the term means that Jesus is the head or the chief over all things (Ps 89:27). He has the right of the firstborn son.

Besides Satan, many members of the heavenly council have rebelled against God. That is why Paul reminds the church that its struggle "is not against flesh and blood, but against the rulers, against the authorities, against the powers of this dark world and against the spiritual forces of evil in the heavenly realms" (Eph 6:12).

Fortunately, Jesus is superior to the members of the heavenly council. When Christians align with him and do his work, they are also superior to them. In fact, eighteen times New Testament believers are called the sons or children of God. In truth, when Christ returns, they will be equal to or higher than the Watchers because they will be made into the image of Christ himself (1 John 3:1–3). Even now, God has made the saints alive together with Christ and has raised them up with him, so that they are already seated with him in the heavenly realms (Eph 2:5–6). When Christians own that truth, it enables them to claim their identity and do God's kingdom work with authority and power.

All of us have down days when we are overwhelmed by evil supernaturalism and the hardships of this life. In those times, we are tempted to forget who we are, to take our eyes off Jesus, and to stop pursuing the prize that awaits us. To win the battle, we have to run the race and fight the good fight with patient endurance (Rev 12:14). When I want to give up, I remember Philippians 2:9–11. "God exalted [Jesus] to the highest place and gave him the name that is above every name, that at the name of Jesus every knee should bow, in heaven and on earth and under the earth, and every tongue acknowledge that Jesus Christ is Lord, to the glory of God the Father." This applies to every creature from the Watchers in the deepest abyss to the sons of God in the highest heaven. Someday, even the demons will bow before King Jesus.

11

High Gods and Territorial Spirits

From ancient times, peoples from all parts of the world have believed in a high god who presided over a council of lesser gods. Some say that the universal existence of a high god in every culture establishes the hypothesis of original monotheism.[1] The theory argues that polytheism devolved from primitive monotheism as the pantheon of lesser gods and ancestor spirits increased.

A highly acclaimed anthropologist by the name of Wilhelm Schmidt argued for original monotheism. To gather the necessary data, he sent researchers throughout the world to document the high god or sky god myths. The resulting ethnographic researched showed that most polytheistic traditions had high god myths. To their surprise, in most cases, the high god wasn't of any current significance. Rather, the people fixated on the lesser gods and spirits who interacted with their daily lives. It seems that folk religion developed in relationship to the appeasement of the lesser gods.

When examining ancient pantheons, some variation of the following pattern is consistently observed. The earth goddess and the sky god produce

---

1. Nineteenth-century anthropologists subscribed to evolution of religion theories. Most believed that primitive peoples lived in fear of nature. In time, they associated spiritual powers with natural phenomena. They used magic and ritual to control outcomes and manipulate spirit beings. For the evolutionists, religion mitigated anxiety. Polytheism grew out of this. Eventually, as a given culture advanced, monotheism replaced polytheism. Adherents to the evolution of religion theories believed that nonreligious rationalism (atheism) would eventually replace monotheism. Anthropology no longer accepts this theory for the same reasons that it rejects the evolution-of-culture theory. Still, social scientists mostly ignore the theistic origins of religion and posit naturalistic explanations for the development and practice of religion.

a child who lives on a tall mountain. Eventually, the mountain god is joined by siblings. In time, they kill the sky god. In the aftermath, the elder child presides over a council of gods from his high place on Earth. The other gods are a part of his family and they are bound to each other through filial ties. They also rule over aspects of his kingdom.[2] The people of the land over which the gods rule are bound to the gods. Sacrifice, worship, and service empower the gods.[3]

Gods from one region may fight with gods from another region. When this ensues, war happens on two fronts. On the ground level, the human armies battle. In the heavenlies, the gods battle. The outcome of the human battle is decided by the divine battle. When the gods of one region beat the gods of another region, the people who belong to the beaten gods worship the new gods. The defeated gods are either banished or assimilated into the pantheon of the victorious gods. People on Earth are bound to the gods who control the land on which they dwell.[4]

The Bible employs a modified version of the above concept. God is the God of the Jews. They are to have no other gods before him (Exod 20:22). He is a jealous God who has picked the Hebrew children to be his treasured possession in the land that he gave to them (the Promised Land). The land is God's portion and the Jews are God's people. They must serve the Lord in accordance with the covenant he made with them. If they serve other gods or do evil, God will spew them out of the land and bring calamity on them. Serving other gods is spiritual adultery.

If his Jews are faithful, God fights for them when they are aggressed by an enemy. When the Jews are unfaithful, God allows them to suffer defeat in the hopes that they will repent and return to him. Unlike the stories from

---

2. Witzel, *Origins of the World's Myths*, 128–32, 160–65.

3. Daniel Block shows the intricate relationship between the nation gods, the land, and the people who live in the land. He makes the following points: God assigned the sons of God to be nation gods; each had jurisdiction over a geographic territory and the people who lived in it; the nation god was to care for his people and land; the nation god was to defend his land and people from other gods/nations who attacked it (to take the land or attack the people was to attack the nation god who was assigned to that place); the people were to serve their nation god; the land over which the nation god ruled was to produce a good harvest; a disaster happens when the tie between the nation god, the land, and the people is disrupted. Israel does not have a nation god. Its God is the Lord of lords. However, God does for Israel what the nation gods do for their peoples (Block, *Gods of the Nations*, 162–68).

4. Alan Tippett coined the term "power encounter" to describe how the people of the South Pacific became Christians through a process by which they tested and rejected their ancestral gods when Jesus proved to be more powerful. Charles Kraft explains the process and expands it. See Kraft, *Power Encounter in Spiritual Warfare*, 1–16.

the other myths, the God of the Jews is omnipotent. His people can't be beaten unless Yahweh allows it to happen.

The Exodus Example

The Exodus story shows how this worked. As the cries of God's people ascended to heaven, God heard their moaning and desired to set them free. However, before he acted, he sought to partner with a person. The sovereign God selected Moses. Even though Moses battled with Pharaoh, the primary battle was between God and the spiritual powers behind the Egyptian system of oppression.[5]

Looking back on the story, one can see that God had already selected Moses when he rescued baby Moses from the reeds. After saving him, he prepared Moses for his task by causing him to live as a prince in Pharaoh's court (Exod 2:1–10). It's doubtful that the gods of Egypt realized what Yahweh's was doing or they would have intervened.

Later, God developed Moses' pastoral skills when Moses tended Jethro's sheep in the wilderness (Exod 3:1). At the right time, God appeared to Moses, told him what he wanted to do, and invited him to be the one through whom he would accomplish his work (Exod 3). If Moses would have said no, God would have found another partner.[6] Thankfully, Moses agreed to go to Egypt.

The episodes in which the Egyptian magicians mimicked Moses' miracles show that the Egyptian gods wielded spiritual power through their servants (Exod 7:11; 22; 8:7). Yes, the gods of Egypt were real spiritual beings who wielded extraordinary power through selected people in the land over which they ruled. The ensuing confrontations between Moses and Pharaoh gave witness to a battle royal in which God and the Egyptian gods fought it out through a contest of signs and counter signs.

In time, the servants of the Egyptian gods couldn't duplicate or stop God's miracles. The plagues that targeted specific Egyptian gods showed the superiority of Yahweh over the gods of Egypt. When the God of the Israelites (Yahweh) defeated the Egyptian gods, he destroyed the might of Egypt and the Israelites went free. In the aftermath, God saved the Hebrew people from their taskmasters and the wicked Egyptian gods who worked through the Egyptians to bring them into despair and ruin.

---

5. See Payne, "Discerning an Integral Latino Pentecostal Theology," 87–106.

6. Blackaby, *Experiencing God*, 51–64. See his model for the seven realities for experiencing God.

After the Hebrews left Egypt, the humiliated Pharaoh had a change of heart and sent his army after the fleeing Israelites. When the Hebrews were stuck between the sea and the advancing Egyptian armies, it appeared that they would be destroyed. However, God fought on behalf of his people. When Moses raised his rod, God divided the sea and the Angel of the Lord positioned himself between the Israelites and the Egyptians (Exod 14:13-14).[7] After the Hebrews crossed over on dry ground, the Lord destroyed the Egyptian army. The victory was complete. Throughout the exodus story, Moses is an actor in a war that God is fighting with and through the hosts of heaven. God is a warrior God (Exod 15:3).

The same idea is continued when the Hebrews fight their way into the Promised Land. Joshua is the human leader. However, God declares that he will fight for the people if they obey him. "My angel will go ahead of you and bring you into the land of the Amorites, Hittites, Perizzites, Canaanites, Hivites and Jebusites, and I will wipe them out . . . Worship the Lord your God, and his blessing will be on your food and water. I will take away sickness from among you, and none will miscarry or be barren in your land. I will give you a full life span" (Exod 23:23–26).

The promise came with a condition. God strictly warned the Hebrews to avoid the gods of that land. In fact, he told them to demolish the *Elohim* of the land and break their sacred stones to pieces. Every high place was to be torn down. None of the practices of the Canaanites or their gods could continue. God was going to displace them as he cleansed the land of their vile pollution. This was necessary so that Yahweh could fully dislocate the old gods and establish his rule over that land (Exod 23:20–26).

Why Did God Destroy the Canaanites?

God loves human beings so much that he refused to destroy Adam and Eve when they sinned. From the beginning, the Lord planned to rescue humankind from their sin and captivity to false gods. In fact, redemption was foreshadowed in the Garden of Eden. As such, it is hard to understand

---

7. Moses used his staff to perform miracles—e.g., turned it into a snake, parted the waters with it, and made water come out of a rock with it. When Aaron's rod sprouted, Moses gathered the other staffs that were in the Lord's presence and distributed them to the leaders of Israel (Num 17:9). Evidently, other Jewish prophets carried empowered staffs. Elisha had Gehazi lay his rod on the face of the dead Shunammite boy (2 Kgs 4:31). Even angels could use a staff to do a miracle (Judg 6:21). Isaiah 10:26 says that God will raise his staff over the waters as Moses did in Egypt. Elijah and Elisha both parted the Jordan River with a cloak symbolic of the prophet's office (2 Kgs 2:8; 14). In the New Testament, oil and prayer cloths were used in healing.

why God told the Israelites to annihilate all the people in Canaan when he brought them into the Promised Land.

Three responses to this question will be considered. First, Jubilees 7:7-17 gives additional details about the sin of Ham, the curse of Canaan, and the reason why God evicted his descendants from Canaan (ref. Gen 9:22-28). After Ham sinned against his father, Noah didn't curse Ham. Instead, he cursed Ham's youngest son, Canaan. The text doesn't say why Noah cursed Canaan. Because Noah cursed Canaan, Ham moved his family away from his father.

Later, while looking for a place to settle, Canaan stole the land that had been allotted to Shem's descendants (Jub. 10:27-34). When Canaan wrongly claimed the Promised Land and desired to establish his family in it, his father and brothers warned him, "Do not dwell in the dwellings of Shem because it came to Shem and his sons by lot. You are cursed and you will be cursed more than all the sons of Noah by the curse we swore with an oath before the holy judge and before Noah, our father" (Jub. 10:32, Charlesworth). After Canaan took the land, it was named the Land of Canaan.

Retaining one's allotted ancestral land is a sacred obligation in the Hebrew Scriptures. Not even the king can steal the ancestral land of a Jew. For example, when King Ahab confiscated Naboth's land, God cursed him with no descendants and said that the dogs would lick up the blood of his wife.[8] When viewed from this perspective, the children of Shem (the Jews) had an obligation to drive out the Canaanites from the Promised Land because they were claiming the inheritance that had been stolen from them. The Canaanites were interlopers who had no right to the land.

An interpretive lens called the missional hermeneutic uncovers the second response to the question. The hermeneutic reads the Bible to discern a grand narrative that reveals God's mission (*missio Dei*). From the beginning, God was working his plan. The Scriptures give witness to God's plan and how it was being played out at any given time. As God works his plan, the Evil One also works his plan in an effort to corrupt and disrupt God's desired outcome. Satan also has a plan and a will. Even though God suffers setbacks, his plan continues to unfold. The life, death, and resurrection of Jesus are central to God's plan of redemption, renewal, and restoration. The plan is still playing out in this age. Like Scripture, history also gives witness to God's missional purposes.

---

8. In 1 Kings 21, King Ahab attempted to buy Naboth's vineyard. Naboth would not part with it. He said, "The Lord forbid that I should give you the inheritance of my ancestors." Jezebel had Naboth stoned and Ahab confiscated his property. When the Jews entered into the Promised Land, it was divided by lot, and it belonged to the families to whom it was given.

The Exodus story reflects God's mission and points to his long-term plan. After the fall and the continued corruption following the flood, the Lord needed a place and a people from which he could re-establish his rule and his name in the earth. Following the Tower of Babel calamity, God called Abraham, Isaac, and Jacob to be his chosen ones, the people through whom he would reveal his Name, give his Law, and establish his covenant. They were the children of Shem. However, Jacob and his family were a small people living in the pagan Land of Canaan.

To keep the Hebrew children from intermarrying with the Canaanites and assimilating into their evil ways, God sent them to the Land of Goshen for 430 years. While in Egypt, the Hebrew people were segregated from the Egyptians. During this time, they became a large people.

At the right time, God called Moses to deliver the Hebrews from Egypt. When the might of Egypt was destroyed, Moses led the children of Israel to the Promised Land, the land from which they had migrated when Jacob took his family to Egypt. Passing through the Red Sea into the Promised Land represented the birth of the nation.

Even though God had promised the land of Canaan to Abraham and his children, the Canaanite peoples filled it. In order for God's purposes to go forward, the Canaanites and everything related to their evil ways had to be purged from the land. Without a land, God would have no place to plant his people, reveal his name, and establish his rule on the earth.

The need to displace the Canaanites makes sense when seen in light of God's missional purposes. Additionally, the Canaanites were a wicked people who worshipped false gods. For the same reason that God sent a flood on the evil world of Noah, God had a right to destroy the wicked inhabitants of Canaan. Afterward, God warned the Jews that the land would vomit them out if they followed the wicked ways of the Canaanites.

At this point, it is necessary to reiterate the larger purpose of clearing the land and calling the Jews. Israel was not chosen because God hated the nations and only loved the Hebrew people. God had an instrumental purpose. Israel was called to be a holy people and a nation of priests who mediated God to the world (Exod 19). The Jews were a light unto the nations. As the gentiles encountered faithful Israel, they would encounter God. The Queen of Sheba and Naaman illustrate this. Foreigners and sojourners who sought the Lord had a protected status in Israel because of God's missional design. In fact, God directed the Jews to build a court for the gentiles in the temple so that the nations would have a sanctioned place to bring offerings to God and worship him there.

As long as the Jews remained faithful and kept the covenant, God's missional purposes moved forward. Whenever the Jews abandoned God or lapsed into sin, the purposes of God were threatened. Over and over, God called wayward Israel back to him. Time after time, God saved a faithful remnant through whom his plan continued. The unfaithfulness of the Jews was the biggest obstacle to God's missional plans. Hence, the Jews became God's Achilles Heel. Satan is an expert archer.

Some spiritual warfare thinkers have proposed a third option. God sent the flood to kill all corrupted flesh. Only Noah and his family found grace in the eyes of the Lord. They were pure children of Adam. In order to preserve the seed of the woman, God needed to eliminate the Nephilim and those who had been morally and genetically contaminated. They were the seed of the serpent (Gen 3:15). They spread evil in the world. In the post-diluvian reboot, the evil seed would be destroyed and Noah and his family would continue the seed of the woman.

When Noah's family disembarked from the ark, Ham uncovered Noah's nakedness when he was drunk. The grievous sin harkened back to the wickedness of the previous era. It shows that he had been morally corrupted by that world. However, instead of cursing Ham, Noah cursed Canaan, Ham's son (Gen 9:21–25). Why would righteous Noah curse an innocent child for the sin of its father?[9]

Consider this. After the flood, Canaan settled in the land of Canaan. His children occupied that land. After the exodus, Jewish spies reported that the land was filled with giants and the Nephilim, the descendants of Anak (Num 13:32–33). Deuteronomy 23:9, describes them as "strong and tall." The Bible refers to the Emim, Zuzim, Rephaim, Anakim, and Nephilim as clans of giants. Og, Goliath, Ishbi-Benob, Saph, Lahmi, Ahiman, Sheshai, Talmai, Anak, and Arba are names of giants. The Bible describes other giants without naming them. Some had six digits on each extremity. The term "gibborim" (mighty, valiant, of great stature) is used to describe the giants.

Most of the giants are associated with Canaan the person and Canaan the land. Giants lived in the antediluvian world. Somehow the descendants of the giants reemerged in Canaan after the flood. Did they come through Canaan?[10] That is unknown. However, the Bible associates Canaan with the existence of giants in the postdiluvian world.

9. According to Derek Gilbert, Ham "uncovered the nakedness of Noah" by having sex with his mother. This signaled his desire to usurp Noah and his brothers. He wanted his bloodline to be greater than that of all others. Reuben had sex with Jacob's concubine (Bilhah) for the same reason. Also, Solomon had sex with David's concubines in order to show that he claimed authority over his father (Gilbert, *Great Inception*, 48–50).

10. Some internet sites have proffered alternative explanations regarding Noah cursing Canaan and the second rise of the giants. One, Noah cursed the child Canaan instead of Ham because he saw something in him that reminded him of the old world. For example, he could have had six fingers. Six fingers are associated with giants. That

Unlike Noah, the Canaanites were corrupted in flesh and in conduct. Before the conquest of the land, the children of Israel weren't allowed to exchange brides with them. Both Isaac and Jacob went to Abraham's homeland to get brides. Abraham said that he didn't want Isaac to get a wife from among the Canaanites (Gen 24:3). The Canaanites were rejected because God didn't want the seed of Canaan to contaminate the seed of Abraham. Esau was condemned for taking wives from among the Canaanites. His seed was rejected.[11]

After God selected Jacob and his children to be his people, he sent them into Egypt so they wouldn't interbreed with the Canaanites. As long as the children of Israel remained as a tiny family in Canaan, they would have had social intercourse with the Canaanites. Eventually, the Canaanite DNA would have entered their family tree. That is why God moved them to Egypt. For 430 years, they only married each other. While in Egypt, the Israelites became a large people who could fill the Promised Land and displace the Canaanites from it.

God had already determined that the Nephilim and their seed must be wiped from the face of the earth. The conquest of Canaan continued the judgment of the flood. Most were killed by Joshua. Some retreated to the land of the Philistines. Finally, the last of the giants was killed by King David and his troops. First, David killed Goliath. Then he killed all the relatives of Rapha, giants with six fingers on each hand (2 Sam 21:15–22). The struggle against the giants is well documented in the conquest narrative. For example, Anak and his children are mentioned eighteen times.[12]

---

would mean that Ham's wife continued the bloodline of the giants when she and Ham entered the ark. Two, some of the Nephilim escaped the flood by going to Lebanon. Noah's flood didn't reach them there. Three, King Og of Bashan was a giant from the "generation of the flood." Deuteronomy 3 says he was the last of the Rephaites and that his bed was 13.5 feet long and six feet wide. He survived the flood by hanging onto the ark. Afterward, he repopulated the giants. Four, the giants reemerged in the same way that they originated. Angels mated with women after the flood. Five, it was a regional flood, and the giants that the Jews found in Canaan came from another region after the flood. Most likely, they were related to the seafaring Philistines. Six, Noah and his children were very tall. After the flood, people and animals became smaller. Giants were people who didn't get short as fast as other people. Seven, the epic hero Gilgamesh is often styled as a giant demigod who survived the flood. He is the Babylonian counterpart to Noah. The same sources say that Nimrod was a giant. For more information, see "How Did Nephilim Reappear after the Flood"; Colavito, "How the Nephilim Survived"; Skiba, "Moses tells us Exactly How"; Snelling, "Flood"; and Daily Renegade, "FINALLY! The TRUTH!"

11. In a popular Jewish Midrash, King Nimrod is a wicked man of superhuman abilities. He is called a son of Canaan. Because he is the seed of the serpent, he conspires to kill Abraham, the seed of the woman (Ginzberg, *Legends of the Jews*, 90–94).

12. Even though archeology has not discovered extensive physical evidence for

Nation Gods

The Torah believes that Yahweh is Israel's God. It calls him the God of Abraham, Isaac, and Jacob. Additionally, the Hebrew Scriptures refer to "the God of Israel" 195 time. Evidently, God was okay with this. In the Decalogue, he stipulates, Yahweh is your God and you shall have no other gods before him (Exod 20:2–3). Other gods may exist in the world and in the land into which you are about to enter, but Yahweh is your God. Don't worship other gods.

God uses the metaphor of marriage to illustrate his covenant of spiritual monogamy. Worshipping other gods is like having sex with a person to whom you are not married. That is why he calls faithless Israel an adulteress (Hos 3:1). Judges 2:17 says that the Jews went whoring after other gods, demons, and idols. Repeatedly, God uses graphic imagery to describe Israel's unfaithfulness to him.[13] In an environment in which the gods of the nations attempted to seduce the Jews, the people must be as devoted to God as a chaste wife is to her husband.

Like the nation gods, Yahweh attached himself to his people and to his land. The story of Elisha and Naaman illustrates this idea. In 2 Kings 5:1–19, God healed the Aramean general of his leprosy when he dipped himself in the Jordan River seven times. The river was in Yahweh's territory. The proud general wanted to dip in the clear rivers in his own land. However, the gods of his land couldn't heal him. Perhaps God gave him the leprosy so he would be drawn to him. Ultimately, the general had no choice but to obey Yahweh's prophet and dip in God's river if he wanted to be healed.

After being healed, the general understood what transpired. Since the God of Israel healed him when the gods of his land could not, he converted to Yahweh worship. This is an example of an Old Testament power encounter. When leaving to return to the land where Rimmon reigned, Naaman asked the prophet if he could carry about five hundred pounds of Israelite dirt back to his home country. He reasoned that the ground from Israel

---

giants, they are widely discussed in ancient mythologies and are depicted in ancient art. Anthropologist Andy White assesses the physical evidence in "Ancient Giants." Also, discrete peoples from all over the world, people who had no cultural contact, include similar giant stories in their histories and myths (Witzel, *Origins of the World's Mythologies*, 106–37). Plus, the Jewish historian Josephus claimed that he saw giant bones (*Ant.* 5.2.3). The Dead Sea Scrolls even include a book about giants and their origins (see Stuckenbruck, *Book of Giants from Qumran*). Finally, Philo offers a detailed apologia for the existence of the giants in his "On Giants."

13. Other explicit references to whoring after other gods are Exodus 34:15–16; Leviticus 17:7; 20:5–6; Numbers 15:39; Deuteronomy 31:16; Judges 8:27, 33; 1 Chronicles 5:25; 2 Chronicles 21:13; Palms 73:27; 106:39; Ezekiel 6:9; 23:30; and Hosea 4:12; 9:1. Some translations use "prostitute themselves" for whoring after other gods.

belonged to the God of Israel. When he laid it out in his own land, it would become an outpost for Yahweh because God is attached to his land. In order to worship Yahweh in that foreign land, he believed that he needed to stand on God's soil. In some sense, the concept parallels the modern idea of embassies. They fly the flag of the home country and are considered the sovereign territory of that country. The Bible doesn't endorse Naaman's perspective. However, it was a common understanding because people believed that national gods were joined to their land and their people.

Jonah's story shows how the Jewish understanding of Yahweh and his land evolved over time. Jonah thought that he could escape from God and God's command by fleeing from Israel to the far side of the world. However, he discovered that God wasn't a territorial god like the gods of the other nations. His rule extended to the oceans and included the entire world. As proof of this, when God upset the seas, even the Gentile sailors prayed to him. Ultimately, Jonah realized that Yahweh was the Lord of heaven, the one who created both the seas and the dry ground (Jonah 1:9; 16). This understanding of monotheism became very important during the Babylonian exile when the Jews were displaced from their land.

David voiced this same truth when he said, "Where can I go from your Spirit? Where can I flee from your presence? If I go up to the heavens, you are there; if I make my bed in the depths, you are there. If I rise on the wings of the dawn, if I settle on the far side of the sea, even there your hand will guide me, your right hand will hold me fast" (Ps 139:7–10). He came to this conclusion because he had to go to foreign lands that were ruled by other gods when fleeing from Saul. In retrospect, he saw the hand of God wherever he went. God never abandoned him.

In modern terms, the early Jewish understanding of monotheism would be classified as henotheism. It is the worship of a single god while not denying the existence of other gods. As the Jews matured in their faith, they realized that the gods of the nations were not real gods. Yahweh was the only real God. Even though the other gods had power and ruled over a particular people, they were created by God and existed by his will.

In time, the truth of radical monotheism changed how the Jews saw themselves and their task in the world. Wherever they went in their many exiles and deportations, they took God with them. He was no longer tied to a country or a soil. They confessed that the earth and everything in it belonged to the Lord. He created the heavens and all that is in them. As such, the gods of the nations should not be worshipped or invoked when making an oath (Exod 23:13; Josh 23:7; 1 Chr 16:26; Ps 96:5).

They believed that God would eventually destroy the gods of the nations and establish his rule over all the earth (Ps 47; 66; 86–87; 96; 98; 100; 102; Isa 2; Jer 16; Hab 2; Zeph 3; Zech 8; Mal 1). Zephaniah 2:11 gives voice to this belief when it says that Yahweh will destroy the gods of the nations. When he does, all the peoples will worship him in the midst of their own lands.

Don't Worship the Other Gods

Even though the Bible teaches that God is the Lord of the world, it doesn't deny that the gods of the nations exist. A quick word study of "gods" in selected passages from Exodus will show this.

> On that same night I will pass through Egypt and strike down every firstborn of both people and animals, and I will bring judgment on all the gods of Egypt. I am the Lord. (Exod 12:12)[14]
>
> Who among the gods is like you, Lord? (Exod 15:11)
>
> He said, "Praise be to the Lord, who rescued you from the hand of the Egyptians and of Pharaoh, and who rescued the people from the hand of the Egyptians. Now I know that the Lord is greater than all other gods." (Exod 18:10–11)
>
> Be careful to do everything I have said to you. Do not invoke the names of other gods; do not let [their names] be heard on your lips. (Exod 23:13)
>
> They shall not live in your land, because they will make you sin against Me; for if you serve their gods, it will surely be a snare to you. (Exod 23:33)

The New Testament also takes pagan gods seriously. Paul says, "For even if there are so-called gods, whether in heaven or on Earth (as indeed there are many 'gods' and many 'lords'), yet for us there is but one God" (1 Cor 8:5–6). Also, "Formerly, when you did not know God, you were slaves to those who by nature are not gods [false gods]. But now that you know God—or rather are known by God—how is it that you are turning back to those weak and miserable forces? Do you wish to be enslaved by [the gods] all over again?" (Gal 4:8).

Numbers mocks the gods of the nations by identifying them with mere idols of wood and stone (Num 4:28; 28:36; 64). To the Western mind, it

---

14. When we read the story of the final plague, most do not realize that Yahweh also punished the "gods of Egypt" on the same night that he killed the firstborn of Egypt. Exodus does not say how Yahweh judged the gods of Egypt. However, it must have been proportional to the way that he punished the people of Egypt (Gilbert, *Great Inception*, 84–86).

sounds like Numbers believes that there are no real gods, just lifeless idols made by people. Other parts of the Old Testament pick up on this approach. Even though an idol is manmade, the people dedicate the idol to a god, offer sacrifices to it, and invoke the name of the god over it. Through a dedication ceremony, the god is invited to indwell the idol. Afterward, it becomes a material portal through which the god interacts with its people. When they eat the food that they sacrifice to the idol, the god enters the people through the food. In truth, they don't worship an idol. Rather, they worship the god behind the idol.

Paul says, "Do I mean then that food sacrificed to an idol is anything, or that an idol is anything? No, but the sacrifices of pagans are offered to demons, not to God, and I do not want you to be participants with demons" (1 Cor 10:19–20). That is why the Jerusalem Council proscribed the eating of food offered to idols (15:20; 21:25). There is a positive relationship between Paul's understanding of demons and the gods. More specifically, the false gods who operate in the world are demons.

Later, Paul shifts on this. When an unbeliever serves a believer meat, the Christian shouldn't ask if the meat was previously sacrificed to an idol (1 Cor 10:25–27). Rather, he should break any previous attachments between the meat and the false god by blessing it in the name of Jesus. In essence, the believer rededicates the meat to Jesus before he eats it. In an environment where the pagan gods are woven into the daily rituals of life, the ability to break attachments by invoking the name of Jesus over food, objects, and places is an important benefit.

In summary, the Bible acknowledges the existence of other gods. They have power and control over people who are attached to them. They belong to specific lands. Idols embody the power of the gods and mediate the presence of the gods to the people. Sacrifice to the gods connects people to their gods. Even though the whole Earth is the Lord's, the peoples of the earth are in bondage to false gods. Only those who submit to Yahweh are free.

Saying that the gods of the nations don't exist because one affirms monotheism is one way that the modern West has ignored the reality of the gods. Nevertheless, when properly understood, biblical monotheism doesn't teach that other gods don't exist. Rather, it affirms that Yahweh is the only true God. "For the Lord your God is God of gods and Lord of lords, the great God, mighty and awesome" (Deut 10:17). The other gods aren't divine in the same way that Yahweh is God.

Who Are the Gods of the Nations?

When the descendants of Noah got together, they decided to make a name for themselves by building a city and a tower into heaven. Twice they proclaim, come let us do this or that (Gen 11:3-4). God witnessed the Tower of Babel and knew what it represented. Using the same cohortative structure as the people, he also stated, "Come, let us go down and confuse their language so they will not understand each other" (v. 7). When God said this, he wasn't talking to himself. Rather, he was talking to the heavenly council. Afterward, the Lord scattered humankind to other lands so they could no longer be a united humanity. Then he called Abraham to be the person through whom his plans would go forward.

Deuteronomy 32:8–9 offers additional insight into the scattering of humankind.[15] After God dispersed the nations at Babel, he claimed Israel as his portion and appointed the sons of God to rule over the various nations.[16] Sirach parrots this when it says that God appointed a ruler over each nation, but he picked Israel to be his portion (17:17). The sons of God became the nation gods. Since they exist in the heavenly council with God and exercise royal authority, they are divine beings. However, they are not gods in the same way that Yahweh is God. In reference to them, Deuteronomy 4:19 commands the Israelites not to worship the heavenly array. They have been appointed to the nations. However, Israel must only worship God. Heavenly array refers to divine beings. In the Bible, star is a common euphemism for angel or son of God (see Job 38:7).

Even though God picked Israel, one must assume that God intended that the *elohim* would care for the other peoples on his behalf. They had a stewardship from God.[17] Instead, at some time, they transgressed their

---

15. "Yahweh, who is here identified by the lofty title, Elyon, not only separates the sons of God into their respective peoples; he also apportioned for each, as a politically identifiable entity, a territorial possession, specifically establishing the boundaries thereof . . . The sons of God whose number provided the basis for the division of the nations, should be seen as members of God's heavenly court" (Block, *Gods of the Nations*, 14–15, 18). Block offers a detailed apologia to support this interpretation of Deuteronomy 32. For an in-depth analysis of this text, see Heiser, "Deuteronomy 32:8 and the Sons of God."

16. This refers to the table of nations listed in Genesis 10. There are seventy nations.

17. In reference to the Sons of God in Deuteronomy 32:8, Michael Green says the "Jews resolved the problem of the one and the many. There was only one God, and he was their God for ever. All other spiritual forces, be they good or bad, were ultimately under his control and assigned as tutelary deities to other nations" (*I Believe in Satan's Downfall*, 79). Green describes the relationship between Yahweh and the gods of the nations as a suzerainty; a relationship whereby a sovereign has control over a subordinate state that has internal autonomy.

mission by following the example of Satan. They wanted to be worshipped and become like God.

Even though Paul calls the gods demons (1 Cor 10:20), others have referred to them as territorial spirits. They rule over geographical areas (nations) and claim lordship over certain peoples. They are the thrones, rulers, and powers in the heavenly places to which the New Testament refers. They are assisted by other gods and demons.[18]

In summary, even though the earth is the Lord's and he is the only true God, other divine beings who God created took rulership over lands and peoples when God scattered the peoples. God chose Israel to be his portion. Through Israel, God orchestrated a counterattack that started with the selection of Abraham. Israel became God's witness in the world. Ultimately, Jesus was born through Israel. After his death and resurrection, God sent the church into all the world to make disciples of every nation by calling the people back from the false gods to the true God.

In this age, God is seeking to win all the nations back to him. That means, the church must work with God to dislodge the gods of the people by proclaiming the reign of God and leading people into a relationship with Jesus. In this sense, evangelism is spiritual warfare. It leads people out of their bondage to the false gods and into the reign of the one true God. When the people come to God, the power of the gods is checked. For God's kingdom to flourish on Earth, the gods who were given stewardship over the nations must be dethroned.

Practical Application

Harold Caballeros is a giant in the field of spiritual warfare. While seeking to identify and neutralize the ancient powers and principalities that have ruled the spiritual topography of Guatemala, the Spirit led Caballeros and his team of intercessors to the Grand Snake Mount of the Valley of Guatemala. The god behind it took the form of a feathered snake. He is called Quetzalcoatl.

Through diligent research and spiritual discernment activities, Caballeros and his team discovered that the land and all those who lived on it had been permanently dedicated to this god 200 years before Christ. More important, the god's features were ingrained in the society. Before meaningful revival could go forward in Guatemala, Caballeros knew that

---

18. In *Twilight Labyrinth*, George Otis carefully analyses the history of specific peoples to uncover the spiritual topography so that the reader can understand the aftermath of Babel.

Quetzalcoatl had to be dethroned. Furthermore, since his power had been routinized and passed down from one generation to another by means of the society's prevailing values, beliefs, practices, religion, and worldview, Caballeros' team realized that the culture had to be transformed for a sustainable renewal to take place.[19]

By means of the "Jesus Is Lord of Guatemala" prayer campaign, fasting, deliverance ministry, mass evangelism, Christian education, and discipleship ministries, God began to change the spiritual environment of Guatemala. As a result, the influence of the indigenous religions and syncretistic Catholicism began to wane under the power of a resurgent Pentecostalism. Today, upwards of 50 percent of the population claims to be Spirit-filled. The greatest transformation has happened among the Mayan peoples in the northern highlands. Only 2 percent continue to practice the old ways.[20]

The revival in Almolonga epitomizes the transformation that God has brought to Guatemala. In reference to Almolonga, Caballeros states,

> In this particular case, the process that took place started because of discipleship and prayer, just as in Acts 19. Then it was followed by a consistent practice of deliverance ministry. Through spiritual warfare the demonic powers were broken, and the empire of the territorial spirits was dethroned. This open-heaven brought a great freedom for evangelism. The resulting revival transformed the life and the culture. They changed their habits and abandoned their ungodly traditions. This transformation even went so far as to affect the natural elements, making Almolonga the most fertile land in the whole country.[21]

The process that Caballeros has identified is a model by which faith communities can achieve the sustainable transformation they desire. Since the Bible teaches that the nations were given over to the sons of God and that these "nation gods" corrupted the peoples over which God gave them charge, transformation will happen when the gods over a particular place are fully dethroned and the people are discipled. When this happens, God becomes the God of that land and the people of the land enter into God's reign. That is why the Great Commission focuses on making disciples of every nation (people group). Individual evangelism and the growth of individual churches are important. However, for transformation to happen, the society must reject the old god and embrace Jesus.

19. Caballeros and Winger, *Transforming Power of Revival*, 14–15.

20. Mandryk, *Operation World*, 380–84, and Kimutai, "Religious Beliefs in Guatemala."

21. Caballeros, "Prophetic Pathways," 21.

This is why secular societies that celebrate pluralism, individualism, humanistic values, sexual freedom, and tolerance are very resistant to communal transformation. For revival to seize a community and transform it, the people have to turn from their secular values and embrace the biblical values that enable the kingdom of God to eradicate the works of darkness. In the West, repentance means submitting to the rule of God and rejecting all the values, beliefs, and practices that impede the manifestation of God's kingdom.

12

Introducing Demons

Since ancient times, people have written about demons. The literature has taken the form of legends, myths, sacred texts, magical incantations, psalms, and exorcism rituals. Every ancient society had demon stories. Interestingly, the surviving literature from ancient Israel makes fewer references to demons than the literature of the surrounding nations.

Spangenberg speaks for the academic consensus when he claims that the ancient Hebrews were polytheistic before Yahweh prohibited them from serving other gods. This is in keeping with the evolution of religion theory.[1] During the polytheistic period, the Hebrews would have produced a lot of literature that dealt with the demonic. He argues that the surviving Hebrew literature lacks a robust demonology because the Israelites sanitized its polytheistic literature when they embraced radical monotheism. However, he asserts, hints to its existence can be found in the Hebrew Bible.[2]

The Hebrew Scriptures don't support Spangenberg's main thesis. There is no evidence that the early Hebrew people practiced polytheism. Instead, one can make a case for original monotheism. The Israelites are the children of Abraham, Isaac, and Jacob. Even though they flirted with foreign gods, idols, and the religious practices of the polytheistic peoples with whom they interacted, they never became a polytheistic people.

A quick recap of what was previously discussed will help explain why the ancient Hebrew literature lacks copious references to the demonic. When Jacob lived in proximity to the Canaanite peoples who surrounded

---

1. See chapter 11 for an explanation of this theory.
2. Spangenberg, "Brief History of Belief."

his small clan, his family interacted with the local inhabitants. Over time, through intermarriage and social intercourse, pagan beliefs and practices would have corrupted the radical monotheism that they inherited from Abraham. The stories of Lot and Esau demonstrate this point. The resulting syncretism would have ruined God's purposes for the Jewish people.

To prevent that from happening, God sent the Hebrews to an isolated area in Egypt. After Yahweh dethroned the gods of Egypt, he brought an exceedingly large number of Hebrews back to Canaan. Upon entering the land, he gave them the Ten Commandments and ordered them to drive out the pagans. As they purged the Promised Land, God told them to destroy everything associated with false religions. A radical monotheism that didn't fixate on the demonic ensured as a reaction to the polytheism that they expunged.[3]

Still, a proper understanding of Jewish monotheism doesn't mean that spirits and demons didn't exist or that the gods of the pagans were make-believe. From their experience in Egypt, the Hebrews knew that other spirit beings existed. Moses contended with them. The Decalogue simply told the Jews that they should have no gods before Yahweh (Exod 20:3). The prohibition against other gods included making idols, sacrificing to other gods, learning the ways of the pagans, or flirting with the spirit world. The Hebrews were to stay focused on Yahweh.

This commitment to radical monotheism caused the Israelites to have a diminished literature on demons. Eventually, the tension between monotheism and the growing awareness of demons lessened, especially during the Babylonian Exile. As evidence of this, copious references to demons began to appear in post-exilic Jewish literature. These references informed folk practices. For example, the apocryphal book of Tobit tells Jews how to drive away a powerful demon by using potions (Tob 6:6–16).[4] To be prosperous, a Jew needed to mitigate the harm that demons caused, especially as it related to sickness, misfortune, miscarriage, infanticide, death, infertility, night terrors, the danger of traveling through wilderness areas, and the fear of supernatural beings. In short, belief in one God didn't mean that demons didn't exist or need to be managed in order to live a good life.

---

3. A. Scott Moreau states, "References to the demonic in the Old Testament are relatively scarce. Their existence is never proven; it is simply assumed. The Old Testament focus is not on demons and their schemes but on God and his sovereignty" ("Demon," 163).

4. The Testament of Solomon, a pseudepigrapha book dating to AD 100, is a who's who of demons. It introduces all the main demons by name. It was written by a Jew. It argues for the existence of female demons and shows that magic, folk religion, and astrology intertwined in Judaism.

Around 300 BC, the Septuagint translated the Hebrew word *"sedim"* (tutelary spirits) as demons. Demon is a Greek word with a decidedly Greek meaning that is not the same as the early Hebrew meaning of *sedim*. "As the gods of the nations were demonized, so 'demon' in the dualistic sense is found in the Septuagint as a designation of pagan deities and spirits."[5] This shows that the Jews during the intertestamental period read the Hebrew Scriptures in light of their evolving understanding of evil supernaturalism. Furthermore, the Dead Sea scrolls show that post-exilic Jews had a preoccupation with demons. The Jewish Talmud, Midrashic literature, Kabbalah, the Jewish apocrypha, and the Pseudepigrapha all speak about demons.

The developing demonology wasn't due to progressive revelation. Rather, it emerged as a result of contextual theology. As the Jews read their Scriptures in light of their encounter with the nations, they began to develop a keener awareness of the demonic. This emerging sensitivity to spiritual warfare and the apocalyptic worldview took centerstage in the New Testament.

Like post-exilic Judaism, American culture is saturated with demon-talk. For example, when you type "demon" into Amazon.com, you will get more hits than you can count. A "demon" search on Netflix garnered 308 movies. The most common media genera for demons is horror. However, anime and sci-fi also contain copious references to demons. Exorcism is a popular theme. In addition to *The Exorcist*, you can watch *The Exorcism of Emily Rose*, *The Exorcism of Hannah Grace*, and *The Exorcism of Anneliese Michel*. Even though modern America talks about the demonic, for most, it's a fantasy subject. For that reason, average Americans who watch demon movies don't attempt to minimize the negative influence of the demons who negatively impact their lives in the same way as the intertestamental Jews did. In other words, they lack a theology of demons and corresponding folk practices.

In a similar fashion, advocates of liberation theology use the language of the demonic to undergird a theology of social justice that looks for signs of systemic evil.[6] Instead of identifying the demons behind the systems that oppress, this approach largely demythologizes the language of the Bible so that it can repurpose it. Those who reappropriate the demonic language of Scripture for this cause aren't looking for real demons that have attached themselves to social systems and unjust regimes. Instead, by means of

---

5. Riley, "Demon," 238.

6. For an excellent example of this, see Wink, *Powers That Be*, and Wink, "World System Model," 47–71.

Marxist analysis, they produce political theologies that attempts to fix systemic evil through social interventions.[7]

In evangelical circles, the most influential demon-themed books are Frank Peretti's *This Present Darkness* and *Piercing the Darkness*. In these books, demons and angels interact and struggle for control of people, organizations, churches, and territories. Angels and demons have ranks and assignments. Demons manipulate systems and work through people who do their bidding. By means of spiritual warfare activities, Christians participate in the combat and enable the victory that God desires.

Not only have these books sold millions of copies, they have also aroused the imagination of those who study spiritual warfare. When speaking about these books, Charles Kraft asks, "How well does [Peretti's] portrayal of spiritual warfare correspond to what happens in real life? . . . My thirty-plus years of working in spiritual warfare, during which I have ministered to several hundred demonized people, leads me to grant a high degree of credibility to Peretti's picture of the spirit world."[8]

Sadly, popular evangelical literature often lacks depth or comes to facile conclusions that aren't supported by a robust exegesis of the biblical literature. For example, Paula Price defines a demon as "An unclean spirit with divine and inferior godlike status able to influence humanity and their affairs by bestowing fortunes on people or inflicting suffering upon them. [They] often became worshipped as a god or goddess in ancient civilizations. These beings have their own treasury of fortunes that they distribute

---

7. Liberals have opined that Evangelicals aren't concerned with systemic evil and that they don't address it with their theology or in their praxis. Slavery, poverty, militarism, and global warming are cited as examples. Historically, evangelicalism has been preoccupied with evangelism, world missions, church planting, education, Bible translation, and building the church. They call this the "evangelistic mandate." At the same time, they recognize a "cultural mandate." God desires to redeem culture and those elements of the society that manifest the fall. They differ from liberals because they don't believe that one can achieve the kingdom of God by means of political utopianism. The kingdom doesn't come by means of politics. I speak to this in the last chapter. The Lausanne Movement speaks for global evangelicalism when it addresses systemic evil. "The agenda is warfare against the domination systems that make up our cultures and societies. These systems (cultural, economic, political, religious) are manifestations of what the New Testament calls 'the world' (Greek: *kosmos*): 'The whole world is under the control of the evil one' (1 John 5:19; cf. John 12:31 and 14:30 where Jesus calls Satan the prince of this world). This concept of kingdoms in conflict is also illustrated by Satan's claim of dominion when he offered Jesus the kingdoms of the world (Matt. 4:8–9). The point is clearly that even though God ultimately is the sovereign king of heaven and earth, Satan does exercise significant influence over *kosmos* and its power structures" (Engelsviken, *Spiritual Conflict in Today's Mission*).

8. Kraft, *Evangelical Guide to Spiritual Warfare*, 22.

at will in return for worship and service."⁹ Her definition conflates many ideas and falls short of the biblical understanding of the term. Plus, it draws on New Age concepts.

Demons Are More Common Than You Think

In a recent email with a prominent biblical scholar who teaches that demons are the spirits of the deceased Nephilim who drowned in the great flood, I argued that this popular explanation couldn't account for the high incidence of demonization that deliverance ministers encounter today.[10] In other words, if his theory is correct, we have a math problem. Like other practitioners who write on this topic, I have discovered that demonization is very common.

Without going into specifics, I would argue that most non-Christians have some demonic entanglements. I would also contend that many Christians continue to fall into sin and live with spiritual bondages because they have inherited evil spirits, participated in occult activities, are controlled by addictions, or have deep wounds that need healing. All of the above will open spiritual doors that allow demons to establish a stronghold in a person.

Because demonization is common, early Christianity included exorcism language in its baptismal ritual. Jeffery Russell states, "Until about A.D. 200, baptism was often preceded by a rite of exorcism. Beginning about 200, the exorcism and formal renunciation of Satan were incorporated into the baptismal rite . . . From this time onward, the renunciation of Satan was the first act of baptism . . . The voluntary renunciation of Satan remained part of the tradition, symbolizing as it did the candidate's transition from the army of Satan to that of Christ."[11]

In the baptismal rite of renunciation, the rejection of Satan included the denunciation of demons and all that is evil. Moreover, early church leaders assumed that people coming from the world had entanglements with demons. If they were not expelled when a person confessed Jesus, they would continue to harass and victimize the Christian. That's why Jesus cast out demons from Mary of Magdala and other women before they became close followers (Luke 8:2).

---

9. Price, *Prophets Dictionary*, 157–58.

10. Heiser, "Where Do Demons Come From?"

11. Russell, *Satan*, 101–2. "In 258 AD the Seventh Counsel of Carthage viewed exorcism as a preliminary step toward the re-baptism of heretics. Exorcism also appears before baptism in the Apostolic Tradition" (Sorensen, *Possession and Exorcism*, 200).

Back to the point; if the evil spirits that we encounter when doing exorcisms are the spirits of the Nephilim who drowned in the deluge, there must have been billions of them living in the ancient world because that is the extent of the demon problem today! Since that is not the case, the spirits that we routinely cast out can't be the dead Nephilim. Let me clarify that statement. Since there are more demons than there were Nephilim, most of the spirits that we cast out today aren't Nephilim spirits.[12]

Most Pentecostals and Evangelicals have never considered the Nephilim theory. Instead, they assume that demons are fallen angels who rebelled with Satan. For example, Ed Murphy states that demons, evil spirits, and fallen angels are synonymous terms that refer to the spiritual beings that fell when Satan rebelled.[13] Bob Larson follows suit. After considering origin theories related to a pre-Adamic race and Nephilim, Larson concludes that demons are fallen angels. "In all my years of dealing with demons, I have never encountered a case that contradicts my conclusion about the origin of evil spirits: They are angels who fell from their estate as did Lucifer."[14]

In sum, I acknowledge that angels fell with Satan, that Nephilim spirits may be demons in accordance with the teaching of 1 Enoch 15, and that Jesus cast out demons who "possessed" people. However, I am not prepared to say that fallen angels, evil spirits, impure spirits, and demons refer to the same type of being. Since demon is a generic term, there is room for nuancing.

What Are Demons?

The ancient world gave witness to many types of spiritual beings that are called by many names. In Classical Greek, the term *daimon* served as a broad word that could apply to gods and spirits that were good or evil. Over time, the term became more specific. The members of the Areopagus said that Paul was a preacher of *daimonian* or foreign gods (Acts 17:18). *Deisidaimonesterous* is used in Acts 17:22 and 25:19. It is translated as reverence for the gods, fear of the gods, overly religious, or superstitious. It was not a pejorative word.

---

12. In a creative twist, Price distinguishes between devils and demons. She says that devils refer to the angels who fell with Satan and demons refer to their offspring when the Watchers sired children with women before the flood (*Prophet's Dictionary*, 158). Even though the Scriptures distinguish between the Watchers and the spirits of the dead giants, the way Price uses the words is not correct. Some English translations prefer "devils" and others use "demons."

13. Murphy, *Handbook for Spiritual Warfare*, 21–22.

14. Larson, *Larson's Book of Spiritual Warfare*, 46.

In common usage, demon referred to the lesser gods or ancestor spirits who watched over human affairs (tutelary spirits). They were morally ambiguous in that they could be good, bad, or a combination of the two. In this way, the word aligns with the Muslim use of jinn. The term didn't become associated with evil spirits in league with the devil until the Jewish exile when the covenant people encountered dualism.[15]

The canonical Scriptures never say what or who demons are. In fact, the vaunted King James Version never uses the word. Instead, it translates "demonized" (*daimonizomai*) as one who is possessed by devils (Matt 4:24; 8:16; 28; 33; 9:32; 12:22) and demon as devil. The proper term for the devil is *diabolos*, the one who slanders and accuses. Because of its word choice, the King James translation confuses the issue. In contrast, the New International Version uses demon eighty-two times, impure spirit twenty-six times, and evil spirit six times.

Since "demon" is a Greek transliteration, it does not appear in the Old Testament. *Sedim* is a Hebrew term that has a similar meaning. All the English Bibles translate it as demons or devils. *Sedim* is only used in Deuteronomy 32:17 and Psalm 106:37. In both cases, it refers to people sacrificing to evil spirits. The term can be rendered as "false gods." Other Old Testament words associated with demons are: *seirim*, *'elilim*, *gad*, and *qeter*. Second Chronicles 11:14–15 indicates a close relationship between idols, false gods, and demons.

The New Testament picks up on the "sacrificing to demons" idea when it says that people who sacrifice to false gods or to idols are really sacrificing to demons (1 Cor 10:20). Likewise, the worship of idols is the worship of demons (Rev 9:20). Leviticus 17:7 gets at this meaning when it says that the Israelites can no longer sacrifice to the "goat-demons" to whom they have prostituted themselves as they wandered through the wilderness. The term for goat-demon means goat idol in 2 Chronicles 11:15. Azazel is a type of goat-demon who prefigures Satan in Leviticus 17. By design, the scapegoat is sacrificed to him. In Isaiah 13:21 and 34:13, goat-demons are personified and associated with the desolate wilderness.

In Judges 9:23 and 1 Samuel 16:14–23, God sends an evil spirit to accomplish his work. In 1 Kings 22:22, God sends a lying spirit to entice King Ahab to do something that would lead to his death (also 2 Chr 18:20–22). In these cases, the adjectives evil and lying may refer to the type of mission rather than the type of spirit. Like the destroying angel that killed the firstborn of Egypt, God can use his heavenly beings to do things that are normally associated with demons.

15. See Riley, "Demon," 235.

As a point of reference, in the New Testament demons are called by the action they cause. For example, in Mark 9:25, Jesus addresses a deaf and mute spirit. The spirit was not deaf and mute. Rather, that is how it manifested in the person it demonized.[16]

In general, the Old and New Testaments both deal with the problem of demons. However, the New Testament has a more developed understanding of demons. For this reason, one should not read the New Testament notion of demons onto the Old Testament text. Still, the reality of demons is the same in the Old and the New Testaments. As such, New Testament writers correctly connect Old Testament problems with idols, false gods, and abhorrent things to demons.

The Nephilim Became Demons

I have already mentioned that some believe that modern demons are the disembodied spirits of the Nephilim that were killed in Noah's flood. First Enoch 15:8–12 is the main support text for that belief.[17] Before I address the text, I need to discuss the origins of evil. It undergirds this conversation. Specifically, how did evil enter the world and why does it still exist if God is a good God?[18]

Genesis 1–2 affirms that God is good, creation is good, the heavenly hosts are good, and humankind is good. A good God produces a good

---

16. Kimberly Daniels has identified the following types of demonic spirits mentioned in the Bible: spirit of divination (Acts 16:16–18), familiar spirits (1 Sam 28:5–19), spirit of jealousy (Heb 12:15), perverse spirit (Jas 1:13–15), lying spirit (2 Chr 18:21), spirit of heaviness (Isa 61:3), spirit of whoredom (Hos 5:4), spirit of infirmity (Luke 13:11–13), deaf and dumb spirit (Mark 9:17–27), spirit of bondage (Rom 8:15), spirit of fear (2 Tim 1:7), seducing spirit (1 Tim 4:1), spirit of antichrist (1 John 4:3), spirit of error (1 John 4:6), spirit of death (Heb 2:14–15), and spirit of pride (Prov 16:8) (Daniels, *Dictionary of Demons*, 45–64). Presumably, an exorcist could call out each of these types of spirits by referring to their functional names.

17. Heiser has shown that the Genesis 6 story closely parallels the Mesopotamian story of the Apkallu. Before the flood, the Apkallu were great heroes like the Nephilim (Gen 6:4). In the postdiluvian world, they became giants and evil spirits as in the 1 Enoch 15 account (Heiser, *Reversing Hermon*, 43–47). While reflecting on this theme, Heiser avers that the biblical story of the Nephilim "echoes stories found in every major religion and culture around the world. Mesopotamians, Greeks, Egyptians, African tribes, Native Americans, Asians—they all have a story of beings from the sky or the heavens that came down, had sex with human women, and produced unusual offspring—divine human hybrids—who were given divine right to rule over humanity" (Heiser, *Façade*, 132).

18. See Baker, "Fallen Angels." Baker opines that there are two accounts of the fallen angel story; one for Satan and one for the Watchers.

creation. Good characterizes who God is and what God creates. A good God can't create an evil world. God has never changed. However, the sapient beings that God created were given the ability to do wrong. For a being to be classified as good, it must have the ability to be bad. In time, a disgruntled divine being desired to challenge God. When this happened, he became evil. Through the transgressing being, evil entered creation.

The Genesis 3 narrative tells us that creation was corrupted when the serpent deceived Eve and Adam yielded his birthright to the Evil One who became the Ruler of this World. The serpent was a divine being who decided to become evil. Genesis 6:1–6 adds to the developing story. In that text, some sons of God (Watchers) see that the daughters of Adam are beautiful.[19] According to Second Temple literature, in an act of defiance, they took a vow, came to Earth, incarnated themselves, and chose wives as they pleased. Some said that they veiled themselves with flesh.[20] Afterward, they sired children with their mortal wives. The offspring were demigods. Genesis 6 refers to them as Nephilim. The name may mean "to fall" or "causing others to fall." Others translate it as giants.[21] In any case, the Nephilim filled the earth with evil and corrupted the seed of the woman. They were the seed of the serpent (Gen 3:15). God attempted to destroy them and wash away

19. Two interpretations attempt to humanize the sons of God in Genesis 6. One is called the Sethite view. According to it, the sons of God are the godly children of righteous Seth. They are the ones who called on the name of the Lord in Genesis 4:26. The daughters of men are called the daughters of Cain. They are evil. Seth represents the good seed of the woman, and Cain represents the seed of the serpent. In Genesis 6, the godly children of Seth saw the beautiful daughters of evil Cain and married them. This corrupted the bloodline of Seth and threatened to wipe out the seed of the women. God saved Noah and his family because they were blue-blooded children of Seth. He wanted to reestablish the holy lineage through them. For a fuller explanation of this view, see Byron, *Cain and Abel*, 147–64. Another explanation says that the sons of God were human kings. In the ancient world, a king was considered a son of the nation god. He had a divine right and a stewardship responsibility. The kings erred when they married evil women or entered into plural marriages. A popular take on the "seed of the serpent" approach says that Satan had sex with Eve and was the father of Cain. Adam fathered Abel and Seth. First John 3:12 is often quoted in support of this. It says that Cain belongs to the Evil One. As such, the daughters of Cain had corrupted flesh. They looked beautiful because Satan was beautiful. See Hanegraaff, "Did Eve Have Sex with Satan?" None of the above explanations capture how the Old Testament uses the phrase "sons of God." In the Hebrew Bible, "sons of God" refers to divine beings.

20. According to Heiser, when the sons of God came to Earth, they didn't come to do evil. Rather, they "were trying to reformulate Eden, where the divine and the human coexisted, in their own way. They presumed to know better than God what should be happening on Earth, just like the original enemy had. Alteration of God's plan to restore his rule ends up making a bad situation worse" (*Unseen Realm*, 41).

21. Heiser explores the etymology of this term. He follows the lead of the Septuagint translators and calls them giants (*Reversing Hermon*, 15–17).

their vile influence by means of the flood. Sadly, the Nephilim reemerged in Canaan after the flood.

Are the accounts in Genesis 3 and 6 separate attempts to describe how evil entered the world? That is, one story says it came through the serpent and the other says it came through the Watchers.[22] Or, does the story of the Watchers in Genesis 6 demonstrate that the powerful members of God's divine council continued to defect after Satan rebelled? Later chapters will expand on these ideas. At this point, we must understand that the Jews of the intertestamental period struggled with this question.

First Enoch 15 attempt to resolve the tension.[23] "The giants who are born from the (union of) the spirits and the flesh shall be called evil spirits upon the earth, because their dwelling shall be upon the earth and inside the earth. Evil spirits have come out of their bodies ... They will become evil upon the earth and shall be called evil spirits" (1 En. 15:8–10, Charlesworth).

In Jubilees 10, the spirits of the dead Nephilim are called demons. After the flood, they were blinding people, causing sin, and killing humans. These are things that demons do. In desperation, righteous Noah asked God to intervene. Upon hearing Noah's plea, God gave orders to bind the demons so they couldn't do more harm. However, the head of the demons bargained with God. "Leave some of them before me, and let them obey my voice. And let them do everything which I tell them, because if some of them are not left for me, I will not be able to exercise the authority of my will among the children of men ... All the evil ones, who were cruel, we bound in the place of judgment, but a tenth of them we let remain so that they might be subject to Satan on the earth" (Jub. 10:8; 11, Charlesworth).

First Enoch and Jubilees demonstrate that Judaism grappled with the problem of demons in the centuries before Christ. No longer are allusions to them hidden in their texts. They become key players. The Dead Sea Scrolls also refer to them in practical ways.[24] Because exorcism was needed to counter the demons, the community provided tools for that. By the time of

---

22. Paul says that sin entered the world through Adam (Rom 5:12). Through Adam's disobedience, all people became contaminated by sin. Mortal death is the result of human sin.

23. Jubilees 5:2 declares that the children of the Watchers were giants. Furthermore, the corruption went beyond human flesh. It extended to all flesh. The text implies interspecies hybridization. That is why God determined to destroy "all flesh" (Jub. 5:3). The idea of interspecies hybridization may have been influenced by Greek mythology.

24. The Dead Sea Scrolls include an exorcism formula that frees a person who suffers from a fever demon, a chills demon, and chest-pain demons. The ritual targets demons that cause a variety of problems, including killing babies. Sleep demons were a vexing problem (Wise, "Exorcism," 566–67, 4Q560). Another section of Dead Sea Scrolls includes psalms and songs to disperse demons (Wise, 588–89, 11Q11).

Jesus, the Jews knew what demons were, what they did, and how to protect themselves from them.[25] However, the view that demons are the spirits of the Nephilim is not mentioned in the canonical Bible or endorsed as a doctrine of the church.

Some could argue that the Gospels make a subtle reference to the Nephilim when the demons said, "What do you want with us, Jesus of Nazareth? Have you come to destroy us? I know who you are—the Holy One of God!" (Mark 1:24); and "'What do you want with us, Son of God?' they shouted. 'Have you come here to torture us before the appointed time?'" (Matt 8:29).

"Holy One of God" and "Son of God" are heavenly council phrases that fallen angels and Nephilim would have known. They are reserved for the Lord of the Armies of God. The demons who are exorcized know who Jesus is and associate his appearance with their torment. Their desperate pleas reflect a commonly held expectation that the Messiah would send the Watchers to hell on the Day of the Lord. This expectation is alluded to in the Old Testament prophetic books, Jude 6, and 2 Peter 2:4. However, 1 Enoch 1 makes explicit reference to this. "The God of the universe, the Holy Great One, will come forth from his dwelling. And from there he will march upon Mount Sinai and appear in his camp emerging from heaven with a mighty power. And everyone shall be afraid, and the Watchers will quiver. And great fear and trembling shall seize them . . . Behold, he will arrive with ten million of the holy ones in order to execute judgment on all" (1 En. 1:4–5; 9, Charlesworth).[26]

Attributes of New Testament Demons

As was previously noted, in the New Testament, demons, evils spirits, and impure spirits are used interchangeably. Demons are expelled in all the Gospels and in Acts. Casting out demons and healing the sick defined Jesus' ministry. Jesus says, "Go tell that fox, I will keep on driving out demons and

---

25. For an in-depth study of Jewish exorcisms, see Bohak "Jewish Exorcisms," 277–300. He introduces the reader to all the relevant literature on this topic. He also writes on Jewish magic practices. The Acts of the Apostles introduces us to Jewish magicians. Magic is a type of folk religion.

26. First Enoch 1:9 is quoted in Jude 14–15. "Enoch, the seventh from Adam, prophesied about them: 'See, the Lord is coming with thousands upon thousands of his holy ones to judge everyone, and to convict all of them of all the ungodly acts they have committed in their ungodliness, and of all the defiant words ungodly sinners have spoken against him'" (Charlesworth).

healing people today and tomorrow, and on the third day I will reach my goal" (Luke 13:32).

Jesus gave his followers the authority to cast out demons in his name so that they could duplicate his ministry and give witness to the expanding kingdom (Matt 10:8; Mark 6:6; Luke 9:1; 10:17; Acts 5:16; 8:3). As the kingdom of God grew, it displaced the reign of Satan. Sometimes the disciples used oil to heal and cast out demons (Mark 6:13). At other times, they used cloth that had touched a spiritually powerful person. "God did extraordinary miracles through Paul, so that even handkerchiefs and aprons that had touched him were taken to the sick, and their illnesses were cured and the evil spirits left them" (Acts 19:11-12).

On one occasion, the disciples were not able to cast out a demon until Jesus intervened (Matt 17:19; Mark 9:28). Still, people who were not following Jesus could cast out demons when they invoked his name (Matt 7:22; Mark 9:38). However, when Jewish exorcists altered their ritual to include a reference to Jesus, the demons attacked them and hurt them (Acts 19:1-20).

Those who opposed Jesus' power ministry claimed that the demons had a ruler. They call him Beelzebub (Matt 9:34; 12:24; 27; Mark 3:22; Luke 11:15). Because Jesus had absolute authority over demons, the Jewish opposition accused him of being possessed by a strong demon. That is, the demon that he channeled was more powerful than the ones he cast out. Others said he was in league with Beelzebub (John 7:20; 8:42-52; 10:20-21). The people were amazed that the demons obeyed Jesus (Mark 1:27; Luke 4:36). Sometimes the demons shook their victims when they were cast out (Mark 1:26; 19:26; Luke 9:42). At other times, they did not.

Often, Jesus and the apostles "healed" people who were afflicted by demons (Matt 4:11; 8:16; 15:22; 17:18; Luke 6:18; 8:2; Acts 5:16; 8:7; 8:31). The word selection assumes that the demons were linked to the disease that was cured. People suffering from dumbness, blindness, vexing pain, fever, epilepsy, lunacy, paralysis, back problems, and lameness were healed when their demons were expelled (Matt 4:11; 7:21; 12:22; Mark 5:15; 9:32; 12:22; Luke 4:39; 8:36; 9:42; 11:14; Acts 5:16; 8:3; 19:12). For example, "A woman was there who had been crippled by a spirit for eighteen years. She was bent over and could not straighten up at all. When Jesus saw her, he called her forward and said to her, 'Woman, you are set free from your infirmity'" (Luke 13:11-12).

Not only did Jesus cast demons out of people, he could also cast them out of a storm. "A furious squall came up, and the waves broke over the boat, so that it was nearly swamped. Jesus was in the stern, sleeping on a cushion. The disciples woke him and said to him, 'Teacher, don't you care if we drown?' He got up, rebuked the wind and said to the waves, 'Quiet!

Be still!' Then the wind died down and it was completely calm . . . [The disciples] were terrified and asked each other, 'Who is this? Even the wind and the waves obey him!'" (Mark 4:37-41).

In this case, a demon caused a storm by manipulating the water and the surrounding air in an unsuccessful effort to kill Jesus and his disciples. Jesus recognized the "demon in the storm" and cast it out. Afterward, the waters were calm. Right after this episode, Jesus sends a legion of demons into pigs who drowned themselves in the same body of water (Luke 8:32-33).

Did One-Third of the Angels Fall with Satan?

Much of the evangelical literature on demons argues that one-third of the angels fell with Satan. These became the demons. I agree with Charles Kraft when he states that large numbers of angels fell when Satan rebelled. However, one cannot use Revelation 12:4 to argue that one-third of the angels of heaven fell with Satan.[27] The Bible doesn't say how many angels fell. Furthermore, it doesn't say if they fell at the same time.[28] Have other angels defected over the eons? Additionally, the Bible doesn't say that the demons who possessed people in the New Testament were fallen angels.

The scriptural basis on which Evangelicals argue that one-third of the angels are demons is not convincing. Revelation 12:4 says that the Great Red Dragon swept its tail and knocked a third of the stars out of the sky and flung them to the earth. Stars in the sky is a normal way for the Bible to refer to angels. In this case, the heavenly stars didn't join Satan's revolt. Rather, they were assaulted by him. He knocked them out of heaven. The text doesn't say what became of them once they were knocked down. A few verses later, the text speaks about a war in heaven. Michael and his angels fought against Satan and his angels. Satan's team lost. In the aftermath, Michael evicted them from heaven, and they were hurled to the earth (Rev 12:9).

The text presents three sets of angels: Michael and his victorious angels, the stars who were thrown from the heavens, and Satan and his defeated angels. The stars of heaven are not Satan's angels unless the ones who were thrown down in verse 4 joined with Satan in verse 9.

---

27. Kraft, *Defeating Dark Angels*, 23-24.

28. Heiser contends that the Bible doesn't endorse the notion that a host of angels revolted against God when Satan rebelled. In the Bible, the angels fell in Genesis 6 (*Unseen Realm*, 324n3).

Since Revelation uses apocalyptic language, the symbolism in this text shouldn't be taken literally. Most likely, the tail imagery in Revelation 12:4 refers to Daniel 8:10.[29]

> Out of one of them came another horn, which started small but grew in power to the south and to the east and toward the Beautiful Land. It grew until it reached the host of the heavens, and it threw some of the starry host down to the earth and trampled on them. It set itself up to be as great as the commander of the army of the Lord; it took away the daily sacrifice from the Lord, and his sanctuary was thrown down. Because of rebellion, the Lord's people and the daily sacrifice were given over to it. It prospered in everything it did, and truth was thrown to the ground.

Since the powerful horn (ruler) attacked the city of God and the temple, the place where God resides, it was attacking God. Wanting to be as mighty as the Lord of Host, it stops the sacrifices to Yahweh. In the ancient world, people believed that a god needed to be nourished by the sacrifices people offered to it. In this way, there was a symbiotic linkage between the blessings that God gives his people and the sacrifices that the people offer back to their god. When Leviticus describes the various offerings (Lev 1–7), it says that the sacrifices must be prepared correctly when served to God. The savor and smell of a choice sacrifice that is properly prepared pleases God. "You are to wash the internal organs and the legs with water, and the priest is to burn all of it on the altar. It is a burnt offering, a food offering, an aroma pleasing to the Lord" (Lev 1:9). Leviticus mentions "food offering to God" fifty-three times. By contrast, in Revelation 5:8, the prayers of the saints rise to God like aromatic incense.

Of course, the eternal God doesn't eat human sacrifices or need them to survive. However, the symbolism is strong. Because of his rebellion, the powerful horn received God's sacrifices, conquered some of the heavenly angels, destroyed the temple, and threw truth to the ground. In Revelation 12, the dragon is the powerful horn. As such, the angels that it throws from the sky with his combat move are not his fallen angels.

Let me add a parenthetical comment. I do not know how angels fight or what happens to an angel when it loses a battle. When speaking of fallen angels, the Bible declares that they are bound, put in chains, thrown into

---

29. Aune, *Revelation 6–16*, 685–86. The allusion to one-third of the stars could refer to the number who fell with the Watchers in Genesis 6. First Enoch indicates that two hundred Watchers came to Earth. The author of Revelation knows what 1 Enoch teaches on this topic. Aune avers that the throwing down of the Dragon is a retelling of the Isaiah 14 story. It represents Satan's fall. However, Aune doesn't suggest that the stars that were thrown down were coconspirators in his rebellion.

Tartarus, or cast down to the earth. In the end, they will be thrown into the Lake of Fire. Whatever we think about the topic of heavenly warfare, the Bible says that divine combat has taken place in the heavenlies. God has a heavenly army. It has a commander. Jesus had the right to summon it before he went to the cross (Matt 26:53). Satan fights against it. There are winners and losers. When making this observation, I am not endorsing dualism or the idea that God is not omnipotent.

To use Peter Wagner's terminology, I believe that fallen angels are associated with strategic-level spiritual warfare.[30] Others call this cosmic-level spiritual warfare. This has to do with nation gods, territorial spirits, and those who are assigned to certain industries. For example, Hollywood and the media to include the pornography trade have high ranking fallen angels assigned to them. If I am correct, fallen angels are not likely to attach to an individual person unless that person had great strategic value. Satan attached to Judas. In the end times, Satan will also attach to a person through whom he will control the governments of the world. I assume high ranking fallen angels attached to Hitler, Stalin, and other notoriously wicked political leaders through whom Satan advanced his kingdom and did great evil.

At this point, I affirm that there are fallen angels and that they do the bidding of Satan. A fallen angel is morally corrupted and has been thrown down from heaven. Some are bound in Tartarus. Others are free to roam in the same way that Satan roams the earth (1 Pet 5:8). Most likely, some rebelled after Satan won his initial encounter with Adam. Others may have fallen at various times. The nation gods are fallen sons of God who work with Satan (Deut 32:8–9). They can be described as territorial spirits. Since there are various ranks and levels of heavenly beings, there must be ranks for fallen angels.[31]

From Where Do All the Demons Come?

Wagner writes that ground-level spiritual warfare is the practice of deliverance ministry with individuals. It is casting demons out of people and

---

30. Wagner, "Strategic-Level Deliverance Model," 179–81. "What Wagner and others are calling 'strategic-level spiritual warfare' (SLSW) is praying against these territorial spirits, seeking to 'map' their strategies over given locations by discerning their names and what they use to keep people in bondage and then to bind them in turn so that evangelism may go unhindered" (Engelsviken, *Spiritual Conflict in Today's Mission*).

31. For a detailed explanation of the types of heavenly beings, see Heiser, *Angels*, 1–27 and Walton, "Demons in Mesopotamia," 229–46.

freeing them from bondages so that they can serve God and live holy lives.[32] This is what Jesus did when he expelled demons and set the captives free. Charles Kraft differentiates between ground-level and cosmic-level spiritual warfare. He believes that cosmic-level spirits have authority over ground-level spirits (fallen angels). They assign and rule over the ground-level spirits (demons) that we cast out.[33]

If these demons aren't fallen angels, who are they? Previously, I discussed the Nephilim option. There's no reason to doubt that Nephilim spirits operate as demons. Most likely, they are of a higher order than a common evil spirit. Yet, that cannot be the full answer because too many people have demonic attachments. At most, there could have been 100,000 Nephilim spirits after the flood.

In order to determine why there are so many demons, we need to explore every option. First, as strange as this sounds, fallen angels could be mating with women and siring more Nephilim spirits. In Genesis 6, the sons of God who incarnated themselves copulated with women. In the Old Testament, angels incarnated themselves when they visited Abraham and blinded the people of Sodom. Daniel saw the angel Michael. Angels also appeared to Mary, the shepherds, people in prison, and to others. Hebrews 13:2 reminds us that we could entertain angels unaware. If angels can appear like humans, should we assume that fallen angels can appear human? If they take on human bodies, can they do what humans do? The angels that visited Abraham ate the food he prepared for them. If fallen angels have been mating with women over the centuries, they could have produced a lot of Nephilim who became demons when they died.

To add to this imbroglio, I have cast incubi spirits out of dozens of women. An incubus is a type of sex spirit who rapes a woman. I have also cast out succubae spirits, the female counterpart to an incubus, from men. These are powerful spirits who can be felt by the victim. I will share one example.[34]

Last year, a woman with whom I had done inner healing called me. She sounded desperate and very scared. She reported that she had been attacked by a spirit. The spirit held her down and had sex with her several times. The first time, it appeared to her as a beautiful and seductive prince. When this happened, the woman was angry at her husband. Because of this,

---

32. Wagner, "Strategic-Level Deliverance Model," 179.
33. Kraft, *Evangelical's Guide to Spiritual Warfare*, 235–51.
34. In Hebrew folklore, Lilith is a succubus spirit who mated with Adam. "When Adam, doing penance for his sin, separated from Eve for 130 years, he, by impure desire, caused the earth to be filled with demons, or shedim, lilin, and evil spirits" (Kesler, *Demonology 201*, 183). Folk tradition also states that Samael (a type of Satan) mated with Eve and produced Cain. Cain fathered "sons of divinity" who became demons (Dennis, "Cain," 74).

she allowed the spirit to have access to her. She called me because it wouldn't stop. It came to her every night. The spirit said that he owned her and that she was his bride. He said that he would produce progeny through her. The woman was physically wounded by the violations. The physical evidence included tearing, bruising, and seminal fluid. The woman also developed a very bad vaginal infection.

Many women have reported similar attacks. One woman who came to me for help was physically molested while I was talking to her. Even though I couldn't see the entity, I could see the indentations on her. Normal demons don't do this. Two women told me that they could see dark little creatures that came out of them after they were attacked by an incubus. They believed that the beings were new demons.[35]

Second, others have gone the route of alien abduction.[36] Christians who believe this will offer examples from the Bible to bolster their case. In most abduction stories, the aliens bring a person to a ship, restrain the person, and do things to their reproductive organs. They target males and females. Many abductees claim that they are mating with the aliens to create hybrid creatures. A large percentage claim that they saw hybrid children who look part human and part alien.[37]

Here is an excerpt from the *Harvard Gazette*. The recounted story is typical of those who have been abducted by aliens.

> Mark H. says he was abducted by aliens. He clearly remembers awakening one night, unable to move anything but his eyes. He saw flashing lights, heard buzzing sounds, experienced feelings of levitation, and felt electric tingling sensations. Most terrifying were the nonhuman figures he saw by his bed.
> Mark believes they were aliens.
> Later, he underwent hypnosis to try to recall exactly what had happened to him. Under hypnosis, Mark remembered being whisked through an open window to a large spaceship. He was very frightened when aliens took him into some kind of medical examining room. There he had sex with one of them.[38]

---

35. For more on this, see Payne, *Adventures in Spiritual Warfare*, 23–25.

36. For a popular understanding of this, see Eggert, *Ancient Aliens*, and UAMN TV, "New Alien Abduction Documentary."

37. An alien abduction will usually follow a pattern: capture, examination, and procedures. The procedure will include having sex with an alien or having eggs or sperm removed from the abductee. Often, the person will meet a hybrid creature that resembles them, (Appelle, "Alien Abduction Experiences," 76–77).

38. Cromie, "Alien Abduction Claims Examined," paras. 1–3.

In chapter 2, I explored why some people are more likely to believe in UFOs than spirit beings. I critiqued a worldview that made assumptions about reality without properly evaluating the evidence. In the case of alien abduction stories, those who have been abducted offer similar stories that conform to a pattern. Since thousands of people have shared their stories, one should remain open to the possibility that they are recounting a real event. If the aliens who abduct the people are fallen angels, the resulting offspring would be Nephilim. Of course, some Christians have gone overboard when they assert that fallen angels disguised as aliens are creating a Nephilim army to battle against God's people in the last days. While being open to the evidence, I don't believe that the alien abduction theory solves the presenting problem.

Third, of those who claim to have had a near-death experience, 28 percent describe hellish encounters. I have collected stories from these people. In December 2018, a woman came to me for inner healing and deliverance. She had attended a lecture that I gave and felt a demonic manifestation as I spoke. She wanted to reclaim her life. I told her story in chapter 6. Allow me to recap what she said. She described piercing darkness, searing pain, a burning furnace beneath her, and vile creatures who tore her body. She said that she would do anything to avoid that place. In the most ardent voice, she said that she never wanted to go back to hell.

Hell is as real as heaven. I have argued that Satan is Beelzebub, the Lord of Gehenna. People who die in his service remain in his bondage when they go to hell until the final judgment. God doesn't manage hell. If people who go to hell belong to Satan, could Satan send them back to torment other humans? If many of the ground-level demons were disembodied people from hell, it would explain why they lack the great intelligence of fallen angels, do not speak a lot of foreign languages, and are attached to a specific area.

Additionally, from ancient times people have believed that ancestor spirits can interact with the living. They may protect the tribe or give blessings to individuals. At times, they need to be appeased. If they are not appeased or if they are ignored, they can hurt people and cause social discord. Some have argued that demons are dead people who were unjustly treated or killed in a violent way. They have unfinished business with the living and can't rest until they have satisfied their vendetta. Others say that they are the ghosts of the wicked dead.[39]

Based on my interactions with demons while doing deliverance ministry, this option fits what I have experienced. If my observations are correct, fallen angels are high-level spirits and demons are ground-level spirits. The

---

39. Riley, "Demon," 238.

ranks of the demons may be augmented by the spirits of the departed dead who went to hell and are sent back to do Satan's work. Possibly, Nephilim spirits serve as overlords. C. S. Lewis alluded to this type of teacher/student relationship in his *Screwtape Letters*.

If the common evil spirits that we cast out are dead humans from hell, it explains why they understand the family to which they are attached and why they fear those who have assigned them to their jobs. Those who go to hell will do anything to escape the suffering, even if it means haunting their human family. A person who escapes hell as an evil spirit doesn't want to return to hell.

In *Hungry Souls*, Gerard van den Aardweg gives many examples of dead people who have returned as spirits. In his research, he distinguishes between souls from Purgatory, damned souls from Hell, and demons who disguise themselves as human souls. As I mentioned to in chapter 2, because most evangelical Protestants assume that all apparitions are demons and many folk religionists assume that conjured spirits are deceased loved ones, his cautionary tone is important. Even though I do not espouse the "doctrine of Purgatory" as it is described by the Roman Catholic Church, I believe that Aardweg is on to something.

Aardweg attributes all spirits that manifest during trances, seances, hypnosis, or anything dealing with the occult as demonic. Even still, "damned human souls from Hell, who manifest themselves . . . should not be mistaken for 'demons.'"[40] He devotes an entire chapter to stories of damned souls from Hell who have returned to hurt and haunt people. The fact that it is difficult to differentiate between the spirit of a dead person who has returned from Hell and a demon adds credence to my theory. Whether one is dealing with a bona fide demon or departed person, the end result can be the same.

The idea that some ground-level demons are the spirits of the departed dead who have returned from Hell is conjecture. The Bible doesn't say this. Likewise, the Bible doesn't say why we have so many demons. I have offered this speculation because the prevalence of demons needs to be explained.

---

40. Aardweg, *Hungry Souls*, 17. Aardweg attempts to deal with Protestant objections to spirits from Purgatory (20–21). He is a psychotherapists (PhD) who collects stories about Near-death experiences and the paranormal from his patients in much the same way that I collect the same type of stories from those with whom I do ministry.

In Perspective

I will end this chapter by reminding the reader of a story I shared in chapter 3. I know a respected seminary professor who lost his beloved wife to Alzheimer's. He cared for her during the last ten years of his life. When she died, she did not recognize him. Her death left him empty and lost. He couldn't move on from it. One day, God sent his wife back to him so that he could have closure. The encounter was riveting and life-changing. When she returned for a short visit, she had no traces of disease, remembered all the details of their life together, encouraged him to follow Jesus, and told him to trust God. God gave him the closure that Alzheimer's stole from him.[41] I know that the story is true. If God can send good people back to Earth on a special mission, I assume that Satan can do the same with those who are in hell.

---

41. Crick and Miller, *Journeying with Jeanette*, 233–52.

13

The Fall

YEARS ago, I asked my confirmation students to describe the Garden of Eden. An eleven-year-old boy said that it was a tropical wonderland on an isolated island with exotic birds and lots of fun things to do. Out of curiosity, I prodded him for more details. He replied, "Adam and Eve were naked and last summer I saw naked people on an island when we went on vacation. People in America have to wear clothes because it gets cold but people who live on islands don't have to wear clothes because it's warm all year long." The "without clothes and unashamed" (Gen 2:25) aspect of the garden caught this boy's imagination.

What comes to your mind when you think about the garden? I imagine a loving God, a lush paradise, walks in the cool of the evening, a trickster serpent, a sacred tree, Adam's sin, a divine curse, and a flaming sword. In the fall story, these narrative threads weave themselves together like sulfur, charcoal, and potassium nitrate mix to make gunpowder. They make for a volatile concoction. The story's climactic explosion left humankind broken and separated from its Creator. To add insult to injury, Adam's progeny had to endure his punishment, inherit his fallen nature, and bear his corrupted image.

It gets worse. The cosmic blast that shook the foundations of the garden wasn't limited to humankind. It damaged the entire creation to include the divine realm and every aspect of the material world. Romans 8 captures the enormity of the tragedy when it states, "For the creation waits in eager expectation for the [sons] of God[1] to be revealed. For the creation was

---

1. In this text, "sons of God" doesn't refer to the Watchers or the heavenly host.

subjected to frustration, not by its own choice, but by the will of the one who subjected it, in hope that the creation itself will be liberated from its [slavery to corruption] and brought into the freedom and glory of the children of God" (Gen 19–21).

In their revolt against God, the heavenly beings who sided with Satan became evil. Furthermore, one may surmise that Satan became the leader of the fallen angels in the same way that he became the ruler of the earth when Adam and Eve gave him their allegiance. Unlike fallen people, the demons are eternally bound to Satan and to his fate. They cannot repent, be redeemed, or escape their coming doom. Interestingly, the Watchers trying to repent and be reconciled with God is a main theme of 1 Enoch.

Is the Fall Story a Myth?

This book assumes that Adam and Eve were real humans and that the Genesis fall story describes a past event. Bible scholar John Walton sums up my position when he locates Adam and Eve in history. "When we identify Adam and Eve as historical figures, we mean that they are real people involved in a real past. They are not inherently mythological or legendary, though their roles may contribute to being treated that way in some of the reception history. Likewise, they are not fictional."[2]

Richard Averbeck comes to a similar conclusion about the universal conflict that is portrayed in Genesis 3. He states, "No matter what one believes about the historicity of the Bible and its claims to truth, the way forward . . . is to read myth as analogical thinking about history and reality. We are not talking about some kind of alternative truth system, but a different way of talking about what was and is in fact true, historically and experientially."[3]

Analogical doesn't mean that every aspect of the fall story is literal. Rather, it argues that a narrative based on the collective memory of a past event tells a divinely inspired story that conveys a universal truth. It is revelation. When reading the Genesis fall story, the only way to discover the truth that it avers is to engage the tale because the truth is embedded in the narrative history.[4]

In the New Testament, the believers are called holy ones and sons of God. They will become members of the reconstituted heavenly council in the resurrection when they reign together with Christ. That is when the sons of God will be revealed.

2. Walton, *Lost World*, 101.
3. Averbeck, "Ancient Near Eastern Mythography," 355.
4. The Western impulse to demythologize the Bible is based on a naturalistic

When myth is understood as a sacred story that conveys a literal truth, one can affirm that the fall story is mythological. As a literary device and technical genre, myth doesn't imply make-believe or fairytale. Early Jews believed that God created people in his image and that the proto-humans fell when they sinned against God. Genesis tells the covenant people how it happened. Furthermore, it places the events in the context of a larger, unfolding story of good versus evil. Christians call this "salvation history." In the end, God wins and those who side with God are saved. The fall story is real in the same way that God's progressing plan of salvation is real. It took place in time and space. The characters have names.

Furthermore, the study of comparative mythology shows that the fall story is a universal myth with similar characters and overlapping themes that include a snake and people who lose immortality because they are beguiled.[5] To be sure, the Genesis account is unique in many ways. However, the tale that it uncovers is not unique. The fact that the fall is a universal myth with a similar structure suggests that there was an original story from which the variations diffused over time. I affirm that the Genesis account

---

worldview that assumes that theophanies, demonic encounters, and miracle stories didn't happen and that they don't happen today. In *Confronting Powerless Christianity*, Charles Kraft analyzes this worldview and those who import it into Christianity. Proponents of demythologizing biblical text believe that science is the best way to know truth and that the miracle stories in the Bible are not literally true. As a Christian, I affirm that miracles happen today and that they happened in the ancient past. (For a convincing academic examination of this point, see Keener, *Miracles: The Credibility of the New Testament Accounts*.) For example, I believe that Jesus died and was literally resurrected. Since many ancient myths talk about the resurrection of a hero from the dead, the resurrection of Jesus can be described as a mythological story. However, that doesn't mean that it didn't happen like the biblical writers said it happened. Furthermore, Jesus and the New Testament church expelled demons. In fact, shamans and religious specialists from all over the world interact with spirits and cast them out of people. I also cast out demons on a regular basis. They speak to me and manifest in predictable ways. The same people who demythologize the Bible would say that what I and others do can't happen. They are wrong on all accounts. Once you allow for the interplay and overlapping of the natural and supernatural realms, the events of sacred narrative can be received and interpreted in terms of the given genera. Not all biblical stories are meant to be understood as literal events. For example, Jesus was an expert at employing parables to convey deep theological truths. How do the writers of the story of the fall intend that it be interpreted? A literal interpretation does not preclude the use of allegory. Like an allegory, the portrayal of a real event can be done in such a way as to reveal a hidden meaning.

5. "The study of myth certainly gives the [Christian] believer something to think about. The parallels between the myths of our traditions and those of vastly different cultures offer parallel myths of the Fall, virgin births, resurrections, and so on—often strikingly similar to our own sacred stories" (Bierlein, *Parallel Myths*, 308). The author offers a theological response to the fact of parallel myths (308–14).

gives voice to the original myth from which all the variations are imperfect memories.

The following excerpt from Joseph Campbell helps to make this point. Even though the quotation doesn't refer to the fall story, Campbell and others affirm the fall as a universal myth.[6]

> The comparative study of the mythologies of the world compels us to view the cultural history of mankind as a unit; for we find that such themes as the Fire-theft, Deluge, Land of the Dead, Virgin Birth, and Resurrected hero have a worldwide distribution, appearing everywhere in new combinations, while remaining, like the elements of a kaleidoscope, only and always the same. Furthermore, . . . [the tales] appear also in religious contexts, where they are accepted not only as factually true but even as revelation of the veritas to which the whole culture is a living witness and from which it derives both its spiritual authority and its temporal power.[7]

As a point of comparison, what the Bible says about heaven and our future glorification is also real even though the colors with which the story is painted seem as exotic to the modern hearer as the Garden of Eden tale. Read Revelation 22:1–5 out loud and pay careful attention to how the writer uses colorful language to describe the undoing of the fall.

> Then the angel showed me the river of the water of life, as clear as crystal, flowing from the throne of God and of the Lamb down the middle of the great street of the city. On each side of the river stood the tree of life, bearing twelve crops of fruit, yielding its fruit every month. And the leaves of the tree are for the healing of the nations. No longer will there be any curse. The throne of God and of the Lamb will be in the city, and his servants will serve him. They will see his face, and his name will be on their foreheads. There will be no more night. They will not need the light of a lamp or the light of the sun, for the Lord God will give them light. And they will reign for ever and ever.[8]

The prophetic tradition in the Old and New Testaments affirms that God is going to correct the fall and free the creation from the curse he placed upon it. Imagining the renewal of all things requires that one reach beyond the language of everyday life. Common vocabulary cannot capture the wonder

---

6. Campbell explores the fall-story motif in *Mythic Dimension*, 198–202.

7. Campbell, *Mythic Dimension*, 15.

8. God and his throne are in the midst of the new Eden. Heiser has argued that God's throne was also in the original Eden (*Supernatural*, 27–28).

of what will be revealed. Hence, the exotic words of Revelation 22 give voice to a universal longing that people from every time and place have felt.

Even though the fall story is written with the language of myth, it describes something that will actually happen. Hence, by means of symbolic language, the Bible paints a picture of a future reality that reveals a hidden truth beyond the scope of the ordinary imagination. Paul captures this when he states, I "was caught up to paradise and heard inexpressible things, things that no one is permitted to tell" (2 Cor 12:4). During his time in heaven, he saw reality as it really was but was unable to use our language to describe it.

People who have near-death experiences often say that they lack the vocabulary to describe the landscapes and vibrant colors that they saw in heaven. In some sense, the fall has dampened our ability to perceive reality as it really is. When one is released from the physical body, the biological filters are removed. Those who go to heaven during their near-death experiences say that you can talk without speaking, that love pulsates from Jesus' radiating body, and that the city of God is real. The otherworldly experience causes them to declare that Revelation accurately captures the reality of heaven.[9]

In sum, in order for there to be a future renewal, there had to be a past fall. The fall story in the Bible uses the language and myth of the original hearers to describe the fall. In the same way that the future restoration will happen, the fall actually happened. Modern theologians interpret the fall story using exegetical tools in order to say what it means. I believe one can't understand the meaning of Genesis 3 until one affirms its language and imagery.[10] It tells a real story.

Why Did Satan Rebel?

When the early church appraises the fall, it remembers that Satan was the first sinner. The fall began with the heavenly beings, not with humans. Humankind would not have fallen if Satan had not rebelled. So, why did the Evil One turn on God and entice Adam and Eve to sin? A pseudepigraphal book called "The Life of Adam and Eve" answers this compound question.

---

9. I recommend Roth and Lane, *Heaven Is beyond Your Wildest Imagination* if you are interested in the afterlife that awaits the children of God.

10. Murphy comes to a similar conclusion when he uses the terms *literal* and *symbolic* to describe the genera of Genesis 3. "Genesis 3 is both an historical and a pictorial account of the fall of humanity. It actually happened the way it is recorded. There really was an historical Adam and Eve" (*Handbook for Spiritual Warfare*, 34). When describing the historical-symbolic approach, Murphy says that the historical events that are portrayed are "given in story form and with vivid imagery and symbolism" (35).

In the book, Adam and Eve are struggling to survive in the post-idyllic world. Despite their hardships, Satan is still pursuing them. After succumbing to another trick, an exacerbated Eve asks Satan why he continues to assault them. Satan's response shows that his malice was motivated by jealousy, pride, annoyance, and insolence. Speaking to Adam he says,

> When God blew into you the *breath of life* and your countenance and likeness were made *in the image of God*, Michael brought you and made (us) worship you in the sight of God . . . I said to him, "Why do you compel me? I will not worship one inferior and subsequent to me. I am prior to him in creation; before he was made, I was already made. He ought to worship me." . . . And the Lord God was angry with me and sent me with my angels out from our glory; and because of you, we were expelled into this world from our dwellings and have been cast onto Earth. (LAE 13–16, Charlesworth)[11]

The text is important because it proffers a reason for Satan's fall. Additionally, it ties the fall of Satan to the creation of humankind when it says that the vivification of Adam triggered Satan's jealousy and disobedience. Moreover, it shows why Satan has great malice toward people. Furthermore, it intuits that Satan's greatest anger is toward God. He believes that God betrayed him and other angels when he created Adam. Satan portrays himself as a victim who is seeking to get even by tormenting the people God loves.

Charles Kraft follows this line of thinking when he argues that the creation of humankind was the event that pushed Satan to rebel.[12] Before the creation of Adam, Satan reigned as heaven's leading light. As the anointed cherub, he basked in the glory of a perfect relationship with the Almighty for uncounted eons. He had no rivals.

Michael Heiser says that Satan became angry when God told the heavenly council that he would create people in our own likeness (Gen 1:26–28) and give them dominion over the natural world. He identifies the Serpent with Satan and calls him a malcontent from Yahweh's council. As a member of God's entourage, he accompanied God to Eden and had full access to it and to Eve.[13]

---

11. The writer of the Life of Adam and Eve wrongly believed that Hebrews 1:6 referred to the creation of Adam as the firstborn of this world. "For to which of the angels did God ever say, 'You are my Son; today I have become your Father'? Or again, 'I will be his Father, and he will be my Son'? And again, when God brings his firstborn into the world, he says, 'Let all God's angels worship him'" (Heb 1:5–6).

12. Kraft, *I Give You Authority*, 21–36.

13. Heiser, *Unseen Realm*, 73–75.

Michael Green suggests that Satan was the angelic administrator of the earth before the creation of Adam.[14] However, the creation of humankind threatened his privileged position. Moreover, it shifted the spotlight from him to humankind.

Not only were Adam and Eve the delight of God's eyes and made in his image, they also had physical bodies that connected them to the material world. Moreover, since God created them to tend the garden and have dominion over the material creation, they would have become full members of the divine council had they not sinned. Once they had matured in their rulership role as the masters of the Earth, they may have supplanted Satan as God's leading lights. Perhaps that is why Satan tempted them while they were still trainees.

Adam Created to Have Dominion

According to Genesis 2:5–7, because there was no earthling (*adam*) to care for the earth (*adamah*), God formed the earthling from the earth (v. 7). Then God put Adam in the garden that he planted and placed him in charge of its care (v. 15). The ground needed to be tended. Afterward, as a sign of his authority to steward the creation, God brought all the animals to Adam so he could name them (vv. 19–20). In the ancient world, a father named the child over whom he had authority and for whom he had a nurturing responsibility. With authority comes responsibility. As such, the naming of the animals by Adam represented God giving Adam authority over them and tasking him to care for them.

Following the naming of the animals, God gave Adam a helpmate to join him in his divine task of nature-care (Gen 2:18–19). Eve is more than a wife. She is his soulmate and a partner in his labors. Adam comes from the ground and is tied to it. Eve comes from Adam and is tied to him (v. 23). They become one flesh (v. 24).

Genesis 1:26 says that God made humankind (male and female) in his image and his likeness so that they could exercise dominion over the material creation to include animals and plants. Sirach captures this when it says that God granted them authority over everything on Earth (17:2). "Exercising dominion over all living things" is more emphatic than tend the ground or manage the garden (Sir 17:28–30). Moreover, the dominion that God gave to Adam and Eve extended to their children.

As a sign that God had not abandoned his purposes for "adamkind" after the flood, he directed Noah's children to be fruitful, multiply, fill the

---

14. Green, *I Believe in Satan's Downfall*, 47.

earth, and increase upon it. What's more, God restated that Noah and his children still had a limited dominion over the animals and plants (Gen 8:17; 9:1; 7). All of them are given to people for food. In addition, all creatures will fear and dread human beings (Gen 9:2). Animals aren't permitted to kill people. God will judge all that do.[15] People aren't allowed to drink the blood of animals (Gen 9:4–5).

Psalm 8 refers to the divine right that God gave to people in Genesis 1:26. "What are human beings that you are mindful of them, mortals that you care for them? Yet you have made them a little lower than God, and crowned them with glory and honor. You have given them dominion over the works of your hands; you have put all things under their feet" (Ps 8:4–6, NRSV). Following the example of Genesis, the psalmist emphasizes that humankind has dominion over the land animals, birds, and the fish (Ps 7–8).

Verse 5 is often translated "You have made him a little lower than the angels." The term is *elohim*. The Scripture could be translated, you have made him a little lower than God, the gods, or angels. In this case, the Septuagint translates *elohim* as angels (Ps 8:5). The writer of Hebrews follows that translation when he quotes Psalm 8. However, when translating verse 5, he adds an important caveat. You have made them lower than the angels "for a little while." He understands that people will be higher than the angels in the resurrection. Regardless, when God said, "Let us make humankind in our image, in our likeness" (Gen 1:26), he was talking to the *elohim*. This presumes that God, the Watchers, and humans share a common image and are kindred beings.

Before the creation of Adam, the heavenly *elohim* were made in the image of God and shared authority with God to include power and rulership. Psalm 8 declares that God intended to place all things under humans as they exercised God's authority. Does "all things" include the heavenly *elohim* or does it only relate to things in the material world? Psalm 8 doesn't address this issue because it isn't talking about a hierarchy between people and angels. Still, Paul reminds us that the saints will judge angels (1 Cor 6:3).

In truth, God doesn't pit people against angels. The example of Satan shows why God's family shouldn't be pulled by sibling rivalry. God created both people and angels as sapient beings. Both share aspects of God's character and his glory. Both enjoy God's pleasure and are called to serve him. They are on the same team and belong to the same family. For ages to come, they will live together in the halls of heaven and go to the vast reaches of the

---

15. In "Fire Ants and Demons: Knowing Our God-Given Dominion," I expound on the meaning of this command in practical ways. People still have authority over the wild animals (Payne, *Adventures in Spiritual Warfare*, 99–110).

universe to do God's bidding. Even now the holy angels work alongside the saints to accomplish God's work.

I strongly affirm that God didn't intend the garden to be the final residence of Adam and Eve. Rather, it was a training ground close to the throne of God.[16] After they grew into their role as God's coregents, they would have embraced the larger office for which God created them. After they sinned, God denied them access to the Tree of Life out of mercy. Living eternally in a fallen body would have been a fate worse than death (Gen 3:22–24).

Jesus' Temptation as an Example

Why did God allow Satan to tempt Adam and Eve? To answer this question, we should examine the temptation of Jesus. Jesus is called the Second Adam (1 Cor 15:45). He came to undo the calamity that the first Adam wrought through his sin. When Jesus refused Satan's temptations, he defeated Satan.[17] The temptations of Adam and Jesus can both be described as a test.

When Jesus returned from his temptation triumph, the response of a belligerent demon demonstrated his total victory over Satan and his evil hosts. "Go away! What do you want with us, Jesus of Nazareth? Have you come to destroy us? I know who you are; the Holy One of God!" (Luke 4:34).[18]

---

16. "An ancient Israelite would have thought of Eden as the dwelling of God and the place from which God and his council directed the affairs of humanity" (Heiser, *Unseen Realm*, 47). "In many ancient religions, luxurious gardens and inaccessible mountains were considered the home of the gods. The Bible uses both descriptions for Eden. Eden was God's home and, therefore, where he conducted business. It was his headquarters, or home office" (Heiser, *Supernatural*, 28). More will be said about the mountain image when I discuss Mount Zaphon and Satan's desire to ascend to the throne of God.

17. In the garden temptation of Eve and the wilderness temptation of Jesus, Satan misrepresented the word of God, attempted to confuse the person, and divined a half-truth. He told Eve that she would become like God (an *elohim*) if she ate from the Tree of Knowledge of Good and Evil. He told Jesus that he would give him all the kingdoms of the world if he worshipped him. In both cases, the half-truth appealed to the person. However, the promises were designed to bring the person under Satan's dominion. For more on this, see chapter 15.

18. The Old Testament prefers "Holy One of Israel." Isaiah uses the phrase twenty-seven times. It always refers to Yahweh. On the other hand, "holy ones" refers to the Watchers and is used in parallel with sons of God and morning stars. It can also refer to angels. In the Gospels, "Holy One of God" refers to the Messiah and is only used for Jesus. Demons uttered the phrase right after Jesus defeated Satan in the temptation battle. Peter must have heard them say it because he also employs it. "We have come to believe and to know that you are the Holy One of God" (John 6:69). It's possible that 1 Enoch is the primary reference for Holy One of God. It says, "The God of the universe, the Holy Great One, will come forth from his dwelling. And from there will march

The demons recognized Jesus as the one who could torment them (Matt 8:29). They had to obey him because he could destroy them. The befuddled Jews marveled at Jesus because he exercised complete authority over the demons (Mark 1:22–27). As the second Adam who remained true to the will of the Father, Jesus became the master of the demons.

Would Adam and Eve have gained authority over Satan in the same way that Jesus did when he resisted temptation if they had repelled Satan's temptation and remained true to God? The answer is yes! Additionally, they would have moved from the category of innocent to the category of righteous. As sapient beings with free will, they had to choose to submit to God in order to become righteous. Before the temptation, they were innocent but they weren't righteous. After they failed the temptation, they ceased to be innocent and didn't become righteous. Instead, they became fallen sinners. The same fate would have seized Jesus had he given into Satan's temptation.

Binary oppositions demonstrate how language is structured (light-dark, high-low, hot-cold). When one names the extremes, gradation can be noted. Based on this, good is only known when seen in the light of evil. As such, without the possibility of sin, there cannot be good because good requires that one rejects evil. That is, being good is a willful choice to side with God because God is the epitome of good (Mark 10:18). Righteousness is knowing God and doing his will.

Good can't be the result of a computer program that determines outcomes. It must be a willful choice. Innocence may be beautiful, but it isn't a moral good. In the fall, Eve was deceived but Adam chose to follow Satan. He made a decision with dire consequences (1 Tim 2:14). The human fall is traced to him.

John Wesley defines sin as the willful violation of a known law of God. Sin is an act of the will that reflects an inbred defect in the moral being of fallen humanity.[19] Today, people aren't condemned because they are born

---

upon Mount Sinai and appear in his camp emerging from heaven with a mighty power. And everyone will be afraid, and Watchers shall quiver" (1 En. 1:3–4, Charlesworth). According to 1 Enoch, when the Holy Great One comes, he will execute judgment on the rebellious Watchers and the Nephilim who became evil spirits when they died in the flood. The title "Holy One of God" indicates that Jesus is the greatest among the holy ones (Nickelsburg, *1 Enoch*, 143–45). In a similar way, 1 Enoch refers to the "Chosen (elect) One of God" fourteen times. Luke 9:35 borrows that term to describe what the Father said to Jesus during the transfiguration, "This is my Son, the Elect One of God" (Lumpkin, *Book of Giants*, 43). It's a messianic term that connects Jesus to the Divine Council.

19. Leviticus 4 specifies that a person is guilty for unintentional sins. It prescribes an offering to atone for the guilt. All sin, intentional or unintentional, is a violation of the Torah. Wesley focuses on volitional sin because his doctrine of sanctification is tied to it. One can only achieve sinless perfection (full sanctification) if sin is defined as an

with a fallen nature or are innately prone to sinful behavior. They are condemned because they sin and rebel against God's rule. To be clear, all have sinned (Rom 3:23; 1 John 1:8–10). In truth, the church must emphasize getting people saved and the process of getting them converted. The first happens when one encounters the gospel message, repents, and turns to Christ in faith. The second happens as the new believer submits to the lordship of Christ and bears the fruit of the Spirit. A good tree can't bear bad fruit (Matt 7:18).

Satan, the fallen angels, and Adam are willful transgressors who rebelled against God's rule. Satan is a sinner! In the regeneration that comes through Christ, God enables repentant people to reject willful sin as he transforms them by the power of his indwelling Spirit. Believers can't excuse willful sin because they have a fallen nature. Tolerating sin is the pathway to defeat and demonization. Sin must be conquered. A good God invites wayward people to become like him by striving for holiness and sanctification.

In the same way that Adam yielded to Satan, the saints are free to reject Satan and align with Christ when they fall under the drawing power of the Holy Spirit. When people give themselves to Jesus, God gives himself to them. At that time, they are no longer under the dominion of sin or the power of Satan. Sadly, willful sin works against God's plan and enables Satan to maintain access to the believer. Sin equals bondage.

---

act of the will. Once the will is in full submission to God, the person can be sanctified. This is a work of the Spirit in the believer. As long as one lives in a fallen human body, one cannot escape from unintentional sin. While unintentional sin is serious, this type of transgression doesn't appear in the New Testament vice lists. Rather, on the Day of Judgment, the motives of people's heart will be revealed (1 Cor 4:5).

14

The Serpent in the Garden

> Now the serpent was more crafty than any of the wild animals the Lord God had made. He said to the woman, "Did God really say, 'You must not eat from any tree in the garden'?" The woman said to the serpent, "We may eat fruit from the trees in the garden, but God did say, 'You must not eat fruit from the tree that is in the middle of the garden, and you must not touch it, or you will die.'" "You will not certainly die," the serpent said to the woman. "For God knows that when you eat from it your eyes will be opened, and you will be like God, knowing good and evil." (Gen 3:1–5)[1]

Having a snake in the garden is a serious problem. Many years ago, my newlywed wife and I lived in a parsonage that had a lush garden foyer. To get to the front door, we had to open a patio gate and walk on a path through the tropical shrubbery. We enjoyed pulling weeds and nurturing the plants. One day, my wife saw a rattlesnake in the garden. After that, she would no longer use the front door or work the garden. Certainly, a snake is a universal archetype that arouses fear. With the possible exception of crazy

---

1. Wenham offers five possible interpretations for the phrase "knowing good and evil." Knowing good and evil is (1) knowing the consequences of obeying and disobeying God's commandments; (2) knowing the difference between right and wrong (having moral discernment); (3) having knowledge about sex and sexuality; (4) having omniscience; and (5) acquiring wisdom (*Genesis 1–15*, 63–64).

python hunters in the Florida Everglades, most sane people try to avoid snakes.

Why Did Eve Talk to the Serpent?

Humankind wouldn't have fallen when it did if the serpent hadn't waylaid Eve by the Tree of the Knowledge of Good and Evil. Why did Eve talk to a slithering snake since most people would have fled from it? Why didn't the talking serpent offend Eve or arouse fear in her? Why didn't she call out to Adam? Answering these questions will lead to a deeper understanding of Satan's fall.

Jubilees and Josephus say that the garden animals talked before the fall.[2] C. S. Lewis runs with this idea in his creation parody, *The Lion, the Witch and the Wardrobe*. In his allegory, a talking lion (Aslan) is a Christ figure. A wicked witch is a Satan figure. An unwitting son of Adam has fallen under the domain of the wicked witch when he listened to her cunning, ate her Turkish Delight, and betrayed his siblings. To redeem the errant son of Adam from the witch's cruel custody, Aslan freely gives himself as a sacrifice. The witch thinks that she has won when Aslan dies. However, Aslan is raised from the dead because he died a righteous death on behalf of another person. In the end, with the help of the talking animals, the witch's reign is dismantled and the children of Adam assume their rightful role as the lords of Narnia (earth).

If the animals in the Garden of Eden talked, Eve wouldn't have been afraid of a speaking serpent since she and Adam had dominion over the animals. Since the breath of life (*nephesh*) is in all animals (Gen 1:30; 6:17; 7:15; 22) like it is in humans (Gen 2:7), and since the animals fell at the same time that humankind fell, it's possible that they were sapient beings at one time. Certainly, the animals in the garden obeyed Adam. Even today, pet owners know that a dog has a personality, shows emotions, and can think. I have watched my beagles make deliberate decisions to disobey. When they disobey, are they sinning?

In the restoration, the Bible says that animals will live at peace with humans and each other. In some sense, they will be renewed just like people are renewed. If they talked in the garden, it's possible that they will talk in the revitalized world. Still, the Bible doesn't affirm that the garden animals talked. It says that the serpent talked. Plus, in the natural world in which we presently live, snakes don't have the physical apparatus or mental capacities

---

2. Jub. 3:28–29 and Josephus, *Ant.* 1.1.4

to talk like a human. Based on this, I conclude that the creature that talked to Eve couldn't have been a normal snake.

To the extent that a donkey talked to Balaam (Num 22:21–39), one could argue that the serpent in the garden could have talked under the right conditions or that a deceiving spirit possessed the snake and spoke through it. This would allow for the plain reading of the text. If one went with this interpretation, one would have to identify the spirit that possessed the snake. In the New Testament, the python spirit possesses diviners (Acts 16:16).

Moreover, it is not clear if Genesis 3:1 actually says that the snake was one of the wild animals that God created. It says that it was more crafty than any of the creatures of the field which God had made. Even though it is called a snake, the talking serpent may not have been one of the field creatures. While the "possessed snake" explanation is biblically tenable, there are better interpretations.

We know that God talked with Adam and Eve when he walked in his garden in the cool of the evening (Gen 3:8). Before creating Adam, God was in the garden with his heavenly council when he said, "Let us create man in our own image" (Gen 1:26). Did the members of the heavenly council also talk with Adam and Eve?

I think that the heavenly *elohim* interacted with Adam and Eve for four reasons: First, some from their group intermingled with humankind in Genesis 6. For some reason, they wanted to have physical bodies like people and were sexually attracted to mortal women. Second, extra-biblical texts say that they taught Adam and Eve how to tend the garden (Jub. 3:15). Someone needed to teach Adam and Eve the art of horticulture. That task seems perfectly suited to angels, the helpers of God. First Enoch says that the heavenly *elohim* taught people many things (7:1; 8; 9:6; 10:7; 65:11). Third, people and angels are spiritual cousins. Both are made in the image of God. Before the fall, the veil that separates angels from humans hadn't been drawn. Fourth, since Eve wasn't repulsed by the talking snake, she must have spoken to other beings besides God.

In sum, I conclude that the *elohim* to whom God spoke in Genesis 1 interacted with humans in the garden. In part, this explains why Eve was willing to speak with a talking serpent who may have resembled a type of divine being in the garden.

The Serpent Was a Seraph

In the section, I will argue that the serpent was Satan, that he appeared in his normal form, and that the term that Genesis uses to describe the snake can be interpreted in ways that allow for multiple explanations.[3]

Satan was at the scene of the crime and he had a motive. As has been claimed, Satan was a member of the heavenly council before his fall. Ezekiel says he was a cherub who was in Eden, the Garden of God (28:12–16).[4] Most likely, he was present when God created Adam. Based on the previously mentioned works of Charles Kraft, Michael Green, Michael Heiser, and the Life of Adam and Eve, I have already noted a possible motive for Satan's treason. I will expand on that motive in a later part of this chapter.

The Bible depicts cherubim as creatures (Ezek 1; 10; 1 Kgs 7:29; Rev 4:7). On the ark of the covenant, cherubim are commonly portrayed as humanoids with two outstretched wings. However, the Old Testament never describes how the covering cherubim appeared except to say that their wings should be spread upwards (Exod 25:18–20). Ezekiel 1:11 says that they have four wings. Supposedly, those who sewed their images into the tapestry of the Tabernacle knew how they appeared. Egyptologists say that sphinxes are the original cherubim. Besides cherubim and seraphim, no other heavenly beings in the Bible have wings.[5]

Seraphim and cherubim do the same thing. They protect the sanctity of God's holy presence and serve as throne guardians.[6] In the canonical Bible, seraphim and cherubim never appear together. When the words appear together in deuterocanonical literature, they are not clearly distinguished. For example, the heavenly scenes in 2 Enoch 19–21 don't distinguish between seraphim and cherubim. They look the same and do the same thing. For practical purposes, the functionally equivalent names refer to winged divine

---

3. Even though the New Testament is clear that the serpent is Satan, Second Temple literature is mixed. First Enoch 69:6-7 says that a fallen Watcher named Gadreel deceived Eve. Walton argues that the original hearers would have identified the serpent as a chaos creature. "Deception, misdirection and troublemaking are all within the purview of chaos creatures" (*Lost World*, 134). Wenham doesn't attempt to identify the snake with a personal being. Instead, he says it is an anti-God symbol that is connected to other serpent images of chaos (*Genesis 1–15*; 72–73). Heiser says, "The dark figure of Genesis 3 was eventually thought of as the 'mother of all adversaries,' and so the label *satan* got stuck to him." Heiser doesn't believe that the original hearers would have identified the serpent with a fully formed understanding of Satan (*Unseen Realm*, 57). Others point to a parallel in the Gilgamesh story in which a snake stole a plant that would have given the hero immortality (Coleman, *Dictionary of Mythology*, 198–99).

4. Fred Dickason makes this case (*Angels*, 127–29).

5. Heiser, *Angels*, 164–67.

6. Heiser, *Angels*, 25–26.

beings who protect the holy presence of God. Even though the root words may be different, the descriptions of the beings are similar.[7]

The term seraphim is only used in Isaiah. Other parts of the Old Testament may make indirect references to them when speaking about serpentine creatures. Cherubim is a commonly used term in the Torah and historical books.

The *Dictionary of Deities* calls seraphim winged serpents with some human attributes.[8] Heiser sees a connection between the Hebrew seraphim and the Egyptian Uraeus serpent who protected pharaoh by breathing out fire.[9] Even though burning is the Hebrew meaning of seraph, before the Masoretic text inserted vowels into the Hebrew Bible, serpent and burning were spelled the same (*srph*). In Numbers 21:6, *nechashim* (snakes) and *seraphim* (burning ones) are used together to mean fiery serpents or poisonous snakes. Two verses later, Numbers 21:8 conflates the terms and *saraph* translates as fiery serpent. Isaiah 14:29 says that a fiery flying serpent (*saraph*) will come from the root of the snake (*nachash*). A fiery flying serpent could be an ancient term for dragon or seraph type creature.

Tannin is translated as serpent when Moses throws his rod before Pharaoh in Exodus 7:8-12. The resulting snake would have been the size of Moses' rod. In Canaanite religion, Tannin is the name of a snake-like god that the high god, Baal Zaphon, defeated. In Isaiah 27:1, *tannin* translates as a coiling dragon. It's associated with Leviathan, the premortal sea monster. Isaiah says that the *tannin* will be executed by Yahweh on "that day." Isaiah 51:9 indicates that Rahab, the ancient water dragon from the abyss, is a *tannin*.[10] Even though the Bible refers to these titan creatures of a bygone era, not much is known about them.

A previous chapter showed that Revelation 12 calls Satan by the following serpentine names: Ancient Serpent, Dragon, Great Dragon, Great Fiery Dragon, and Serpent. From this list, one can see that both the Old and New Testaments portray a relationship between snake, serpent, burning one, dragon, and Satan. In short, the Bible describes Satan as a serpentine creature.[11]

---

7. Dickason attempts to distinguish between cherubim and seraphim. However, the distinction feels contrived (*Angels*, 61-67).

8. See Stolz, "Seraphim," 742-44.

9. Heiser, *Angels*, 26-27.

10. See Heider, "Tannin," 834-36.

11. Witzel discusses how the serpent/dragon image is woven into the vast majority of creation myths (*Origins of the World's Mythologies*, 148-54). The fact that it is a global archetype that conjures fear in the subconscious of most peoples points to its vast distribution.

In Genesis 3, the term for snake is *nachash*. As a noun, the word describes an ordinary animal. When different vowels are used with the root *nchsh*, it can mean diviner or one who divines.[12] For example, in Acts 16:16, the slave girl from whom Paul cast out a python spirit had clairvoyant abilities. The "spirit of python" is the spirit of divination. The mythological python that lived at Delphi can be described as a dragon-like creature associated with prophecy and dispensing hidden knowledge.[13]

When used as an adjective, *nchsh* is associated with copper or bronze. In Numbers 21:9, the bronze serpent that Moses made is called *nechash nechosheth* (the copper serpent). As you can see, the root words for snake and bronze are the same. The wordplay is obvious to the native speaker. Also, Daniel uses the copper term when he describes the divine being that stood before him. "His body was like topaz, his face like lightning, his eyes like flaming torches, his arms and legs like the gleam of burnished bronze [*nechosheth*], and his voice like the sound of a multitude" (Dan 10:6).

In sum, the root word *nchsh* can refer to snake, diviner, or the appearance of shining copper. If all the meanings are held together in the mind of the original hearers, they would capture how the Bible describes the serpent in the Garden.[14] Based on this, I conclude that the snake in the Garden refers to a serpent-like divine creature called a seraph. In this regard, I am using seraph and cherub loosely, believing that they may be different ways to describe the same type of divine being.

Furthermore, I believe that the seraph in the garden was Satan. Eve recognized him as a divine being and was happy to converse with him just like she did with other divine beings in the garden. Perhaps she looked upon him as a teacher and trusted him because the other divine beings taught her and Adam how to care for the garden. As a member of the heavenly council, he had free access to the garden.

---

12. Heiser, *Unseen Realm*, 87.

13. In Greek mythology, the spirit of divination is associated with a python spirit. It possesses those who divine at the Oracle of Delphi. Originally, it lived at Delphi to protect the premortal earth goddess, Gaia. In addition to being a snake, it is also described as a dragon-like creature. Apollo, the god of prophecy, did battle with it (see "Python" in *Prophet's Dictionary*, 458). For a different take, see Franklin, *Spirit of Python*.

14. "The serpent (*nachash*) was an image commonly used in reference to a divine throne guardian. Given the context of Eden, that helps identify the villain as a divine being. The divine adversary dispenses divine information, using it to goad Eve. He gives her an oracle: You won't really die. God knows when you eat you will be like one of the *elohim* [with whom she had regular contact in the garden]. Lastly, a shining appearance conveys a divine nature. All the meanings telegraph something important" (Heiser, *Unseen Realm*, 88).

While I suppose that Eve interacted with the *elohim*, I can't say if she had previous interactions with Satan. Nevertheless, I don't believe that Satan was a stranger.[15] First, he knew the exact wording of the command that God gave to Adam regarding the trees of life and knowledge. Second, Satan had studied Eve so that he targeted her in a specific way. He knew her weak spots and how to best tempt her.

Even though the text says that Adam was "with her" when she gave him some of the fruit to eat, it doesn't mean that he was standing beside her during the temptation (Gen 3:6). The context implies that Adam was in the proximity of the temptation, but not involved with it until Eve had eaten from the tree and brought some of the fruit to him. Otherwise, as the head, Satan would have included him in the conversation. Also, Adam knew what God commanded. Most likely, he would have corrected Eve and the serpent if he would have been involved in the conversation. If Adam and Eve had routine conversations with the *elohim* in the garden, one shouldn't be surprised that Adam ignored Eve's conversation with the serpent being.

Apparently, Eve heard God's warning secondhand through Adam. To keep it simple, she and Adam had turned the commandment into "don't eat or touch the fruit." Basically, they ignored the sacred trees. Satan's temptation made Eve take notice of the forbidden fruit, created a desire for it, played on her confusion, and guided her into rebellion. Previously, in her innocent state, she was aware of the forbidden fruit but she wasn't attracted to it. In her case, the seed of sin was planted in the soil of mistruth and ripened as the fruit of lust. Eventually, the craving that Satan created in her overwhelmed her inhibitions. Satan fomented evil desire and led Eve into sin.

Apples in Paradise

Throughout the ancient world, people believed in magical fruit, sacred trees, and guardian creatures. For example, the Norse gods ate golden apples from an orchard guarded by Idun in order to stay young. For the Greeks, the golden apples in the Garden of Hesperides were guarded by Ladon, a serpent-like dragon that wrapped itself around the apple tree.[16] They grant-

---

15. According to the Life of Adam and Eve, God appointed two angels to guard Adam and Eve. It doesn't say why they needed a guard or what threat God perceived in his garden. When the angels took leave to worship at the throne of God, the devil came and seduced Eve (LAE 33:1–3). In Jubilees, Satan tells Eve that she will become like one of the *elohim* if she eats from the forbidden fruit. That assumes that she knew the *elohim* (3:19).

16. Snakes are also villainous creatures in modern cinematology. Consider the role of Kaa, the python, in the Disney adaptation of Rudyard Kipling's *The Jungle Book*.

ed immortality to the one who ate them. One of them led to the start of the Trojan War. In Egyptian mythology, the sacred tree of life was guarded by a sphinx-like creature (cherub).

According to a Micronesian myth, when humans were created, two trees existed in a garden.[17] They were guarded by a premortal creature named Na Kaa. Men lived under one tree and gathered its fruit. Women lived under the other tree. One day when Na Kaa was away, the men and women came together. When he returned, Na Kaa said that they had chosen the Tree of Death, not the Tree of Life. For their sin, they were expelled from the garden and became mortal.

In the biblical account, it's possible that the serpentine creature was guarding the Tree of the Knowledge of Good and Evil when he tempted Eve. That would explain why the serpent was at the tree. Also, it would align the story with other sacred tree myths. Perhaps, Eve was working in the vicinity of the tree and the serpent called to her from the midst of the tree. Even if the serpent wasn't guarding the tree when he tempted Eve; after she and Adam were expelled, God posted cherubim to guard the way to the Tree of Life (Gen 3:24).

There are obvious parallels between the Bible's garden story and ancient myths. When one considers what the Bible teaches about the sons of God and the origins of the nation gods, I expect to find parallel stories in world religions. That being said, in Genesis 3, the knowledge of good and evil didn't come from fruit. It came from an act of disobedience. In the story, eating the fruit was the mechanism by which Eve became aware when she disobeyed God. The fruit didn't impart the knowledge of good and evil to her.

After hypnotizing Mowgli from the safety of his tree, he slowly wraps his coils around him and hoists him up into the tree so he can eat him. In *Harry Potter and the Chamber of Secrets,* Harry Potter must battle an enormous basilisk in order to save his friends. In *Indiana Jones and the Raiders of the Lost Ark,* Jones says that he hates snakes as he repels into a room filled with them. A popular site lists 419 modern movies that feature snakes.

17. Coleman, *Dictionary of Mythology,* 239. Coleman lists ten separate Tree of Life myths from Africa, Central America, the East Indies, India (Hindu), Ireland, Mesopotamia, Siberia, Tibet, West Indies, and Israel (*Dictionary of Mythology,* 461). This is not an exhaustive list. Like the flood, the sacred tree myth is also universal in its reach. For a detailed analysis of trees in creation myths, see Witzel, *Origins of the World Mythologies,* 132–37.

What Would Have Happened If Adam Would Have Rejected the Fruit?

Did Eve have to convince Adam to eat the fruit? After partaking and before giving some to Adam, was Eve already aware that she had fallen? Were her eyes opened like the serpent said they would be? Did she give Adam the forbidden fruit because she had a new self-awareness and wanted him to have the same sensation?

The text doesn't indicate that Adam was tempted when he ate the fruit that Eve offered to him. Did he realize the tremendous consequences of what he was doing when he ate the fruit? Adam's obligation to obey God's commandment assumes that Adam had the capacity to recognize sin and reject it. However, we don't know to what extent his moral awareness had developed. Up until this moment, obeying God's commandment wasn't an issue. Adam and Eve obeyed because they had not been tempted to disobey.

If Adam had an underdeveloped sense of right and wrong, Adam could have eaten the fruit because he was gullible, innocent, and easily persuaded by Eve's example. In this case, Adam and Eve would have been like two children sharing a stolen candy bar on a school playground. At some level, they knew it was wrong, but the act didn't feel bad when they did it. That is why society doesn't hold children to the same level of culpability as adults. This may be one of the reasons that God determined to redeem fallen humanity.

Newly minted sapient beings have to grow in self-awareness and learn critical thinking skills. Adam and Eve may have been created with adult bodies, but they weren't created with adult minds because they lacked the life experience and intelligence of a mature adult. That is why extra-biblical sources say that the divine beings schooled them. Even Jesus had to grow in wisdom and stature so that he increased in favor with God and others (Luke 2:52). The fact that Adam and Eve were morally immature could explain why Adam and Eve ate the fruit.

This line of thought begs a simple question; how developed was Adam? He had significant life experience before Eve was created. Genesis 2:19–20 says that God created the animals and brought them to Adam so he could name them. This implies that Adam had ongoing interactions with God before the creation of Eve. The time between Adam's creation and Eve's creation could have been many years. To some extent, we must assume that Adam had more moral awareness and cognitive development than Eve. Based on this, it's possible that Adam was fully aware of his actions, the commandment of God, and the consequences of following Eve into sin when he chose to eat the fruit. If this is the case, he wasn't tempted. He made a willful choice to sin.

Definitively, the Scriptures don't tell us why Adam sinned. In fact, no one knows what would have happened if Adam would have said "no" when Eve offered him the fruit. In my mind, the two thoughts are connected. Could it be that Adam loved Eve so completely that he disobeyed God so he could remain with her? Even though that sounds horribly romantic, it may be true. She was made from him and was his helpmate. They were created for each other. Before dismissing this sentimental idea, one should remember that God loved humans so much that he gave himself for them (John 3:16). Even though he didn't sin, he became sin so he could save fallen humanity from the consequences of their sin (2 Cor 5:21).

Let me state the proposition as a series of three related questions. Did Adam sin so he could stay with Eve? Did he think he could save her by casting his lot with her lot? If faced with Adam's choice, what would Jesus have chosen? I can't excuse Adam for his sin. However, when one considers Christ's sacrificial love for lost people in bondage to Satan and the command that men should love their wives like Christ loved the church (Eph 5:25), Adam's choice would seem noble if he made it so he could stay with Eve. In some way, it reflects the way Paul describes *agape* love.

Related to the above line of reasoning, Adam may have feared that he would lose Eve forever when she faced the judgment of God after her sin if he abandoned her to her sin. For that reason, he followed Eve into sin because he believed that God would save them from their folly if he stayed with her. In other words, past experience with God caused Adam to believe that God would fix this problem because he knew that God loved them.

Possibly, humankind wouldn't have succumbed to Satan's deception if Satan would have tempted Adam instead of Eve. This is why Satan singled out Eve. She wasn't as well prepared for the encounter. Paul seems to get to this when he teaches that Adam wasn't deceived. Rather, Eve was deceived (1 Tim 2:14; 2 Cor 11:3).

Would God have redeemed Eve from Satan if Adam never fell? There is no way to know. It's possible that God could have made Adam another helpmate if Eve was taken from him. Still, Adam loved Eve and was intensely bonded to her.

Unlike Eve, Adam's temptation pitted his desire to remain true to God against his fear of abandoning Eve. He was caught between the proverbial rock and a hard place. Calling out to God for help would have left Eve in her fallen state. In his mind, he was checkmated. Adam did what Satan expected him to do when he ate the fruit and surrendered his birthright. If this is correct, Satan developed a brilliant strategy by tempting both Eve and Adam at their weak points.

In sum, I suspect that Adam was morally developed, he knew what was at stake, and he made a rational decision to sin. Additionally, I believe that Satan played Eve so he could get to Adam. The temptation of Eve was penultimate to the real temptation. Moreover, Satan went through Eve because a direct approach wouldn't have lassoed Adam. He was the prize because the rulership of this world was attached to him.

The Esau and Jacob Parallel

A possible parallel to the garden temptation may be found in the story of Esau and Jacob (Gen 25–27). The characters are different, but the outcome is similar. The narratives are connected by structure and the use of the same Hebrew cognate (*adm*). The word *adm* is spelled with three Hebrew consonants (aleph, dalet, and mem). The aleph is a silent consonant to which a vowel is attached. When written, each of the cognates share the same *adm* structure.

When Esau was born (Gen 25:25), he was covered in reddish hair. Red (*adem*) became his nickname. After Esau and Jacob became men, a famished Esau found Jacob eating red stew as he was returning from the field. Joseph agreed to give Esau some of the red, red (*adom adom*) pottage if Esau gave him his birthright. The stew is called *adom*, Esau is called *edem*, and the land where Esau lived was called Edom. The name "Adam" shares the same three consonants with the other words. Remember, Hebrew words didn't have vowel pointing when Jacob and Esau lived. A native speaker who read the Esau story in Genesis without vowel notations would have noticed that all the above-mentioned names were written the same as Adam. Does the story intend to portray Esau as an Adam figure? If so, in what way was Esau an Adam figure?

When Isaac, the father of Esau and Jacob, was about to die, Jacob deceived him so that Isaac mistakenly gave him the blessing that was meant for Esau (Gen 27). Jacob means "supplanter."[18] The deception story paints Jacob in a very devious light. He deceived his father and stole his brother's birthright. In a similar way, Satan deceived Eve so he could steal Adam's birthright. In this case, both Adam and Esau sold their birthrights in a foolish way.

---

18. Jacob had to be converted before he could become the man that God wanted him to be. His redemption happened when he fought with the "Angel of God" in the night (Gen 32:22–31). Afterward, God blessed him and changed his name to Israel (ruling with God).

The use of the Hebrew noun *adm* connects the stories to each other.[19] Esau was a type of Adam when he gave away his birthright. Furthermore, when Jacob was redeemed, he ruled with God. When the children of Adam are redeemed by Christ, they will rule with God. If the Esau story is a parallel to the temptation story, it shows that Adam gave away his birthright without being deceived in the same way that Esau gave away his birthright to get something he wanted. Esau wanted food. Adam wanted to stay with Eve.

Why Did God Allow Satan to Tempt Eve?

There are two approaches to the above question. One approach was already discussed. Namely, Adam and Eve needed to be tested so they could move from the category of moral innocence to the category of moral righteousness. Before dismissing this idea as being out of God's character (Jas 1:13), one should recall that God drove Jesus into the wilderness to be tempted by Satan (Mark 1:12–13) and worked in conjunction with Satan to tempt Job (Job 1:8—2:8). In both cases, God allowed those being tested to be stretched to their limits. Neither temptation was fair. Jesus wasn't permitted to eat for forty days leading to his temptation. He was physically weak and a bit delirious. God allowed Satan to kill Job's children and take away his health as a part of his trial. In the end, Jesus gained authority over Satan as the second Adam and God rewarded Job because he wouldn't curse God.

Abraham was also tempted beyond reason when God told him to sacrifice his son Isaac (Gen 22:2).[20] The testing proved his faithfulness and became the means by which God declared him righteous. Abraham passed the test because he knew God and believed that God would keep his promise to make Isaac his heir (Rom 4:18–22). His righteousness combined faith in God with deeds that gave evidence to his faith. Ultimately, the aborted sacrifice of Isaac points to the Father's sacrifice of his own Son. With Abraham, Christians affirm that God will provide himself a lamb for the sacrifice (Gen 22:8).

Lest one forgets, throughout the ages the saints of God have been tempted to abandon Jesus Christ in times of intense persecution. Repeatedly, they have witnessed to their faith in the hour of trial and temptation by sacrificing themselves for Jesus. Jesus expects this and promises to reward this sacrifice (Matt 10:33). Attempts to avoid the suffering or save one's life

---

19. Mullen has an extended discussion on the name *adam* (see *Assembly of the Gods*, 243–44).

20. In Jubilees 17:15–18, Mastema (Satan) encourages God to test Abraham by telling him to sacrifice Isaac to see if he is really good.

by compromising with sin or denying Christ is cause for judgment (Mark 8:35).

Another approach argues that God didn't "let" Satan tempt Eve and he didn't work in conjunction with Satan to test Adam and Eve. Rather, Satan acted in defiance to God when he seized an opportune moment to ply his malevolence. If this is correct, God let the temptation move forward. An omniscient God can't be fooled.

In the Scriptures, God doesn't protect people from temptation. Rather, when temptation arises, God energizes their free will so they can say no to temptation by submitting to God and resisting the devil (Jas 4:7). Eventually, as people submit to God and live in harmony with him, the Holy Spirit enables them to say no to temptation. Holiness is a fruit of the Spirit and a sign of Christian maturity (Gal 5:22–23).

If option one is the case, the temptation was a setup in which God and Satan cooperated in much the same way as God and Satan cooperated to tempt Jesus in the wilderness. God knew what the outcome would be even if Satan didn't. For that reason, when Adam and Eve failed, the cross wasn't a backup contingency plan to save the people he loved from the consequences of their sin. Rather, it was God's predetermined plan of action from the beginning. As such, God chose the route of the cross because the ultimate benefit from it was greater than the losses that he incurred when humankind fell.

Options one and two aren't mutually exclusive. First, I don't believe that God predetermined that Adam would sin or told Satan to tempt Eve. God honors free will and doesn't program angels or people to act like puppets. Second, I don't believe that God sanctioned Satan's encounter with Eve. Because Satan had free will and great leeway as a guardian cherub, he took advantage of an opportunity when he tempted Eve. Third, since the sovereign and omniscient God knew the eventuality, he had an eternal plan of salvation in place before Adam sinned. Fourth, Satan may have been aware of the salvation plan. In fact, he may have been playing into it. As they say, there were wheels within wheels at work in the temptation narrative.

An Audacious Proposal

At this point, I will offer a bold proposition. The temptation scene in the garden portrays the fall of Satan. On the day of the temptation, Satan put into play a carefully planned rebellion. The temptation of Eve was the first act of his mutiny against God. Before the temptation scene, Satan had not fallen. After the scene, he, humankind, and creation had fallen. In the aftermath, Satan became the lord of this world.

Many reasons lend credence to the above proposal. Some have already been discussed. First, Satan had a motivation to rebel. The creation of humankind provoked his defiance. He didn't want people to rule over the material creation and he didn't want them to be the kingpins of creation. Previously, he enjoyed the exalted status as the guardian cherub who was closest to the throne of God.

Second, the temptation story shows that Satan had free access to the garden. Even if the aforementioned "option one" is correct, it doesn't explain why God would have permitted a fallen cherub to roam freely in his paradise garden over a prolonged period so he could devise a strategy to target Adam and Eve. After the fall, God had to post cherubim to guard the entrance to the garden. Cherubim with flaming swords are overkill for Adam and Eve. I assume that the sword-wielding cherubim were stationed to keep a fallen Satan out.

Third, the temptation was a carefully planned act that set-in motion a series of events that led to a full revolt. When Satan won his tactical victory in the garden, he claimed lordship over the world and invited the other angels to join in his victory. He told them they would share his power. He also convinced them that they would win the final battle. The ancient angels with vast intelligence must have believed him or they wouldn't have joined with him in his rebellion. I assume that they resented God's design related to humankind and shared Satan's grievance. Even though they wouldn't have acted on it by themselves, once Satan won the first round they were lured into it. Their pride and unsettled grievance gave them motivation to rebel. If this be the case, the fall of the angels happened after the fall of humankind.

Fourth, since the Bible doesn't say when Satan rebelled, one is free to speculate about the timing based on the information that the Bible offers. Consider these Scriptures. "Do not let anyone lead you astray . . . The one who does what is sinful is of the devil, because the devil has been sinning from the beginning" (1 John 3:7–8). The author says that the saints shouldn't be led into sin. The imagery harkens back to the temptation story when Satan led Eve into sin. Then it says that the one who sins is of the devil because the devil has been sinning from the beginning. This also reaches back to the temptation of Eve. The connection between the temptation story and "sinning from the beginning" stands out. We know that Satan didn't sin from the beginning of creation because he was a chosen cherub for countless eons. Since "from the beginning" refers to the garden story, Satan fell when he tempted Eve.

Jesus uses a similar phrase when speaking about the devil. He says that Satan was a murderer from the beginning (John 8:44). Since the Bible doesn't support angelicide or say if immortal angels can be killed, one must assume that the phrase "Satan was a murderer from the beginning" refers to the unlawful killing of humans. In this case, Satan's actions led to the ultimate physical death of Adam and Eve and played into Cain's murder of Abel. Cain is of the serpent's seed. Satan is the inspiration for murder. As such, the phrase "the devil was a murderer from the beginning" probably refers to the fall story in the garden. Before that, he wasn't murdering.

Revelation 12:7–9 says, "Then war broke out in heaven. Michael and his angels fought against the dragon, and the dragon and his angels fought back. But he was not strong enough, and they lost their place in heaven. The great dragon was hurled down—that ancient serpent called the devil, or Satan, who leads the whole world astray. He was hurled to the earth, and his angels with him."[21]

In this text, the war in heaven and the casting of Satan to the ground happened at the same time. Those who read Revelation in a dispensational way insist that the above Scripture refers to a future event. However, the context of Revelation 12 includes the fall of the demons and the election of Israel to give birth to the promised Messiah. Both are past events. From the perspective of John the Revelator, the one who was cast down to Earth leads the whole world astray. Clearly, Satan has been leading the world astray from the time of the garden. Most likely, after the garden scene, the rebellion continued in heaven when other angels aligned with Satan. It was at that time, that they were cast down to the ground.

Isaiah 14:12 says that the Morning Star (Satan) has fallen from heaven and was cast down to Earth. When the seventy-two disciples returned to Jesus in Luke 10:18, they declared that the demons had to submit to them when they invoked the name of Jesus. In response, Jesus said that he saw Satan falling like lightning from heaven. Being hurled to the earth like lightning sounds like something that God would do to one who rebelled against him. Either, Satan has been thrown from heaven on numerous occasions or Isaiah 14 and Revelation 12 are referring to the same event.

Afterward, Jesus told the seventy-two disciples that he gave them power to tread on serpents. The "tread on serpent" language points back to the curse that God placed on Satan in the garden when he said that the seed of the woman (Messiah Jesus) would crush his head (Gen 3:15). Stomp

---

21. The hurled-to-the-earth phrase has been discussed in light of Isaiah 14; Ezekiel 28; and Genesis 3. It means that Satan was sent to the underworld. "His angels with him," means that others must have joined with him in his rebellion even though the above texts do not mention them. Until the final judgment, they are the lords of hell.

on him and tread on him evoke the same image. In this case, the defeat of the serpent extends to the seed of the serpent. His seed can be demons, nephilim, evil humans, or a generic term for Satan's kingdom.

The biblical evidence that Satan rebelled when he tempted Eve isn't conclusive. However, neither is the belief that Satan fell at some time before the fall of humankind. In the end, it doesn't matter when Satan fell. Only one thing matters. When Adam yielded to Satan, he transferred his dominion to him. Before that time, Satan wasn't the lord of this world.

The Future Is Sure for Those Who Stand with God

Jesus was the Second Adam. In the wilderness temptation, he defeated Satan and reclaimed creation for God. That is why he exercised authority over demons in his earthly ministry. They had to yield to him because he overcame Satan and reclaimed the lawful authority that Adam ceded when he sinned. Not only did they yield to him, they also feared him.

Yet, the victory wasn't finalized because the seed of Adam was still marred by sin and the creation remained fallen. Ultimately, in the cross Jesus freed humankind from the curse of sin and the dominion of Satan. However, to walk in Christ's victory, people had to repent, turn to God, and consciously align with God by rejecting Satan and sin.

During this in-between time, the battle still rages. Satan continues to ply malice and exercise authority through those who yield themselves to him and serve his cause. By deceit and lies, he continues to blind people to their lost condition as he leads them into destruction. Still, he only has the power that people give to him. He isn't the supreme ruler. The battle may rage, but Jesus is the lawful king. People who surrender to Jesus in this life share his victory and his power over the demonic world.

At a future time, Satan will be fully dethroned, his kingdom will be fully destroyed, and God will free the creation from the curse. Those who have turned to Christ in this world will become coregents with God in the new creation. God wins! God's victory is our victory.

15

The Temptation of God

In the previous chapter, I argued that the temptation of Eve was secondary to the temptation of Adam. In this chapter, I propose that Satan intended to test God via the temptation of Eve and the fall of Adam. Specifically, the fall of humankind set in motion a series of moves by which Satan hoped to checkmate God.

Here I use "temptation of God" tongue-in-cheek. The God of heaven can't be tempted. However, the incarnated God was tempted. The temptation of Jesus happened because of a decision that God made when Adam and Eve fell. Satan rightly anticipated that God would redeem his beloved children. That decision made God vulnerable to a future temptation. From the beginning of his scheming, Satan was aiming for God. The fall of humankind was the means to get to him.

Isaiah 14:13–14 offers insight into Satan's purposes.[1] In the original context, King Nebuchadnezzar attacks Jerusalem. Jerusalem is Mount Zion, the abode of Yahweh. As such, the king is attacking God. A myth about a god attacking Baal's pantheon on Mount Zaphon provides the imagery by which Isaiah describes Satan's (*helel*, the shining one) desire to attack Yahweh in heaven. In sum, the Isaiah text uses Nebuchadnezzar's attack on the City of God to connect to a Canaanite myth that conveys a story about Satan's desire to attack God's throne.

According to the text, Satan wanted to rise above God and those who sit with him in the heavenly council. "You said in your heart, 'I will

---

1. For a more detailed analysis of this text, see "Satan before His Fall" in chapter 9 and Day, *Yahweh and the Gods*, 151–84.

ascend to the heavens; I will raise my throne above the stars of God; I will sit enthroned on the mount of assembly, on the utmost heights of Mount Zaphon. I will ascend above the tops of the clouds; I will make myself like the Most High [*El Elyon*, the supreme God]." The New International Readers Version rightly nuances the text as "I'll sit as king on the mountain where the [sons of God] meet." Ironically, Satan wanted to ascend to the highest heaven and rise above the heavenly potentates. Instead, he was cast to the lower underworld where the Rephaim (dead giants or shade spirits) rise up to greet him (Isa 14:9).

Because of the reference to Mount Zaphon and ascending to heaven, the place where the sons of God meet with the Most High, the text may have reminded the original hearers of the epic battle between Typhon and the gods. Baal Zaphon (the god of Zaphon) governed Mount Zaphon. When Mount Zaphon was called Mount Kasios (Casius in modern times), Zeus was the high god who ruled on top of it. They called him Zeus Kasios. As such, Zeus is Baal Zaphon, the god of Zaphon.[2] In the story about Typhon, the dragon monster attempted to ascend the sacred mountain, destroy Zeus, and rule the pantheon.[3] The parallel between Satan in Isaiah 14 and the Typhon story in mythology is close.

---

2. The reference to Mount Zaphon (Isa 14:13) adds intrigue to the text. Some translations substitute "north" for Mount Zaphon because that is the meaning of the Hebrew word. Zaphon is north of Jerusalem and became associated with the cardinal direction. To go toward Mount Zaphon was to go north. In the verse, Zaphon refers to the mountain (Day, *Yahweh and the Gods*, 108). Likewise, Psalm 48:2 uses Zaphon as a place when it states, "like the heights of Zaphon is Mount Zion, the city of the Great King." In the psalm, Mount Zion, the city of God, is compared to Mount Zaphon, the place where Baal Zaphon reigns over his pantheon. He and his mountain are identified with other high gods to include Zeus on Mount Kasios. Mount Kasios is another name for Mount Zaphon (Niehr, "Baal Zaphon," 152). Also, there are etymological and mythological connections between Typhon and Baal Zaphon. According to Day, some scholars believe that the name Zaphon lies behind the monster Typhon (*Yahweh and the Gods*, 108 n33). In Greek mythology, Typhon was the bane of the gods. The giant storm monster attempted to conquer Mount Olympus. Eventually, Zeus subdued him with lightning and hurled him to Tartarus. He has a snake-like body, wings, and spits fire. He is a great fiery dragon, much like the Leviathan that is described in Isaiah 27:1 (van Henten, "Typhon," 879). Like Typhon was the bane of Zeus, Satan is God's nemesis. He wants to ascend to heaven where God reigns so he can dethrone him. However, God throws him down to the ground (underworld) like lightning falling from heaven (Luke 10:18). Revelation 20:3 locates him in Tartarus, the same place where Typhon resides. Based on the similarities between Satan and Typhon, one can appreciate why Isaiah utilized the myth language to illustrate Satan's design and his fall.

3. Day believes that the shining one who attacks Mount Zaphon, the abode of the high god, refers to Athtar, the morning star, who attempted to take Baal's place (Day, *Yahweh and the Gods*, 110). Others say that the story is similar to a Hurrian myth in which the sky god (Teshub) eventually defeats the underworld god (Ullikummi) after

Satan almost won. When Adam deliberately disobeyed God by eating the fruit, he ceded his dominion to Satan. At that time, the Evil One became the god of this world. He wasn't God or superior to God. However, he walked in the authority and position that God had given to Adam. We can't realize the authority that Satan had until we comprehend the standing that Adam gave away. Chapter 5 reviewed a host of rulership titles that the Bible ascribes to the devil. They included God of this World, Power of Darkness, Prince of the Power of the Air, and Ruler of this World. Those epithets give clear evidence to the authority that Adam yielded to him.

When Satan won his tactical victory, God was fully aware of his plan. At that point, God could have destroyed Satan and the fallen creation. He could have started from scratch. Satan didn't believe that God would do that. After spending an eternity with God and watching the creation of Adam, he knew God's weak spot. God's "fatal flaw" was his love for humanity. As he played out his chess game, Satan believed that God would "sacrifice his queen" in a gamble to win back his beloved from Satan's domain. In short, Satan tempted Adam and Eve because he wanted an opportunity to tempt God directly. He desired to own Jesus, the eternal Son of God with whom he had many previous dealings in the heavenly council.

God Indicates His Plan

When Adam and Eve sinned, they realized that they were naked (uncovered). Afterward, they attempted to cover-up their nakedness by sewing together fig leaves (Gen 3:7). In later commentary, this represents works righteousness. One cannot atone for one's own sin. That is why God intervened and provided animal skins to cover the nakedness (sin) of Adam and Eve (Gen 3:21). To get the skins, God had to kill innocent animals.

In biblical language, covering means atonement (*kippur*). The sacrificing of the animals from which the covering was made pointed to Jesus dying on the cross. He is the atoning sacrifice for our sins (1 John 2:2). He is the Lamb of God who takes away the sin of the world (John 1:29). In the Old Testament, animal sacrifices pushed back the inevitable judgment, but they didn't satisfy it. The price (ransom) wouldn't be paid until God died on the cross in the place of lost humankind. In other words, God played into Satan's hand when he killed flesh to provide a covering to hide the nakedness of Adam and Eve (Gen 3:21). The provision of a covering for Adam and Eve was a token that said God planned to redeem Adam and Eve by giving himself as their ransom.

---

he ascended to the heavens. Oriental myths are full of similar stories.

Our Ransom

Jesus is the Lamb of God who takes away the sin of the world by dying on behalf of the sinners (John 1:29). During the Last Supper, Jesus made it clear that he was the Passover Lamb. His body would be killed and his blood would be poured out as an eternal sacrifice. The imagery harkens back to the exodus story. When the death angel visited Egypt and killed the firstborn in every house, he passed over the houses on which the blood of the sacrifice had been properly applied. Jesus is the Lamb of God who gives his life as a sacrifice for fallen humankind. When his blood is applied to a sinful believer, that person passes from judgment unto life (John 5:24). This is called the substitutionary theory of atonement. It's core theology in the Gospels and foundational to how evangelicals preach salvation.

The New Testament also affirms the ransom theory of atonement. Accordingly, Jesus satisfies the debt and pays the ransom to redeem people from their bondage to Satan. Mark 10:45 declares that the Son of Man came to give his life as a ransom for many. "There is one God; there is also one mediator between God and humankind, Christ Jesus, himself human, who gave himself a ransom for all" (1 Tim 2:5-6, NRSV). "You know that you were ransomed from the futile ways inherited from your ancestors, not with perishable things like silver or gold, but with the precious blood of Christ, like that of a lamb without defect or blemish" (1 Pet 1:18-19, NRSV). "You are worthy to take the scroll and to open its seals, for you were slaughtered and by your blood you ransomed for God saints from every tribe and language and people and nation" (Rev 5:9, NRSV).

Ransom and redeem are used interchangeably. Both mean to set free by means of paying a price. Ransom language is associated with paying a debt, covering sin, or buying someone out of slavery. For example, a man whose bull killed someone could redeem his life from death by paying the required price (Exod 21:30). If a Jew was sold into slavery because of a debt that he couldn't pay, his next-of-kin could manumit him and his family by paying his debt for him. The owner of the slave had to release the slave once the price was paid. If the next-of-kin couldn't pay it, another kin could do it (Lev 25:47-55). The person who has the right to ransom the relative is called a kinsman redeemer.

In the story of Ruth, Boaz is a kinsman redeemer for Ruth when she came back from Moab with Naomi (Ruth 2:20). Even though Boaz was not the next-of-kin, Leviticus 25:49 makes it clear that an uncle, cousin, or any blood relative can redeem a person. In order to redeem Ruth, Boaz purchased the land that had belonged to Naomi's late husband and returned it to the family in accordance with the redemption rules of Leviticus 25:23-28.

He also married Ruth and raised up a son for her late husband so that the land would remain with the family.

Interestingly, Deuteronomy declares that God redeemed the Israelites from slavery in Egypt because they were his inheritance and his people. He didn't pay the Egyptians money when he ransomed them. Instead, he redeemed them by his great power because the Egyptian Pharaoh would not release them (Deut 7:8; 9:26; 15:15; 24:18).

Exodus 13:13–14 makes the point when it says, "Therefore, say to the Israelites: 'I am the Lord, and I will bring you out from under the yoke of the Egyptians. I will free you from being slaves to them, and I will redeem you with an outstretched arm and with mighty acts of judgment'" (Exod 6:6).

God's redeeming action culminated on the night in which he killed the firstborn of people and animals. The Jews were spared this fate when they offered a sacrifice and painted the door with its blood. Afterward, in commemoration of this, they had to "redeem" their firstborn sons and animals by means of a sacrifice (Exod 15:13–15).

The Torah says that a Jew must be released from slavery in a jubilee year. A jubilee occurs every fifty years. Since the Egyptians held on to the Jews for 430 years (Exod 12:40), they lost their right to enslave them (Lev 25:54). At that point, God had a right to redeem his people with force. The Lord was their redeemer (savior). Repeatedly, the Old Testament emphasizes this point. God redeemed the children of Israel from slavery because they are his people.

Jesus Is Our Kinsman Redeemer

Jesus took on the role of being the kinsman redeemer of humanity. As the creator of all people and the firstborn over all creation, he is everyone's next-of-kin. He became flesh so he could pay the price for everyone's redemption since no human could pay the price or redeem humankind. No other person had the universal standing or moral purity to be the holy sacrifice since all have sinned. Fallen humankind needed to be redeemed by a human but no human could redeem it until God became human.

Before the garden encounter with Satan, God had foreseen this inevitability. The cross was God's purpose from the very beginning. Ephesians 1:4 says that God chose us in Christ before the foundations of the world. First Peter 1:19–20 refers to Jesus as a perfect lamb without blemish who was chosen to die for us before the creation of the world. Revelation 13:8 refers to the Lamb of God who was slain before the foundations of the earth. What a sobering thought. Before humankind rebelled, God already had enacted a plan to save them. That plan required that he enter the creation, become a human, and die a horrific death as the scapegoat.

Paul builds on this theme when he declares that God planned for the glory of humankind before time began. He calls it a mystery that was hidden from the rulers and powers. If they had known about it, they would not have crucified Jesus (1 Cor 2:7-8). In truth, no eye has seen, no ear has heard, and no human mind has conceived the things God has prepared for the redeemed in glory (1 Cor 10:9). Matthew 25:34 and Revelation 17:8 both affirm that God planned for our salvation before the foundation of the earth. When speaking about our salvation, 2 Timothy 1:9-10 says, "His grace was given us in Christ Jesus before the beginning of time, but it has now been revealed through the appearing of our Savior, Christ Jesus, who has destroyed death and has brought life and immortality to light through the gospel."

Imagine this. Billions of years ago, before the creation took form, God already was thinking about humankind. In fact, he created the universe in order to create people! From the beginning, his heart was turned toward humans and his love poured out for humankind. People aren't an accident of evolution. They are the predetermined result of a purposeful creation! Knowing this should cause humans to fall before God in praise and thanksgiving. They should trust him and know that he won't abandon them or forsake them. His love for people is eternal and his desire for humankind is sure.

Satan's negative reaction to God's love for people shouldn't surprise anyone. Human experience shows that this is a normal response. For example, when a person realizes that the one he adores loves another one more than she loves him, he may feel rejection. If that happens, his anger may boil and a desire for revenge may take root. This creates an emotional wound. Like people, angelic beings are emotional creatures who can feel the spectrum of emotions. Likewise, God is also an emotional being who feels love, anger, jealousy, joy, satisfaction, compassion, and the like. God may have kept his plans for humankind secret from the heavenly council because he anticipated how they would respond. Even though they were with him when he created the world, they didn't hear about people until God informed them that he would make them in "our image." I have already argued that the creation of humankind triggered Satan's rebellion.

Jesus' Temptations

The temptation of Adam and Eve happened in God's garden. The temptation of Jesus happened in the wilderness. When the Israelites meandered in the wilderness, they traveled through a haunt of demons. Some offered sacrifices to the evil spirits (goat-demons) so they wouldn't harm them (Lev 17:7). Azazel, a demonic prefiguration of Satan, lived in the wilderness outside the camp. On the Day of Atonement, the scapegoat was dispatched to him (Lev 16).

Since the wilderness wasn't "holy" ground, God resided with the Jews in the camp and protected them from the desert demons when he led them through the wilderness. To keep the camp pure, anything evil or unclean was carried into the wilderness (outside the camp) away from the presence of God. That is why the scapegoat was sent away after the people had transferred their sins to it. As such, when Jesus went into the wilderness to meet Satan; symbolically, he went into Azazel's domain.

Second, I assume that God and Satan agreed that Jesus would be tested in the wilderness. Otherwise, the Holy Spirit wouldn't have driven Jesus to his rendezvous with the Evil One (Mark 1:12).[4] Also, I assume that Satan set the condition that Jesus had to fast. He and Jesus were battling for the governorship of this world. In order to become the Second Adam and reclaim Adam's forfeited birthright, Jesus had to undergo the same kind of test that Adam failed. For that to happen, Satan had to be a willing participant. Since Satan wanted to own Jesus, he would have relished the opportunity to tempt him. However, to improve his odds, he may have set some ground rules. Without a doubt, fasting for forty days diminished Jesus. Imagine Rocky Balboa boxing Apollo Creed with one arm tied behind his back.

The Rock to Bread Temptation

After Jesus was weakened from the forty-day fast, Satan threw his first punch when he said, "If you are the Son of God, tell these stones to become bread." Jesus answered, "It is written: 'Man shall not live on bread alone, but on every word that comes from the mouth of God.'" (Matt 4:2–4).

---

4. In Mark 1:12, the Greek uses the verb *ekballo* (to throw out or expel) to denote how the Spirit led Jesus into the wilderness. It can also mean to dispatch someone without force. However, all the English translations use a form of drove, forced, or compelled to translate the verb. If the emphasis is on being compelled instead of being sent out, it would mean that Jesus wasn't keen on the idea. Mathew 4:1 and Luke 4:1 say that the Holy Spirit led Jesus into the wilderness. Likely, Mark used *ekballo* because he wanted to emphasize a point.

Satan began the temptation with a conditional clause that could be understood as a taunt; "If you are the Son of God." The accuser appeared with the sons of God when they presented themselves in Job 1:6. He knew who Jesus was and who he had been. Jesus was not a son of God. He was "the" Son of God, the Commander of the Heavenly Hosts, and the Second Yahweh. He presided with the Father at the divine council. The angels gave full deference to him. In his present condition, Jesus didn't look like the eternal Son of God. Furthermore, the host of heaven couldn't help him. He had to do this on his own in a human body. The irony of the statement may have bit at Jesus.

Moses and Elijah both fasted for forty days in advance of great spiritual events. That may explain why Jesus fasted. However, at a more basic level, Jesus fasted because the Father told him to fast. It wasn't a spiritual discipline that prepared him for a battle of cosmic proportions. It weakened him and made him vulnerable to Satan's attack. What general makes his troops fast before a decisive battle that will decide the war? In order to win, Jesus had to remember who he was and hold on to that identity as he staunchly refused to disobey the Father's commandments.

The rock to bread temptation played on Jesus' extreme hunger. He was so weakened by the fasting that angels had to minister to him when the contest was completed (Matt 4:11). Turning rocks into bread was a real temptation for three reasons: One, Jesus wanted bread. His body needed food. He was at the point of physical death. Two, the round white limestone rocks that lay all around him looked like little loaves of baked bread and reminded him of his hunger.[5] Three, he could turn them into bread.

In Matthew 3:9, right before Jesus was baptized and driven into the wilderness for the temptation, John the Baptist reminded the self-righteous Jews that God could rise up heirs to Abraham from these rocks (Matt 3:9). He was using a hyperbole to emphasize that being a child of Abraham would not save the Jews on the Day of Judgment if they failed to keep God's commandments. Still, one can presume that God could have turned rocks into Jews since he created Adam from earth.

Typically, theologians believe that the first temptation targeted Jesus' awareness of his divine right. Satan had just emphasized that point. If Jesus would have used his supernatural abilities as "the Son of God" to serve his physical needs, he would have disqualified himself from his role as a Second Adam since normal humans don't have access to the same powers when they face temptation or get famished. The Second Adam had to be a real human being who chose to submit to the Father as he rejected the Satanic

---

5. Barclay, *Gospel of Luke*, 51.

temptations. Still, using divine power to fix a natural problem wasn't a sin and it would not have made Jesus the captive of Satan. Repeatedly, Jesus fed multitudes by multiplying bread and fish. Throughout his ministry, he did countless miracles to advance the cause of God and defeat the devil. "When Jesus became human, he emptied himself of his divine right (Phil 2:6–8). In the incarnation, Jesus didn't cease to be God. Rather, in order to be fully human, he laid down his divine attributes. That is why the temptation story represented a series of real temptations."[6]

Even though there is truth in the "you can't use your divine powers to help yourself" interpretation, the real temptation was to disobey God in order to get something that he wanted. If my interpretation of the garden temptation was correct, Adam underwent the same temptation when he chose to disobey God to stay with Eve. God told Jesus to fast. He was not at liberty to eat until the temptation was over. That is why Jesus rebuffed the temptation by saying, Man does not live by bread alone but by keeping the commandments of God (Matt 4:4). When picking between eating or obeying, Jesus chose to deny his physical need in order to obey the Father. Implicit in his obedience was the idea that he trusted the Father and was willing to do what he commanded even though his own desires led him in another direction.

The Jump off the Temple Temptation

The second temptation changes venues. "Then the devil took him to the holy city and had him stand on the highest point of the temple. 'If you are the Son of God,' he said, 'throw yourself down. For it is written: He will command his angels concerning you, and they will lift you up in their hands, so that you will not strike your foot against a stone.' Jesus answered him, 'It is also written: Do not put the Lord your God to the test'" (Matt 4:5–7).

One could argue that Satan gave Jesus a vision and that he was not on the pinnacle of the temple. Since evil spirits can give people false visions and false dreams, Satan could have given Jesus a vision of himself standing on top of the temple. The temple mount is God's property. It's associated with his presence. Why would Satan squander his geographic advantage in the wilderness by taking Jesus to the epicenter of God's sacred ground?

---

6. Payne, *Adventures in Spiritual Warfare*, 41. Because Jesus was a real man who emptied himself of his divine right when he was incarnated, he needed to be baptized with the Holy Spirit to do power ministry. In support of this, the canonical Gospels don't report that Jesus did any miracles before his baptism. The twelve-year-old Jesus who talked with the elders in the temple (Luke 2:41–52) was aware of his identity, but didn't act on it until he was baptized with the Holy Spirit.

I reject the vision interpretation because the temptation requires that Jesus be able to jump off the temple. It implies risk. Will the angels come to his aid and lift him up or will they take the opportunity to join Satan in his rebellion? If Satan took Jesus to the temple, God must have assured him safe passage. Perhaps, a force of fallen angels accompanied Satan, a force that could prevent the holy angels from intervening if Jesus jumped. Jesus can't receive divine intervention during the temptation. Still, why would this be a temptation?

What would have happened if Jesus floated down from the sky with a crowd of angels in front of the worshippers at the temple? You got it. The people would have known that Jesus was the long-expected Messiah from heaven and all would have rallied to him. That is what Jesus wanted. He wanted to be accepted by his people. He wanted the people to love him and serve God's cause. In fact, he was their Messiah and they should have rallied to him.

When he returns the second time, he will return in a way similar to the second temptatioon. Zechariah 14:1–5 indicates that the Messiah will come and set his feet on the Mount of Olives. When he does, the ground will split in half. Acts 1:11 says that Jesus will return just like he ascended to heaven. Every eye will see him when he descends from heaven. Matthew 24:30 says that all will see Jesus return with power and a multitude of white-robed angels (clouds of glory). Revelation 1:7 picks up on the prophecy in Zechariah 12:10. It states, "'Look, he is coming with the clouds [angels],' and 'every eye will see him, even those who pierced him'; and all peoples on Earth 'will mourn because of him.'"

Jumping off the temple plays into that expectation. Unfortunately, the temptation would shortcut God's plan. The Zachariah prophecy clearly states that they will look upon him who they have pierced. The New Testament writers connect that prophecy to the crucifixion. Jesus must complete his mission before he can fly down from heaven with a host of angels.

If this is correct, the temptation is to take a shortcut that God didn't authorize. The deviation may seem like a great idea until the implications are ascertained. Eve discovered this. Eating forbidden fruit can make you aware of good and evil just like the serpent said. However, it also gets you kicked out of the garden. Jesus remained resolute in his determination to follow the Father's will.

Jesus' rejoinder to Satan is poignant. "Don't tempt the Lord, your God!" That put Satan on notice. Even though Jesus was vulnerable in his flesh, he remained Satan's God. In other words, he told Satan to watch what he said and attempted to do. Jesus could have destroyed Satan with the snap of his fingers. After the second temptation, there is no doubt that Satan understood that Jesus was "the" Son of God.

I'll Give You the Nations Temptation

The third temptation was the most revealing. "Again, the devil took him to a very high mountain and showed him all the kingdoms of the world and their splendor.[7] 'All this I will give you,' he said, 'if you will bow down and worship me.' Jesus said to him, 'Away from me, Satan! For it is written: 'Worship the Lord your God, and serve him only'" (Matt 4:8–10).

In essence, Satan tried to trick Jesus into becoming his slave when he showed him the kingdoms of the world and offered to give them to him if he would worship him. When one worships Satan, the devil gains rights over the person. One can only worship God. Since Satan wanted to be worshipped like God and to own God, this was his boldest move.

Why would Jesus be tempted to worship Satan? Because Jesus came to redeem the kingdoms of the world from Satan. They were Satan's and he offered to give them to Christ if Jesus would worship him (Luke 4:6–7). Jesus knew that he couldn't worship Satan without submitting to him. He also knew that he wanted to redeem the world. However, in order to redeem the world in accordance with the Father's plan, he had to die on the cross. That was a very unpleasant thought to him. In short, like the previous temptation, Satan offered Jesus a shortcut. Basically, he promised to relinquish his claim on the children of Adam and let Jesus save them if Jesus worshipped him.

The half-truth was glaring. Satan offered to give Jesus what he wanted without making him die on the cross as the scapegoat. There was no redemption in Satan's offer. It was a mere *quid pro quo*, you give me what I want, and I'll give you what you want. This was very appealing because Jesus didn't want to become the sin-bearer on the cross. However, the scheme would make Satan the master of God. Furthermore, if Satan was Jesus' master, humankind could never be free from his malice.

Even though Jesus said no and remained true to the Father, the angst of the cross still bit at him. When he took his disciples to Caesarea-Philippi,

---

7. The high mountain is not mentioned. I would guess that Satan took Jesus to the top of Mount Hermon. It's 9,232 feet high. It's the highest point on the east coast of the Mediterranean Sea. More importantly, it's the place where the sons of God (the Watchers) determined to rebel against God. First Enoch 6:6 says, "And they were altogether two-hundred; and they descended into 'Adros, which is the summit of Hermon. And they called the mount Armon, for they swore and bound one another by a curse" (Charlesworth).

Peter confessed that he was the Christ, the Son of the living God (Matt 16:13–19). The confession made Jesus happy. Afterward, Jesus told the disciples that he must go to Jerusalem and die on the cross. Immediately, Peter began to rebuke him and tried to talk him out of it. Peter's words stung. When he spoke them, Jesus heard a renewed temptation to avoid the cross. He replied, "Get behind me, Satan! You are a stumbling block to me; you do not have in mind the concerns of God" (Matt 16:23). Yes, the desire to avoid the cross was a real temptation for Christ. Satan knew how to exploit it.

The agony of the pending crucifixion gripped Jesus when he was in the Garden of Gethsemane on the night before his torturous death. He said that his soul was overwhelmed with sorrow to the point of death (Matt 26:38). He was so desperate that he asked the Father to take the cup of his crucifixion and all that it entailed away from him (Matt 26:39). "And being in anguish, he prayed more earnestly, and his sweat was like drops of blood falling to the ground" (Luke 22:44).

Dying a death on a cross is one of the worst ways to die. Yet, Jesus was a strong man who demonstrated an ability to undergo a daunting temptation in which he almost died of starvation and exposure. When one realizes how the pending cross provoked deep emotional anguish in Jesus, one should wonder if there was something more to the cross.

The Scapegoat

During the temptation story, Satan tried to divert Jesus from the cross with a promise and a lie. Toward the end of his ministry, Satan was still trying to dissuade Jesus from going to the cross (Matt 16:23). The "worship Satan option" must have remained a possibility. At some point, Satan changed his strategy. By the time of the Last Supper, Satan started to cooperate with the crucifixion plot. He even entered Judas to push him to do the deed (Luke 23:3; John 13:27). All the evil and unjust events leading up to the crucifixion bear the unmistakable fingerprints of vile Satan. He reveled in Jesus' agony.

Since the crucifixion was the means by which Jesus redeemed humanity, one wonders why Satan collaborated with God's plan. After all, Satan could have thwarted that plan by not cooperating with it. Why did he change his mind? Why did he adopt God's plan? The answer relates to the scapegoat typology.

If Jesus gave his life as a ransom for sin, to whom was the ransom paid? The Bible doesn't answer that question directly. Some have argued that the debt was paid to God. All sin is an affront to God. Others have said that the debt was paid to Satan. Proponents argue that Satan claimed ownership of humankind when Adam sinned and ceded his authority to him. In order to appease that debt, Satan needed to be paid in accordance with Leviticus 25:47–53. He is the owner of the slaves. The money from the kinsman redeemer goes to him.

The Day of Atonement ritual helps to untangle this Gordian knot. Leviticus 16:7–10 states: "He shall take the two goats and set them before the Lord at the entrance of the tent of meeting; and Aaron shall cast lots on the two goats, one lot for the Lord and the other lot for Azazel. Aaron shall present the goat on which the lot fell for the Lord, and offer it as a sin offering; but the goat on which the lot fell for Azazel shall be presented alive before the Lord to make atonement over it, that it may be sent away into the wilderness to Azazel" (NRSV).

This text has a long history of translation. At times, the name Azazel is rendered as scapegoat (the goat that goes away). When it is, the translation adds a footnote that explains that Azazel is a name associated with a demon. Rendering Azazel as scapegoat is forced and doesn't fit the context. However, the thought of sending the scapegoat to a demon is so troubling that many translators prefer the scapegoat translation.[8]

Azazel is the correct rendering of the Hebrew text. Additionally, over fifteen standard translations have opted for "the scapegoat is sent to Azazel in the wilderness." Also, modern scholars and Jewish sources in the time before Christ accepted that Azazel is a proper name and that it should be rendered as such.

In the Dead Sea Scrolls community, Azazel is a leading watcher who teaches people the secret things of heaven (1 En. 9:6). God complains that the whole earth has been corrupted by Azazel's teachings and his actions (1

---

8. Some associate Azazel with Mot, the underworld god of death who prefigures Hades. His name appears often in the Hebrew Bible (Healey, "Mot," 598–603). Others say he is a desert goat-demon (Lev 17:7). The Dead Sea Scrolls affirm this interpretation. In the ransom theory of atonement, Azazel is Satan. That is one of the reasons that the satyr (goat man) becomes a primary image for him (Janowski, "Azazel," 128–31). Heiser recognizes that early Christian ransom theology portrays Azazel as Satan. However, he argues a different interpretation: "During the wilderness journey to the Promised Land, the Israelites had been sacrificing to demons, because they feared evil forces would threaten their camp. The wilderness was, after all, outside the Israelite camp, and therefore it was the place of evil entities. This practice had to stop, and the goat for Azazel accomplished that. The goat for Azazel wasn't an offering to evil gods—the goat was never sacrificed. Instead, sending it into the wilderness was a symbolic way of cleansing holy ground (the Israelite camp) from sin" (*Supernatural*, 82–83). Heiser's reliance on "cosmic geography" construals leads him to this interpretation (*Unseen Realm*, 176–78). Contrary to Heiser, the Jews believed that the scapegoat sent to Azazel was sacrificed to him when it was led outside the camp and thrown over the cliff. I list Azazel as a name for Satan in chapter 5.

En. 10:8). He is so central to 1 Enoch that all of chapter 13 is dedicated to him. In chapter 54, the armies of Azazel resist the armies of God when they come to bind the Watchers and throw them into the abyss.[9] In the Apocalypse of Abraham (a first-century BC book), he is identified as the serpent, standing between Adam and Eve in the garden (Apoc. Ab. 23:12). He's described as a dragon with six wings, having human hands and feet. This is another example that portrays the serpent as a seraph dragon.

In common parlance, Azazel is described as a goat-demon. In popular culture, he looks like a Greek satyr mixed with human features. That image is used in Satanism and is associated with the pentagram. In fact, the goat-demon image is the most common image used for Satan. That is why many have assumed that Azazel, the goat-demon, is another name for Satan.

This is where it gets tricky. On the Day of Atonement, one goat was offered to God because human sin is an affront to God. With it, the priest atones for the people. The other goat is a type of Christ. It is the scapegoat. "Aaron shall lay both his hands on the head of the live goat, and confess over it all the iniquities of the people of Israel, and all their transgressions, all their sins, putting them on the head of the goat, and sending it away into the wilderness by means of someone designated for the task. The goat shall bear on itself all their iniquities to a barren region" (Lev 16:21–22, NRSV). Often, it was thrown over a ridge to a place where people thought Azazel resided.

If this scenario is applied to Jesus, one will understand why Jesus struggled with his crucifixion. First, he becomes the sin bearer. This point is established in Isaiah 53:12 and throughout the New Testament. Because he who knew no sin becomes sin for humankind (2 Cor 5:21), God turns his head from the Son during the crucifixion. To hide the shame, the entire sky became dark.

Second, this is the place where God outplays Satan in his carefully strategized game of chess. Satan agrees to release humankind from its bondage to him when Jesus dies as the sacrificial lamb on the cross because Satan expects to receive Jesus as his payment. The scapegoat belongs to him.

---

9. In Talmudic Midrashic literature, Azazel must bear the sin of Israel on the Day of Atonement because he led humankind into sin. When the two he-goats were sacrificed in the temple on the Day of Atonement, the one for God pardoned the sins of Israel, and the other for Azazel bore the sins of Israel. "But Azazel persisted obdurately in his sin of leading mankind astray by means of sensual allurements. For this reason, two he-goats were sacrificed in the temple on the Day of Atonement, the one for God, that He pardon the sins of Israel, the other for Azazel, that he bear the sins of Israel" (Ginzberg, *Legends of the Jews*, 105). Since the sacrificed goat bears the sins of Israel when it is given to Azazel, it is not clear how Azazel becomes the sin bearer in the Midrash. First Peter 2:24 says that Jesus bore our sins in his body when he was crucified. In Christian typology, he is the true scapegoat on which the sins of the world are placed.

The sacrificed Jesus is the ransom payment. That is why Jesus went into the depths of hell after he was crucified. However, Satan didn't know that he couldn't entrap or hold onto Jesus. Instead, Jesus destroyed the domain of Satan before God raised him up. In short, going along with the crucifixion in order to own Jesus was the biggest mistake that Satan ever made! This is why the early church fathers said that God tricked Satan.

According to Robin Collins,

> Essentially, this theory claimed that Adam and Eve sold humanity over to the Devil at the time of the Fall; hence, justice required that God pay the Devil a ransom to free us from the Devil's clutches. God, however, tricked the Devil into accepting Christ's death as a ransom, for the Devil did not realize that Christ could not be held in the bonds of death. Once the Devil accepted Christ's death as a ransom, this theory concluded, justice was satisfied and God was able to free us from Satan's grip.[10]

John Driver puts it this way.

> All humanity has fallen under the power of the devil who is able to afflict and put to death. He could not be expected to give them up unless he received a ransom in return. Jesus Christ came to offer himself as that ransom for the lives of all who have been taken captive by the devil. Satan, supposing that he could extend his power by killing the Son of God, took Christ in exchange for the lives of humanity and killed him instead . . . However, Christ could not be held, and the drama reaches its climax in the resurrection in which he wrenches himself free from Satan's grasp. The deceiver at last has been deceived.[11]

It was previously noted that God used force to redeem the Hebrew people from Egypt and from the gods of Egypt because they had lost their right to hold on to them. Without a doubt, a proper understanding of the ransom theory includes the use of divine force. God raised Jesus up from the grave by the power of his might. Acts 2:24 says, "God raised him from the dead, freeing him from the agony of death, because it was impossible for death to keep its hold on him." In this case, death has a double meaning. Christ was in the realm of the dead and death was a god named *Thanatos*. The personification of death is common in the Old and New Testaments.

The ransom theory of atonement is the first and oldest Christian theory of the atonement. It is closely related to the Cristus Victor theory

---

10. Collins, "Understanding Atonement."
11. Driver, *Understanding the Atonement*, 41.

of atonement. It dominated atonement thinking for the first 1000 years of the church. Irenaeus, Origen, Gregory of Nyssa, and Augustine affirmed the ransom theory. In their commentaries on the New Testament teaching about ransom, they say that Adam ceded his authority to Satan, Jesus is the scapegoat, God deceived Satan, and Satan couldn't hold onto Jesus.[12]

The following eleven-point recap will help organize all that has been said in this chapter.

1. Because of the sin of Adam, humankind remained in bondage to sin and Satan. It needed divine help. Jesus came as humankind's Savior.

2. Jesus overcame Satan in the wilderness temptation. Afterward, the demons had to submit to him.

3. Jesus' victory over Satan in the wilderness didn't extend to all people. They were still in bondage to Satan and needed to be redeemed.

4. In order to free humankind from Satan, Jesus became the Lamb of God and died as a human sacrifice (scapegoat).

5. Satan thought that he would get Jesus in exchange for letting God redeem humankind. The scapegoat goes to Satan. It is his prize and booty. Since Jesus wouldn't become his slave by worshipping him, the scapegoat plan was a great alternative. That is why he cooperated with the crucifixion.

6. Satan didn't foresee the resurrection. He thought that by means of the sacrifice of Christ on the cross for sin, his claim on the world would be relinquished but he would own Christ. That is, God would be in submission to him.

7. Based on his pending descent into Hades as the scapegoat, Christ demonstrated emotional turmoil while in the garden on the eve of the crucifixion. Perhaps Jesus wasn't fully aware of what would transpire when he was given to Satan as payment for humankind's sin.

8. Satan didn't know that death couldn't hold Christ in the ground. Similarly, he didn't expect that Christ would defeat his domain and set the captives free.

9. Because of the cross, humans are freed from Satan's control when they put their faith in Christ and live holy lives.

---

12. For a fuller understanding of the redemption theory of the atonement, see Colijn, *Images of Salvation*, 144–73 and Pugh, *Atonement Theories*, 1–25;

10. Since the resurrection of Jesus, Christians share in Christ's victory over Satan and the kingdom of darkness. His authority is now their authority.

11. The ransom theory shows that love is the strongest power. For God loved us so much that he risked everything to save us from our sins.

16

Spiritual Warfare in the New Testament

GREG Boyd is one of the most influential spiritual warfare theologians of this time. His *God at War: The Bible & Spiritual Conflict* shows that the apocalyptic worldview of the intertestamental period greatly influenced what Jesus and the New Testament church thought about reality. New Testament leaders read Second Temple literature and they incorporated its theology into their teachings. When we read the Gospels in light of the apocalyptic worldview, we will see that Jesus' countercultural ministry wasn't a form of social and political protest. Rather, it was a form of spiritual warfare.

Even though the phrase "spiritual warfare" doesn't appear in Scripture, the Bible clearly reveals the concept. The notion of two-kingdom conflict goes to its core. When Jesus came preaching the kingdom of God and calling people into that new reality, he confronted the god of this world and set about to undo his kingdom. In the Gospel narrative, God's kingdom displaced Satan's reign wherever Jesus went.

The temptation story is the first round of that struggle (Matt 4:1–11; Mark 1:12–13; Luke 4:1–13). After Jesus defeated Satan in the wilderness battle, he claimed authority over Israel and began to cast out the demons who served as Satan's foot soldiers. However, Satan didn't quit. Luke tells us that he departed until an opportune time after his defeat in the wilderness (4:13). That is, he pulled back in a strategic retreat and looked for opportunities to strike back. His malice is revealed throughout the Gospels. In accordance with the spiritual warfare theme, Jesus' ministry should be seen and interpreted in light of his ensuing conflict with Satan.

When Jesus preached the kingdom of God, he called people to repent of their sins, align with God, bear good fruit, and become his disciples (Matt 4:17; 9:35; Mark 1:14; Luke 4:43). Aligning with God via repentance was necessary because sin separates people from God and causes them to fall under the domain of the Evil One. Without dealing with the sin problem and the alienation that it causes, one cannot enter God's reign.

Jesus' hearers could enter the kingdom of God by believing the good news that he preached and accepting that he was God's Messiah. As he shared the good news of a realized kingdom, the eschatological Messiah actualized God's reign in tangible ways when he healed the sick, cast out demons, cleansed the lepers, raised the dead, fed the hungry, forgave sins, and loved the outcasts. Each of these acts upended Satan's kingdom by freeing people from their bondage to him and from the consequences of the fall that he orchestrated.

The gospel that Jesus preached declares that God is on the move. He is destroying the work of the enemy. Not only does he set the captives free, but he also reestablishes the dominion that Adam and Eve surrendered when they submitted to the Evil One in the garden. Freedom and salvation are at hand for those who receive the kingdom. This is the gospel message and the message of spiritual warfare.

A summary of the first sixty-three verses of Mark reveals the good news, demarks the contours of the emerging kingdom, and shows the spiritual warfare nature of Jesus' ministry. Even though the events in the summary are specific to the opening section of Mark, they reflect the larger pattern of the Gospels.

1. As the one who came to "prepare the way of the Lord," John the Baptist announces the kingdom, anticipates Messiah Jesus, and tells the eager crowds that Jesus will baptize with the Holy Spirit.

2. The Holy Spirit comes upon Jesus. When he does, the Father claims him as his son. This shows the Father's approbation and signals the start of Jesus' public ministry.

3. Jesus defeats Satan in the wilderness challenge. This establishes his role as the Second Adam and grants him authority over Satan.

4. Jesus collects a band of common people who witness his lordship, follow his ministry, and share in his work. He calls them his disciples.

5. Jesus casts out demons who proclaim his identity and acknowledge that he is superior to them. All marvel that Jesus has spiritual authority and exercises complete power over the dark domain.

6. Jesus heals Peter's mother-in-law by commanding the sickness to leave. Afterward, hordes of sick and demonized people stream to Jesus so he can free them from illnesses and demons.
7. Jesus cleanses a leper who was a social outcast. In the kingdom, social pariahs, women, tax collectors, non-Jews, and sinners of all sorts find worth and salvation.
8. Jesus heals a paralytic by forgiving him of his sins. Per Jesus, the man's malady was related to his sins. Sin separates people from God. Jesus has the authority to broach that barrier by forgiving people of their sins. When he forgives people, he takes their sins upon himself. He will carry those sins to the cross.
9. Jesus "saves" a lost tax collector and celebrates with his friends. For this, the self-righteous who reject the kingdom of God and desire to maintain a social barrier between them and others accused Jesus of being a friend of tax collectors and sinners.

In sum, Jesus reveals God's kingdom as he casts out demons, heals the sick, cleanses the lepers, forgives sin, embraces the outcasts, and loves sinners. Each of these acts builds God's kingdom and diminishes the influence of Satan because they strike at his reign and push against the results of the fall that he caused.

Before the fall, Adam and Eve lived in a perfect relationship with God. There were no demonic manifestations or social outcasts. No one was sick, no one had leprosy, no one died, and no one was hungry. In the new kingdom that Jesus proclaims, God's people will be rightly related to God, each other, and the physical environment. In microcosm, Jesus' early ministry manifests what will happen in the consummation when Satan is fully defeated and the kingdom of God is fully realized. For that reason, Jesus' ministry graphically shows spiritual warfare and reveals the contours of the in-breaking kingdom.

Images of Spiritual Warfare in the Gospels

Other texts also point to the spiritual warfare theme in the New Testament. In Luke 4:8-19, Jesus quotes from Isaiah 61:1-2. He says, "The Spirit of the Lord is on me, because he has anointed me to proclaim good news to the poor. He has sent me to proclaim freedom for the prisoners and recovery of sight for the blind, to set the oppressed free, to proclaim the year of the Lord's favor." Not only does Jesus apply the text to himself, he also indicates that each part of it reflects a specific aspect of his kingdom agenda. People are in bondage to Satan. His kingdom of evil oppresses them. Jesus has come to free them from Satan and his malice.

Peter clarifies that Jesus' ministry of healing and doing good were directed at setting the captives free. He states, "God anointed Jesus of Nazareth with the Holy Spirit and power, and he went around doing good and healing all who were under the power of the devil, because God was with him" (Acts 10:38). By means of healings and deliverance, Jesus freed people who lived "under the power of the devil" as he grew the kingdom of God one person at a time.

In Luke 11:14–20, Jesus drove out a demon that caused a man to be mute. Afterward, the man could speak. His adversaries accused Jesus of casting out demons by the power of Beelzebul. Jesus rebuffed their accusations by making a startling claim. The fact that he drives out demons by the finger of God proves that the kingdom of God has come upon them. In other words, his work of exorcism clearly evidences that the kingdom of God has come and that he is more powerful than Satan.

Starting in Luke 8:22, the evil empire looms large. While going across the Sea of Galilee, Jesus is attacked by a spirit who tries to destroy the boat via a violent storm. In response, Jesus rebukes the wind and raging sea. That is, he rebukes the power that is animating a force of nature and using it as a weapon to cause him harm. In the New Testament, a demon is called by the way it is manifesting. For example, there are spirits of infirmity, blindness, and deafness. When Jesus casts out a spirit of infirmity, he rebukes it in the same way that he rebuked the spirits that caused the wind and waves to lash out against him.

When Jesus gets to the other side of the Sea of Galilee, a man with a legion of demons greets him on the shoreline. After a conversation with the demons, Jesus allows them to go into the sea. This is a curious thing because other demons had just tried to kill Jesus by means of the sea. Luke says that Jesus cured the man with the legion of demons. Regularly, the Bible uses "cured" when one would expect it to use "delivered a person from his demons." The distinction between healing and exorcism is often blurred. This has led some to believe that exorcism is a form of healing. In popular circles, it is called "inner healing."

Spiritual Warfare Implied in the Various Great Commissions

As a reminder of what was shown in a previous chapter, after the Tower of Babel was destroyed and the people were scattered, God picked Israel to be the chosen people through whom he would reveal himself and make his covenant. In contrast to the sinfulness of the surrounding nations, God called Israel a holy nation and a kingdom of priests. He placed his name upon them and called them to be a sanctified people. Through them, he intended to move forward his salvific plan, a plan that climaxed in Jesus and the salvation of the nations. Jesus is a child of the Jewish covenant and an heir of Abraham. He is the promised redeemer. Through him, God's plan to bless all the families of the earth will realize its culmination (Gen 12:3).

When God chose Israel, he set the *elohim* over the other nations. "When the Most High gave the nations their inheritance, when he divided all mankind, he set up boundaries for the peoples according to the number of the sons of [god]. For the Lord's portion is his people, Jacob his allotted inheritance" (Deut 32:8–9). The oldest texts render Deuteronomy 32:9 as "according to the sons of God." Sons of God is the same term that is used to describe the members of the heavenly council and those angels who came to Earth in Genesis 6.[1]

In Psalm 82, Yahweh convenes his heavenly council to include all the *elohim* who were ruling over the nations. He calls them gods and the sons of the Most High. He excoriates them because they did wickedly by not leading the people to practice righteousness. Sometime after they were given their authority over the nations, it appears that they set themselves up as gods and sided with Satan. Through them and the consequences of the fall, Satan claimed authority over all the nations (Matt 4:8–9).

In the various missionary charges (Matt 28:18–20; Mark 16:15–16; Luke 24:46–48; John 20:21–23; Acts 1:6–8), Jesus commands the church to take the gospel to the world and preach it to all nations with the intent of making disciples of all peoples. Notice, the calling isn't to save individuals from among the nations and bring them back to the land of Israel. That is an Old Testament theme.

In the old covenant, God manifested himself in Israel. He claimed the Jews as his people. By joining themselves to Israel, Gentile proselytes and sojourners entered into the covenant that God made with Israel. That is why the Old Testament has so many rules about allowing sojourners to come

---

1. See Heiser, "Deuteronomy 32," 52–74.

into Israel. It is also why God commanded Solomon to build a court for the gentiles in the temple. God wanted the gentiles to come to him.

In the New Testament, the mission changes direction. Instead of calling the nations to come to Israel and meet God, Jesus tells the church to take God to the world. That is why the evangelistic mission of the church directs the church to go and disciple the nations. God wants to reclaim the nations that he put under the care of the *elohim* after the scattering through the evangelistic preaching of his church. The heavenly rulers over the nations lose their power when the people of a given nation reject them and make Christ their Lord.

The Day of Pentecost plainly manifests God's intent. It's the reversal of Babel and signals that all the nations will be saved. Not only are representatives from all the known nations present on that day (Gen 10:21–30), each also hears the gospel message in his own language. Additionally, people from each of the represented nations are saved, baptized, and made members of the church. God's counter-offensive against the *elohim* began on the Day of Pentecost.

On that day, the church was given authority and power to complete its global mission. In fact, God gave the church the Holy Spirit and spiritual gifts to enable it to complete God's mission. Without the indwelling Holy Spirit, the disciples cannot fulfill their calling. As they go forward, they preach the kingdom of God and duplicate Jesus' ministry example in the context of the nations. Some would call the mission mandate an invasion of enemy territory rather than a global church planting movement.

In summary, what God gave to the *elohim* at Babel, he reclaims on the Day of Pentecost. Mission is how God takes possession of the nations. Previously, Jesus reclaimed Israel for his kingdom. After his death and resurrection, Jesus sent his disciples to reclaim the nations in his name. They are to challenge the *elohim* who have set themselves over the nations by evangelizing, church planting, disciple-making, and doing power ministry. In their global mission, the apostolic church fights an indirect war against the *elohim* by growing God's kingdom through their ministry on Earth. Their earthly work has heavenly ramifications. As the peoples reject the *elohim* and turn to God in Christ, God claims the people and the land for himself. The *elohim* are dethroned through the evangelistic mission of the church. For that reason, mission is spiritual warfare![2]

---

2. For a helpful perspective on this theme, see Heiser, *Supernatural*, 127–36.

The Interplay between Kingdom Growth and Satanic Persecution in Acts

The Acts of the Apostles also shows spiritual warfare. In the opening chapters, Satan counters power ministry and mass evangelism by stringent persecution in an effort to stop the gospel from spreading. In a way that is strangely reminiscent of the magicians in Egypt, every move of God is met by a satanic countermove. For example, after Peter heals a crippled beggar in front of the temple, many people receive Christ. However, the enraged religious rulers arrest, beat, and threaten Peter and John. Before releasing them, they demand that the apostles stop speaking in Jesus' name (Acts 4:17–18). Despite the persecution, God continued to grow his kingdom as the masses turned to Christ.[3]

Things boiled over when large crowds brought the sick and the demonized to the apostles to be healed (Acts 5:12–16). Once again, the desperate authorities put the disciples in prison. This time, God fought back. In the night, he dispatched an angel to rescue the apostles. The angelic warrior told the apostles to preach the gospel in the temple. When the befuddled authorities discovered the "escaped prisoners" preaching, they wanted to kill them (Acts 5:33).

Despite the brutal persecution, the church continued to grow rapidly (Acts 6:7). The preaching with powerful signs and wonders overwhelmed much of the Jewish opposition. As a consequence, many of the religious leaders joined the disciples. When the satanically inspired opposition couldn't intimidate the followers of Jesus or force them to stop preaching Jesus, they stoned Stephen to death. Afterward, by means of a vitriolic attack, they drove the believers out of Jerusalem (Acts 7–8).

Instead of slowing down the growth of the church, the "great" persecution of the Jerusalem Church accelerated it. As the believers fled the vexation, they preached the gospel and planted new communities of faith wherever they went. Think of it this way. When Satan dropped a persecution bomb on the Jerusalem Church, instead of destroying the work of God, the resulting blast hurled the movement into new mission fields. In other words, Satan thought that he could stop the work of God by destroying the Jerusalem Church through severe persecution. However, God used Satan's attack to expand his work to other locations.

---

3. Growth summary reports are strategically inserted throughout Acts. The reports declare that the church is growing, and that God's kingdom is spreading despite persecution. See Acts 2:47; 4:4; 5:14; 6:1; 9:31; 11:21; 24; 12:24; 14:1; 16:5; 17:12; and 19:20. Yes, the early church counted their converts and celebrated numerical growth. Church growth was a kingdom metric.

This is the nature of spiritual warfare in Acts. In the spiritual realm, Satan battles against the growing kingdom of God. His malice is manifested in the natural realm when religious authorities and government leaders use intimidation and physical maltreatment to oppose the work of God. God fights back by enabling his saints to preach effectively and to do magnificent signs and wonders. At critical junctures, God intervenes in tangible ways when angels give direct assistance to the saints. Even though the believers do God's will and walk in his ways, they still suffer because they are targeted by the Evil One. When the suffering doesn't dissuade them or cause them to deny Christ, Satan is unable to stop the work of God by means of persecution.

The Example of Paul in Acts

Paul demonstrates the above pattern. When commissioned, Jesus told him, "I am sending you to [the gentiles] to open their eyes and turn them from darkness to light, and from the power of Satan to God, so that they may receive forgiveness of sins and a place among those who are sanctified by faith in me" (Acts 26:17–18). Everything about his calling requires him to free people from the power of Satan as he turns them to God. However, when Paul pushed against the darkness, the darkness pushed back. Paul's confrontation with the powers of darkness often left him bleeding, hungry, and in prison.

In 2 Corinthians 11:23–27, Paul laments the afflictions that he endured as he carried out the commission that Christ gave to him.

> With far greater labors, far more imprisonments, with countless floggings, and often near death. Five times I have received from the Jews the forty lashes minus one. Three times I was beaten with rods. Once I received a stoning. Three times I was shipwrecked; for a night and a day I was adrift at sea; on frequent journeys, in danger from rivers, danger from bandits, danger from my own people, danger from Gentiles, danger in the city, danger in the wilderness, danger at sea, danger from false brothers and sisters; in toil and hardship, through many a sleepless night, hungry and thirsty, often without food, cold and naked.

During their first missionary journey, Paul and Barnabas encountered stiff opposition everywhere they went. When they were in Iconium, great numbers of people turned to Christ. To counter this, Satan worked through his people to poison the minds of those who were believing. To counteract what Satan was doing, God enabled the missionary team to do extraordinary signs and miracles as they ministered the gospel. Not to be outdone, Satan's team worked through the leaders to mistreat the believers. In order to lessen the assault on the new believers, the missionary team departed for Lystra (Acts 14:1–7).

The hostility reached a climax in Lystra. After Paul miraculously healed a crippled man in the middle of a large crowd of unbelievers while preaching the gospel with power, the pagan priests tried to attribute the miracle to Zeus and Hermes. When Paul and Barnabas didn't cooperate, they incited the crowd to stone Paul to death. After the rowdy crowds dispersed, the believers raised him up from the dead (Acts 14:8–20).

Later, Paul exorcized a slave girl who had a divining demon that was harassing him and Silas (Acts 16:18). In the aftermath, they were brutally flogged with rods and thrown into the inner jail. Satan thought he silenced them. However, God was not outdone. At midnight, God sent an earthquake that freed Paul and his companions from their chains. As a result, the jailer and other prisoners believed and were baptized.

Paul's ministry demonstrates how God and Satan work through their emissaries. The growth and persecution pattern repeats itself throughout the book of Acts. Clearly, as God's kingdom moved forward, it was always countered by the kingdom of Satan. At times, the saints are killed and pushed backed. At other times, the church has great success.

Three Stories That Show Spiritual Warfare in Acts

Three stories in Acts require special attention. After the great persecution of the Jerusalem Church, a deacon by the name of Philip fled by way of Samaria. As he went, he preached the word of God with signs and wonders. He ministered with such power that demons exited people with crying and loud shrieks. Even the paralyzed and lame were healed. As a consequence, the city was full of joy (Acts 8:7–8).

Because of the miracles, the people listened carefully to his preaching. However, Satan had already claimed this city. He worked through a magician by the name of Simon. Previously, the people eagerly listened to Simon and followed his crooked ways because he amazed them with his magic. The people referred to him as the "power of God that is called great." After seeing the superior power of God, the people transferred their allegiance to Jesus and were baptized. In the end, the magician was also baptized (Acts 8:4–26).[4]

---

4. Charles Kraft calls this power encounter. His model shows that power encounter,

Second, when Paul and Barnabas journeyed to Cyprus and preached all over the island, they encountered a magician by the name of Bar-Jesus. The magician opposed them and tried to turn the proconsul against them. Seeing this, Paul identified the magician as a son of the devil who was filled with villainy. He said that he was an enemy of righteousness and that he made crooked the straight paths of God. In Elijah fashion, he called down judgment on the man. In the aftermath, the magician was blinded, and the proconsul became a believer (Acts 13:4–12).

It should be noted that God also struck Paul down with blindness when he obstructed God's work (Acts 9). It ended in his salvation. However, the cursing of the magician is the only example in the New Testament in which a believer uses spiritual power to curse an adversary while in a direct ministry encounter.[5] The Bible tells Christ followers to bless those who persecute them and to do good to those who treat them badly (Matt 5:44; Luke 6:28; 35; Rom 12:14; 1 Cor 4:12; 1 Thess 5:15; Jas 3:9; 1 Pet 3:9).

Paul may have resorted to this curse because the magician was a spiritual linchpin who held back the work of God. Those who do spiritual mapping have noted that Satan often sets up a key person who keeps an area in spiritual bondage. When that person is converted or removed, the gospel flows to the people. As a matter of practice, those who do spiritual warfare should avoid cursing others unless God tells them to do it. The goal is to free bad people from Satan and bring them into a saving relationship with Jesus.

As was noted, Paul identified the magician that opposed God's work as a son of the devil. Jesus used the same language when he contended with the Jews who rejected him and wanted to kill him. They were sons of the devil (John 8:44). Previously, he told the Jews that they would be set free if they believed in him and became his disciples (John 8:31–35). He who the Son makes free is free indeed (John 8:36). Being set free assumes that they were in bondage and needed to be liberated from it. In the language of the New Testament, those who give themselves to evil are children of Satan.

Third, when Paul ministered in Ephesus (Acts 19), God performed extraordinary miracles through him. In particular, he healed the sick and demoniacs. As his fame grew, Jewish exorcists began to invoke the name of Jesus. Because of their familiarity with Paul's ministry, the sons of Sceva

---

truth encounter, and allegiance encounter go together. For more information, see Kraft, *Power Encounter*, 2017.

5. Paul curses those who preach a false gospel (Gal 1:8–9), and Jesus cursed a fig tree when it did not bear fruit (Mark 11:12–21). In Genesis, God cursed the serpent, the ground, and those who cursed Abraham. Noah cursed Canaan. To understand the power to bless and curse, see Kraft, *Confronting Powerless Christianity*, 164–67, and *Evangelical's Guide to Spiritual Warfare*, 151–54.

adjusted their exorcism formula. They said, "In the name of the Jesus whom Paul preaches, I command you to come out" (Acts 19:13). Regrettably, they didn't walk under Jesus' covering. As a result, the demons beat them up and ripped off their clothing. They fled in terror.

The story spread like wildfire and fear fell upon the people in Ephesus. Those who practiced the dark arts fell under conviction. When they turned to Jesus and repented, the sorcerers publicly destroyed all their magical scrolls and amulets. The burned items cost fifty thousand drachmas. A drachma equaled a day's wage. By American standards, that would equal five million dollars, assuming an average daily income of one hundred dollars.

More importantly, the sorcerers wouldn't have burned their ritual items unless they knew that Jesus was more powerful than the demon gods from whom they derived their power. Otherwise, the demons would have turned on them. In essence, they rejected their demons when they sided with Jesus because he proved to be the stronger god. By means of power encounters with the dark side, the word of the Lord spread widely and grew in power (Acts 19:20). This is another side of spiritual warfare.

Spiritual Warfare in the Epistles

Paul's letters show spiritual warfare themes in direct and indirect ways. The direct references are obvious. For example, he reminds the Roman church that "The God of peace will soon crush Satan under your feet" (Rom 16:12). He counsels the believers at Corinth to forgive each other so that Satan won't outwit us. For we understand his schemes (2 Cor 2:11). Paul desperately wanted to visit the church in Thessalonica but was unable to do so because Satan blocked his way (1 Thess 2:18). He reminds them that "The coming of the lawless one will be in accordance with how Satan works. He will use all sorts of displays of power through signs and wonders that serve the lie" (2 Thess 2:9). He instructs Timothy to counsel those who oppose the truth so they can escape from the devil's trap because Satan has taken them captive to do his will (2 Tim 2:26).

The direct approach isn't limited to Paul. First Peter 5:8 tells the believers to be sober and watchful because "your enemy the devil prowls around like a roaring lion looking for someone to devour." James tells the church to submit to God and resist the devil so that he will flee from you (4:7).

The following examples from letters to the churches in Asia Minor make direct reference to Satan and spiritual warfare. "I know the slander on the part of those who say that they are Jews and are not, but are a synagogue of Satan. Do not fear what you are about to suffer. Beware, the devil is about to throw some of you into prison so that you may be tested, and for ten days you will have affliction. Be faithful until death, and I will give you the crown of life" (Rev 2:9-10). "I know where you are living, where Satan's throne is. Yet you are holding fast to my name, and you did not deny your faith in me even in the days of Antipas my witness, my faithful one, who was killed among you, where Satan lives" (Rev 2:13). "I will make those of the synagogue of Satan who say that they are Jews and are not, but are lying—I will make them come and bow down before your feet, and they will learn that I have loved you. Because you have kept my word of patient endurance, I will keep you from the hour of trial that is coming on the whole world to test the inhabitants of the earth" (Rev 3:9-10).

Judgment is a way by which Jesus quells the work of Satan in the church. He warns those who eat food sacrificed to idols and who engage in sexual sin that he will make war with them if they don't repent (Rev 2:16). He cautions the Church at Sardis to "Remember then what you received and heard; obey it, and repent. If you do not wake up, I will come like a thief, and you will not know at what hour I will come to you" (Rev 3:3).

A woman called Jezebel who styled herself a prophet taught people to eat food sacrificed to idols and practice fornication with her to learn the deep things of Satan. Seekers would ingest food that had been consecrated to a spirit then have sex with the priestess who channeled it. Through this "sacred" rite, they would have a vicarious encounter with the spirit. God will bring great judgment and distress on Jezebel and those who participate with her unless they repent so the churches will know that God doesn't tolerate sin in his church (Rev 2:20-24).

At other times, the reference to spiritual warfare is indirect. Paul envisions a struggle between the believer and Satan. Sometimes, Paul uses "of the world" and "of the flesh" to describe the conflict. Both the world and the flesh are corrupted by Satan. Believers are not to conform to the world or to the world system because they convey the power of Satan. Rather, they are to be transformed by the power of God that resides within them (Rom 12:1-2).

Those who submit to the flesh and live by its standards become enemies of the cross and won't inherit the kingdom of God. For this reason, the saints must put to death the old nature and its sins so that they may be clothed in the new man that is being renewed in the image of Christ. They are encouraged to "take off" their vices and "put on" the virtues. The virtues to which Paul refers are the fruit of the Spirit (Col 3:1-17).

Not only does Satan tempt the believer, he also empowers the person's fallen nature so that it opposes the work of God in the believer. Repeatedly, the believers are told that they must flee from immorality. Sin brings one into captivity to Satan and stunts the work of God. Those who won't stop sinning must be removed from the congregation. They are turned over to Satan for the destruction of the flesh (1 Cor 5:5; 1 Tim 1:20). They are a threat to the church and a means by which Satan leads others into sin. Sin in the church is like leaven in bread. If not removed, it will corrupt the entire batch of dough (1 Cor 5:6–7).

Satan also tries to corrupt the church by means of false brethren and false teaching. Jesus warned about these people. He called them wolves in sheep's clothing (Matt 7:15). They are the emissaries of Satan who are sent to disrupt the work of God. In Matthew 24, Jesus warns that many false prophets and false christs will arise to lead people astray. They will perform lying signs and wonders that will deceive the saints and the masses (v. 24).

The problem of false teaching is so bad that Paul evokes a curse on those who do it. "Evidently some people are throwing you into confusion and are trying to pervert the gospel of Christ. But even if we or an angel from heaven should preach a gospel other than the one we preached to you, let them be under God's curse! As we have already said, so now I say again: If anybody is preaching to you a gospel other than what you accepted, let them be under God's curse!" (Gal 1:7–9).

Paul shows the connection between those who pervert the gospel and the work of Satan when he says, "For such people are false apostles, deceitful workers, masquerading as apostles of Christ. And no wonder, for Satan himself masquerades as an angel of light" (2 Cor 11:13–14). In Galatians 2:4, he contends that "false believers had infiltrated our ranks to spy on the freedom we have in Christ Jesus and to make us slaves."

Second Peter 2 paints a graphic picture of the problem with false teachers. "They will secretly introduce destructive heresies, even denying the sovereign Lord who bought them—bringing swift destruction on themselves. Many will follow their depraved conduct and will bring the way of truth into disrepute. In their greed, these teachers will exploit you with fabricated stories. Their condemnation has long been hanging over them, and their destruction has not been sleeping" (1 Pet 2:1–3). Peter likens the false teachers to the angels who sinned and are reserved in chains for judgment.

In 1 John 4, the church is commanded to test the spirits because false prophets will give perverse messages in the name of God. Evidently, some entered a spiritual state whereby they channeled an evil spirit that spoke through them. They would argue that they were in a divine trance and were speaking words from God via the Holy Spirit. The saints were to test them by asking the spirit that spoke through them to confess that Jesus came in the flesh. The ones who wouldn't confess this were lying spirits or demons that were trying to insert error into the church.

Paul referred to the same phenomenon when he counseled the church that no one speaking in the Spirit ever said that Jesus was cursed and that no evil spirit would confess that Jesus is Lord (1 Cor 12:3). As such, one could test the spirit by asking it to affirm that Jesus was Lord.[6]

The fact that the New Testament church developed ways to test the spirits that gave "divine utterances" shows that this was a big problem. Satanic attack in the guise of false prophesy and false teaching was very effective. It was a Trojan horse in the church. It needed to be recognized and rebuffed. In addition to false prophesy, the New Testament warns the believers against false visions and false revelations.[7]

The most dramatic spiritual warfare language comes from Ephesians 6:10–13. "Finally, be strong in the Lord and in his mighty power. Put on the full armor of God, so that you can take your stand against the devil's schemes. For our struggle is not against flesh and blood, but against the rulers, against the authorities, against the powers of this dark world and against the spiritual forces of evil in the heavenly realms. Therefore put on the full armor of God, so that when the day of evil comes, you may be able to stand your ground."

This text indicates that each believer is required to engage in spiritual warfare. It also avers that the believer's warfare isn't against an undifferentiated spiritual evil that tempts them to do wrong. Rather, it is against

---

6. Karl Payne offers a fascinating experience from his youth in which he successfully tested the spirits. His neighbor confessed that three spirit guides appeared to him when he did ministry. With their help, he could heal the sick. A steady stream of people came to his door because he was successful at what he did. He assured Payne that he did everything in Jesus' name. Finally, the troubled teen went to his house and told him that he wanted to test the spirits to see if they were from God. The neighbor humored him. When he read 1 John 4:1–6, the man was thrown into a trance and his eyes rolled back in his head. A foreign voice spoke to him. It claimed to serve Jesus. When pushed, it acknowledged that it served Satan (*Spiritual Warfare*, 12–14).

7. In "Spiritual Gifts Enable Spiritual Warfare," I document the relationship between spiritual gifts and spiritual warfare (Payne, *Adventures in Spiritual Warfare*, 111–33). On a regular basis I encounter false gifts when doing inner healing and deliverance ministry. False tongues are the most common. Recently, a person who was manifesting a demon began to speak in a very nasty tongue. When she spoke, she stuck out her tongue and made a hissing sound. The person believed that this was her personal prayer language and accepted it. We have already noted that the spirit of Python allowed a slave girl to prophesy (Acts 16:16). Counterfeit gifts and false signs are a huge problem in the church, especially when they are used to validate false teaching. As a general rule, Satan and his emissaries can duplicate every spiritual gift. That is why one should focus more on the fruit of the Spirit than spiritual gifting when attempting to discern if a person is walking with God.

a well-organized army of evil supernaturalism that is aligned with Satan. Since the saints are already seated with Christ in the heavenly realms (Eph 2:6), they need to own that "pneumographic" truth because they have spiritual authority to combat the wicked forces of evil that seek to destroy the church of God.[8]

Colossians 3:1 makes this point clear. Since Christians have been raised with Christ, they are to seek the things that are above where Christ is seated at the right hand of power and authority. Once the saints know who they are in Christ, they can effectively put on the full armor of Christ and do battle against the devil.

---

8. Pneumographic" is similar to geography and topography. I use the word to refer to the spiritual place where we stand with Christ in the heavenlies. There is a divine topography that Christians should understand when doing spiritual warfare.

17

Spiritual Warfare Versus Social Justice: Discerning a Kingdom Approach

RECENTLY, I had a conversation with a Christian leader who firmly rebuffed the notion of spiritual warfare and any "otherworldly" approach to the Christian faith. Instead, he advocated for a present kingdom that demonstrates God's love by means of tangible justice outcomes. Specifically, he strongly disliked the phrase "spiritual warfare." According to him, the idiom wreaked with hostility and wasn't compatible with the nonviolence teaching of the Gospels. He called it oxymoronic because spiritual and warfare don't go together. He believed that love, truth, and good works were the only weapons that a Christian should wield. Moreover, he opined that an emphasis on the "spiritual" diverted attention from the material struggle and the everyday oppression that dominates the lives of the poor and marginalized. For this man, social justice was the mission of the church and the way by which the church should actualize Jesus' kingdom teaching today.

The following dialogue captures the essence of the conversation that I had with this Christian leader.

Man: I don't do spiritual warfare. I am a pacifist. I also reject the myth of redemptive violence.[1] God is a God of peace. He blesses those who make peace. Divine violence does not bring about universal peace.

---

1. The man's theology was greatly influenced by Walter Wink and those who write against the myth of redemptive violence. See Steiner, "Looking along the Line," 73 and Wink, *Powers that Be*, 48. Often Wink mischaracterizes evangelicals and spiritual warfare practitioners.

Me: The Bible shows us that God is a warrior God who fights against the powers and spiritual principalities on our behalf. Certainly, Jesus didn't act as a pacifist when he cast out demons or cleansed the temple. Yes, exorcizing demons is a spiritually violent act. Whenever we claim the kingdom of God in word, sign, and deed, we push back the kingdom of Satan and fight against the darkness. Giving a robust witness to the in-breaking kingdom that Jesus inaugurated requires that we do spiritual warfare.

Man: God doesn't endorse spiritual warfare. In fact, Jesus tells us to pray for our enemies. That includes Satan.

Me: I also pray for Satan. I ask God to bind him and deliver us from him (Matt 6:13).

Man: Why are you so violent? Don't you know that God loves all things and desires that everything be remade by his love? In the end, even the demons will bow before Jesus. God's masterplan includes the redemption of all things.

Me: Does the redemption of Satan happen before or after God throws him into the Lake of Fire?

Man: An omnipotent God doesn't have enemies. Remember, Satan is also a son of God. God is love. He wants Satan to repent and return to a right relationship with him. God's longsuffering is eternal. He never gives up on anyone.

Me: That's a pleasant thought. Until Satan stops opposing God and bows before him, I am going to do what Jesus did. He cast him out and told him to be gone. In his ministry and his suffering, he worked to set the captives free from Satan's malice. That's how he showed us the Father's love. In the end, God can decide what he does to Satan. For now, I am going to work to mitigate Satan's influence by extending the reign of God.

In the ongoing conversation, the man acknowledged the existence of evil and affirmed the work of Jesus to destroy the power of Satan. However, that belief didn't influence his theology or personal ministry. Instead, he described the biblical texts about evil supernaturalism as myths that mirrored the animistic worldview of the people who wrote them. He believed that political interventionism on behalf of the socially oppressed was the modern equivalency to exorcism. In his words, "It's through partnerships with a just state that the church best advances God's kingdom in concrete ways."

C. S. Lewis encapsulates this man's sentiment in *That Hideous Strength*, when a naive Mark has a conversation with an idealistic vicar who has been unwittingly beguiled by the enemy. In the ensuing dialogue, the minister defines God's kingdom in terms of material outcomes. He anticipates a soon to be realized social revolution. However, the mechanism for the renovation that he desires won't be God's Spirit working through the church to change society and free people from their captivity to Satan. Rather, the social transformation will be realized through science and the intervention of an autocratic state that imposes the desired outcomes. They are the tools that God will use to save humans from themselves and their false religions.[2]

At this point, I need to correct a misperception about those who practice spiritual warfare. Practitioners of spiritual warfare don't advocate for "physical" violence. Spiritual warfare and physical warfare are vastly different. When properly nuanced, spiritual warfare theology is compatible with New Testament teachings on nonviolence and peaceful resistance. Nonviolence is a means by which Christians witness to Jesus when evil people attempt to silence the church by force. It's a noble act of resistance. In the encounter, nonresistance shows that the evil perpetrator is not an enemy that needs to be beaten. Rather, he is a person who needs to experience the love of Christ so he can turn from his evil and receive forgiveness.[3] In this guise, nonviolent resistance is an evangelistic tool. In practice, one can discard the doctrine of pacifism without rejecting the lifestyle of nonviolence.

Today, many speak about the larger significance of Jesus' exorcisms in light of structural evil. In truth, many who reduce spiritual warfare to myth are more concerned with political interventionism than personal deliverance. That is why they focus on systemic evil rather than personal demonization. The paradise that they desire doesn't look like the kingdom of God on Earth. Rather, it resembles a political state that embraces the social priorities of progressive Christianity. In some sense, they advocate for a secular theocracy that reflects the ideals of a certain type of all-encompassing socialism that is fully inclusive of everyone but practicing evangelicals. A living faith in Jesus is secondary to the social justice outcomes that they envision. That is why they can work hand-in-hand with practitioners of other faiths or no faith to achieve their goals.

In one sense, the Christian leader is correct. All aspects of human existence bear the mark of the fall. Without a doubt, the social order is corrupted. Satan infiltrates it and works through it to bring entire sectors of society into bondage. Any cursory look at the American public culture will verify this. For example, when one examines a consolidated list of vices that the New Testament condemns, vices that prevent individuals from entering the kingdom of God or receiving eternal life (Gal 5:16–21; Eph 5:5), one will

2. Lewis, *That Hideous Strength*, 98.

3. Charles Campbell captures this when he states, "Jesus is saying, 'Do not *violently* resist an evildoer.' Don't resort to the ways of the world governed by the myth of redemptive violence, which simply perpetuates the cycle of violence. Instead, Jesus counsels creative, imaginative, nonviolence. We get extraordinary examples of turning the other cheek, giving the cloak also, and going the extra mile, which are not acts of passivity but ways of resisting evil nonviolently" ("Folly of the Sermon," 67).

discover that many have become celebrated virtues in America. Progressive Christianity elevates some vices to the status of universal human rights.[4] Surely, the consequences of the fall are imprinted on every facet of the cultural DNA of American society. Bluntly stated, corrupted culture obstructs God's plan to transform society.

Spiritual warfare happens when the kingdom of God seeks to dislodge the kingdom of Satan from individuals, families, churches, communities, and whole societies. Whenever and wherever the kingdom of God grows in this world, spiritual conflict ensues. For this reason, those who advocate for spiritual warfare recognize the problem with systemic evil. Like those who push for social justice, they also desire that the entire society be transformed as the kingdom of God is realized in all spheres of human existence.[5] For this reason, personal evangelism, healing, exorcism, and the like need to be augmented by activities that target systemic evil.

At some level, the two are intricately intertwined and must not be divided. As I have previously noted, a social activism that doesn't proclaim the full gospel, call people to surrender to the reign of God, and deliver them from their personal bondages to sin and Satan won't grow the kingdom of God, fix the social order, or defeat Satan. On the other hand, community transformation under the power of the regenerating hand of God does defeat Satan, grow the church, and expand God's rule in this world.[6]

In brief, God desires to change the social order. However, a divine change in the social order won't take place when the people who compose the social order remain in bondage to their sins and live spiritually alienated from God. Furthermore, the political apparatus of the state isn't a delivery mechanism for the kingdom of God. Moreover, the church cannot release the kingdom on Earth by means of political interventionism.

Herein we can learn from the Gospels. Jesus didn't attempt to change the Roman Empire or the Jewish state by means of military action or direct political intervention. Rather, he surrounded himself with a group of

---

4. To review a consolidated list of vices that the Bible condemns, see Just, "Virtue and Vice Lists."

5. As communist Cuba approached its referendum on a new constitution that doesn't guarantee freedom of conscience or the right to practice one's faith in public, Pastor Mario Felix Lleonart accurately captured the evangelical perspective when he said, "Our faith doesn't just free us from the eternal consequences of sin. It also makes us free here on Earth, and that brings us into conflict with a totalitarian regime that restricts our freedoms" (Gjelten, "Religious Leaders in Cuba," para. 14).

6. Many believe that the church is the keeper of society. Liberal Christians want to partner with the state to institute a just social order that establishes their progressive values. Evangelicals want to create a Christian state that reflects their morality. Both approaches confuse the mission of the church with a political outcome.

disciples that he trained to proclaim the gospel of the kingdom in word, sign, and deed. Their mission included preaching the kingdom of God, power ministry, and disciple-making. After he trained them, he sent them into the world to duplicate his ministry, destroy the works of Satan, and grow the kingdom of God.

On the Day of Pentecost and in the many commissions, Jesus transferred the apostolic calling to the entire church. The warrant included breaking down satanic strongholds that kept large populations in captivity. Phillip and Paul demonstrated this when they upended the sway that powerful sorcerers held over regions. Because the early church remained focused on the evangelistic mandate, manifested the kingdom of God, and practiced doing good, the Roman Empire eventually recognized Christ and the culture changed from within. Outside of a national revival, there are no shortcuts to the kingdom or to social transformation.

Discerning the Relationship between Spiritual Warfare and Liberation Theology[7]

All Christians of good faith desire to see the social order transformed. No one likes injustice or celebrates evil. However, those who do spiritual warfare perceive the social climate differently from theologians who mostly emphasize class struggle, economic justice, radical individualism, and structural sin because they believe that the above-listed evils are symptoms of a greater malady.

According to the spiritual warfare hermeneutic, social evil doesn't just happen as an accident without causality. Some years ago, I visited a temple to the Hindu Goddess Kali in Andhra Pradesh, India. Kali is a vicious goddess associated with death, sexuality, violence, and human sacrifice. For years, people died from suspicious car accidents and other unexplained reasons in front of her temple on a weekly basis. Local people lived in fear of Kali. Finally, the local Christians banded together to form around-the-clock prayer vigils to neutralize the spiritual power of Kali. Afterward, the accidents stopped and evangelism exploded. The church located across the street from the Kali Temple is not taking any chances. Prayer intercessors still meet to minimize the spiritual power of Kali.[8]

---

7. For a fuller reading on this topic, see Payne, "Discerning an Integral Latino Pentecostal Theology," 87–106.

8. George Otis tells a similar story about Kali in *Twilight Labyrinth*. My account came from Christians who lived by a different Kali temple than the one that Otis mentions.

The Bible personifies social injustice. It is the external manifestation of a deeper spiritual evil. Like a roaring lion, it roams about seeking whom it can devour (Prov 28:15; 2 Cor 2:11; Jas 4:7; 1 Pet 5:8). It seeks to steal, kill, and destroy (John 10:10). It wants to abolish the work of God in society and make slaves out of God's people. Satan creates evil social structures to further his agenda of controlling society, causing sin, and leading people away from God's kingdom. In sum, the evil parts of the social order have been animated by spiritual wickedness in high places.

For many Evangelicals, this understanding legitimizes spiritual warfare activities on behalf of the institutions where they work and the nations where they live. Spiritual warfare activities move beyond social justice models. By means of them, those who do spiritual warfare form intercessory teams that seek to discern the spiritual terrain and act in concerted ways to minimize the influence of spiritual evil because they know that the work of social welfare, reconciliation, restoration, national healing, and evangelization will move forward more effectively when the powers and principalities are weakened. In other words, in order to achieve the integral liberation of people and society, they believe that they must work on the spiritual and material fronts. Any approach to social problems that ignores the spiritual environment is doomed to fail or only offer partial help. Additionally, approaches that only depend on social science interpretive models often lead to more suffering.

The Exodus example in chapter 11 examined Moses and the exodus story through the lens of spiritual warfare. Liberation theologians also appeal to the exodus story to show how humans should work to throw off the shackles of injustice. The exodus story exemplifies how people use different hermeneutics to understand the problem of social injustice and the end goal of salvation. The social justice approach picks up on the theme of "let my people go." It identifies Egypt as the source of oppression. The analysis of the situation shows that the Jews are slaves because the Egyptians need a cheap workforce. Like exploited tools, they have value only when they are used. The Egyptians deny their human dignity because they benefit from their exploitation. Such a situation is evil and unjust. The system must be challenged.

Because God sides with the oppressed, he raises up Moses to confront the evil structure, organize the people, and build a populist movement. When the conditions are right, Moses leads a revolt, frees the people from slavery, and destroys the system. It is a physical deliverance and Moses is the main actor.[9] The Jews leave Egypt with their dignity and are given gold

---

9. For an excellent example of this type of reading, see Torre, *Reading the Bible*,

to recompense them for years of forced labor. This is God's justice and a sign of his preferential option for the poor.[10] It is also a realized salvation in a material environment. Allegiance to God, personal righteousness, and spiritual powers are not emphasized.

The spiritual approach also emphasizes the "let my people go" theme. However, it argues that the primary war is between God and the spiritual powers behind the Egyptian system of oppression; not between Moses and Pharaoh. Based on this reading, God is the primary deliverer and Moses is the human tool through which he works and manifests his power.

The episode in which the Egyptian magicians mimic Moses' miracles shows that the Egyptian gods wield spiritual power through their servants. Additional signs and wonders evidence the superiority of Yahweh over the gods of Egypt as each of them is dethroned. When the Egyptian gods are demolished with divine aid, the might of Egypt is also destroyed, and the people go free.[11] Salvation is material and spiritual. That is, the people are saved from Egypt and the wicked Egyptian gods are ruined.

George Lucas illustrates the idea that the outcome of the earthly battle is tied to the outcome of the heavenly battle in his adventure thriller *The Return of the Jedi*. In the movie, the rebel forces are frantically fighting on a moon, trying to turn off a forcefield that protects the Death Star. However, the real war is fought in the heavens between Jedi novice Luke Skywalker and Darth Vader, Emperor Palpatine's surrogate. When Luke finally wins the heavenly battle, the rebels on the moon are able to destroy the forcefield that protects the Death Star.

The following illustration depicts the relationships between the Material Approach and the Spiritual Approach from the perspective of the Exodus story.

160–61.

10. For good reason, liberationists feel discomfort with the conquest narratives that follow the Exodus story because some have used them to justify genocide. For example, under the guise of manifest destiny, the United States styled itself as the New Israel. The colonists were the chosen people, America was the Promised Land, and the indigenous peoples were the Canaanites who had to be removed from the land. In this scenario, the liberated oppressed became oppressors. This theme often repeats itself when liberationist movements throw off their oppressors. For an informative discussion on this topic, see Hawk, *Joshua in 3-D*.

11. In Exodus 14:13–14, God "fights for his people" to destroy their enemy. As Moses lifts up his rod to divide the sea, the Angel of the Lord positions himself between the Israelites and the Egyptians. Moses is an actor in a war that God is fighting with and through the hosts of heaven. God is a warrior God (Exod 15:3).

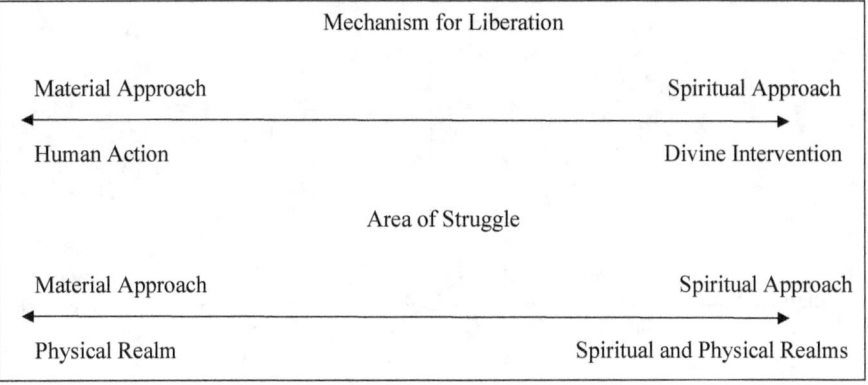

Figure 1. Relationship between Material and Spiritual Approaches to Liberation

The continua deliberately polarize the differences. Both material and spiritual approaches act in definitive ways to change the social environment. The material approach emphasizes the work of the Christian community in solidarity with the poor and oppressed. It sees physical oppression and structural evil as the result of human sin. Often, the sin is systemic and is tied to capitalism and global power structures. God's kingdom brings justice and equality in the physical realm.

The spiritual approach doesn't deny the insights of the material approach. Rather, it emphasizes the work of God on behalf of his called-out people. It declares the existence of spiritual forces of evil that operate in and through the physical realm to enslave God's people and bring them and creation into all manner of bondage. Physical liberation necessitates spiritual deliverance. The material approach without the spiritual approach will fail.

The Contours of a Biblical Model of Liberation

The following illustration combines the axes from the previous one in order to depict an interpretive model based on the materialist and spiritualist readings of the exodus story. The Z axis (diagonal) dissects the X and Y axes. It locates the materialist approach in quadrant II and the spiritualist approach in quadrant IV. However, the spiritualist approach also overflows into quadrants I and III. In this regard, it is more inclusive than the standard materialist approach. Still, a biblical theology of liberation should encompass all four quadrants since each has something important to offer about God, the church, its mission, and social transformation.

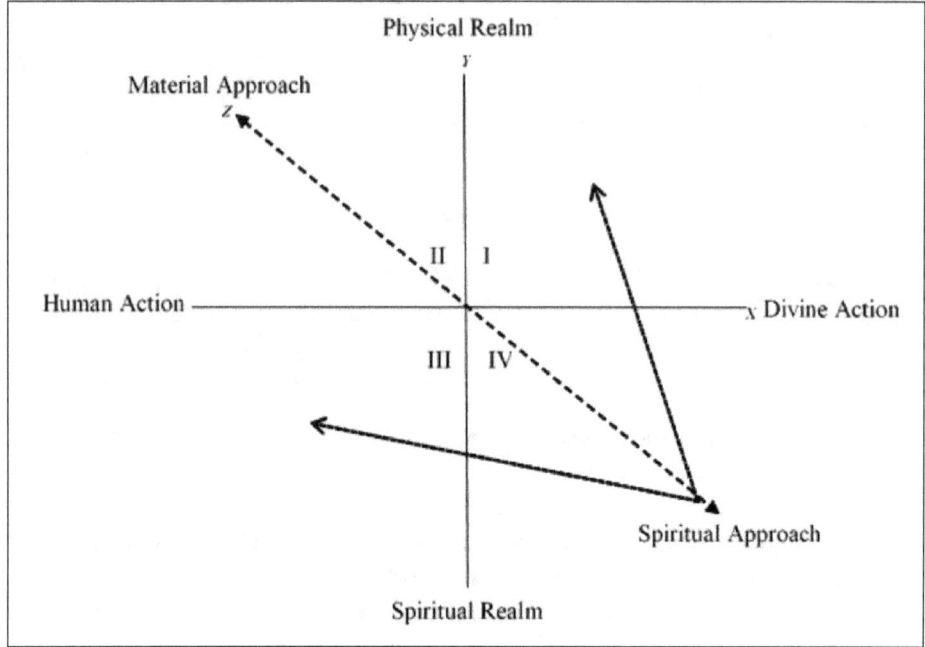

Figure 2. Integrated Model of Liberation

Quadrant I represents divine action in the physical domain. This is seen when God, angels, or demonic powers tangibly intervene in the material world. Quadrant II represents human action in the physical realm. This encompasses everything from feeding the poor to political activity that aims at the reordering of a just society. This is the domain of liberation theology. Quadrant III represents human action in the spiritual realm. It recognizes that God works through and in tandem with his people to fulfill his work. That is why he partnered with Moses. This is the classic domain of spiritual warfare. By means of spiritual warfare, the faith community actively confronts the spiritual powers and attempts to overcome them through the power of the Holy Spirit and the atonement of Christ. Quadrant IV represents divine action in the spiritual realm. Yahweh dethroning the gods of Egypt is an example of this. Activity in this quadrant may be fought in the heavenlies (Rev 12:7–12) or on Earth. In either case, the results of divine combat reverberate in the physical realm. Christians may influence the outcome of divine combat through intercessory prayers and holy living. This is a Quadrant III activity.

Jesus' life, ministry, and teachings about the kingdom of God reveal a holistic liberation that impinges on each of the quadrants. For example,

Jesus cries with the grieving, challenges the religious oligarchy that oppresses the masses, gives hope to those in despair, humanizes the lepers who live as the pariahs of society, respects women, breaks patterns of entrenched xenophobia, socializes with those furthest from the kingdom, and tells his followers that they must reconcile with each other as a condition of remaining right with God. At the same time, he battles against Satan's kingdom by forgiving sins, healing the diseased, casting out the demons, raising the dead, curing the lepers, multiplying food to feed the hungry, preaching repentance, making disciples, empowering his followers with the Holy Spirit, and dying on the cross.

Even though Jesus didn't do direct battle with the Roman government or destroy the evil systems that oppressed the people, he did destroy the power of Satan via his death and resurrection. What began as a Quadrant II event (a human dying on a cross) morphed into a Quadrant IV event when Jesus descended into Hades. The resurrection is the greatest power encounter of all time. Furthermore, when Jesus defeated the spiritual powers of evil, he made it possible for the societies of the world to be set free from Satan's malice. As the church expands the kingdom of God into the realm of Satan, God continues to destroy the power of evil, to set people free, and to reorder fallen social structures. As such, when the church follows Jesus' example, it must embrace spiritual warfare without neglecting to minister to physical oppression and human need.

The Integrated Model of Liberation shows that social justice and spiritual warfare go together. Additionally, it allows the faithful to conceptualize an all-encompassing approach to integral liberation. When the church and ministry practitioners learn to operate in each of the four quadrants, they will be more successful in advancing the kingdom of God in a tangible way.

Bibliography

Aardweg, Gerard van den. *Hungry Souls: Supernatural Visits, Messages, and Warnings from Purgatory.* Amsterdam: Saint Benedict, 2009.

Appelle, Stuart, et al. "Alien Abduction Experiences." In *Varieties of Anomalous Experience: Examining the Scientific Evidence,* edited by Etzel Cardeña and Stanley Krippner, 253–82. Washington, DC: American Psychological Association, 2000.

Arnold, Clinton. *3 Crucial Questions about Spiritual Warfare.* Grand Rapids: Baker Academic, 1997.

Aune, David E. *Revelation 6–16.* Word Biblical Commentary 52B. Nashville: Nelson, 1998.

Averbeck, Richard E. "Ancient Near Eastern Mythology as It Relates to Historiography in the Hebrew Bible: Genesis 3 and the Cosmic Battle." In *The Future of Biblical Archeology: Reassessing Methodologies and Assumptions,* edited by Alan Millard and James K. Huffeier, 328–56. Grand Rapids: Eerdmans, 2004.

Baker, Krista. "Fallen Angels." https://www.deliriumsrealm.com/fallen-angels/.

Barclay, William. *The Gospel of Luke.* New Daily Study Bible. Rev. ed. Louisville: Westminster John Knox, 2001.

Barstad, Hans M. "Sheol." In *Dictionary of Deities and Demons in the Bible,* edited by Karel van der Toorn, et al., 768–70. 2nd ed. Grand Rapids: Eerdmans, 1999.

Bierlein, J. F. *Parallel Myths: A Fascinating Look at the Common Threads Woven through the World's Greatest Myths—and the Central Role They Have Played through Time.* New York: Ballantine, 1994.

Blackaby, Henry T., et al. *Experiencing God: Knowing and Doing the Will of God.* Nashville: Broadman & Holman, 2008.

Bloch-Smith, Elizabeth. *Judahite Burial Practices and Beliefs About the Dead.* JSOT Supplement Series 123. Sheffield: Sheffield Academic Press, 1992.

Block, Daniel I. *The Gods of the Nations: Studies in Ancient Near Eastern National Theology.* Evangelical Theological Society. Jackson: Evangelical Theological Society, 1988.

Blomberg, Craig L. *Interpreting the Parables.* Downers Grove: InterVarsity, 1990

Bohak, Gideon. "Jewish Exorcisms Before and After the Destruction of the Second Temple." In *Was 70 CE a Watershed in Jewish History? On Jews and Judaism before and after the Destruction of the Second Temple,* edited by Daniel R Schwartz and Zeev Weiss, 277–300. Boston: Brill, 2012.

Bowron, Mark. "Seventh Heaven." *Sound Doctrine Ministries* (blog), February 12, 2012. https://sounddoctrineministries.wordpress.com/2012/02/12/seventh-heaven/.

Boyd, Gregory. *God at War: The Bible & Spiritual Conflict*. Downers Grove: InterVarsity, 1997.

———. "The Ground-Level Deliverance Model." In *Understanding Spiritual Warfare: Four Views*, 129–56. Grand Rapids: Baker Academic, 2012.

Burke, John. *Imagine Heaven: Near-death Experiences, God's Promises, and the Exhilarating Future that Awaits You*. Grand Rapids: Baker, 2015.

Byron, John. *Cain and Abel in Text and Tradition: Jewish and Christian Interpretations of the First Sibling Rivalry*. Boston: Brill, 2011.

Caballeros, Harold. "Prophetic Pathways." In *The Transforming Power of Revival*, edited by Harold Caballeros and Mell Winger, 8–21. Buenos Aires: El Shaddai Ministries, 1989.

Caballeros, Harold, and Mell Winger, eds. *The Transforming Power of Revival*. Buenos Aires: El Shaddai Ministries, 1989.

Campbell, Charles. "The Folly of the Sermon on the Mount." In *Preaching the Sermon on the Mount: The World It Imagines*, edited by David Fleer and Dave Bland, 59–68. Saint Louis: Chalice, 2007.

Campbell, Joseph. *The Mythic Dimension: Selected Essays 1959–1987*. Edited by Antony van Couvering. The Collected Works of Joseph Campbell. Novato, CA: New World Library, 2007.

Charlesworth, James H., ed. *The Old Testament Pseudepigrapha*. 2 vols. Garden City: Doubleday, 1983.

Colavito, Jason. "How the Nephilim Survived the Flood." *Jason Colavito* (blog), November 1, 2013. http://www.jasoncolavito.com/blog/how-the-nephilim-survived-the-flood.

Coleman, J. A. *The Dictionary of Mythology: An A–Z of Themes, Legends, and Heroes*. Edited by George Davidson. London: Arcturus, 2015.

Colijn, Brenda B. *Images of Salvation in the New Testament*. Downers Grove: InterVarsity, 2010.

Collins, Robin. "Understanding Atonement: A New and Orthodox Theory." http://static1.1.sqspcdn.com/static/f/38692/208738/1263475937360/Understanding+Atonement+-+A+New+and+Orthodox+Theory.pdf?token=65NPVjq7bsxgcZmefoUBS5KTbX8%3D.

Crick, Robert, and Brandelan Miller. *Journeying with Jeanette: A Love Story into the Land and Language of Alzheimer's*. Oviedo, FL: HigherLife, 2016.

Cromie, William J. "Alien Abduction Claims Examined." *Harvard Gazette*, February 20, 2003. https://news.harvard.edu/gazette/story/2003/02/alien-abduction-claims-examined-2/.

Daily Renegade. "FINALLY! The TRUTH! Dr. Michael Heiser on How the Nephilim REALLY Survived the Flood." *YouTube*, November 12, 2018. https://www.youtube.com/watch?v=L6yJntFNc_c.

Daniels, Kimberly. *The Demon Dictionary*. 2 vols. Lake Mary: Charisma, 2013–14.

Davidson, Gustav. "Samael." In *A Dictionary of Angels: Including the Fallen Angels*, 255–56. New York: Free Press, 1971.

Day, John. *Yahweh and the Gods and Goddesses of Canaan*. Journal for the Study of the Old Testament Supplement Series 265. New York: Sheffield Academic, 2002.

Dennis, Geoffrey W. "Cain." In *The Encyclopedia of Jewish Myth, Magic & Mysticism*, 74. 2nd ed. Woodbury, MN: Llewellyn Publications, 2016.

Dickason, C. Fred. *Angels: Elect and Evil*. Chicago: Moody, 1975.
Dixon-Kennedy, Mike. *The Encyclopedia of Greco-Roman Mythology*. Santa Barbara: ABC-CLIO, 1999.
Driver, John. *Understanding the Atonement for the Mission of the Church*. Eugene, OR: Wipf & Stock, 1986.
Dunbar, Brian, ed. "Finding Life beyond Earth Is within Reach." *NASA*, July 14, 2014. https://www.nasa.gov/content/finding-life-beyond-earth-is-within-reach/.
Eggert, Kaylan, writ. *Ancient Aliens*. Season 5, episode 9, "Strange Abductions." Aired February 22, 2013, on H2. https://www.history.com/shows/ancient-aliens/season-5/episode-9.
Engelsviken, Tormod. *Spiritual Conflict in Today's Mission: A Report from the Consultation on "Deliver Us from Evil," August 2000, Nairobi, Kenya*. Lausanne Occasional Paper 29. Monrovia, CA: MARC, 2001.
Evans, Craig A. *Jesus and the Remains of His Day: Studies in Jesus and the Evidence of Material Culture*. Peabody: Endrickson, 2015.
Franklin, Jentezen. *The Spirit of Python: Exposing Satan's Plan to Squeeze the Life Out of You*. Lake Mary: Charisma, 2013.
Gilbert, Derek P. *The Great Inception: Satan's Psyops from Eden to Armageddon*. Crane, MO: Defender, 2017.
Ginzberg, Louis. *The Legends of the Jews*, Vol. 1. Translated by Henrietta Szold. Philadelphia: Jewish Publication Society, 1909.
Gjelten, Tom. "Religious Leaders in Cuba Outspoken and Critical of Proposed Constitution." *NPR*, February 23, 2019. https://www.npr.org/2019/02/23/697256711/religious-leaders-in-cuba-outspoken-and-critical-of-proposed-constitution.
Green, Michael. *Evangelism through the Local Church: A Comprehensive Guide to All Aspects of Evangelism*. Vancouver: Regent College Publishing, 2012.
———. *I Believe in Satan's Downfall*. London: Hodder & Stoughton, 1999.
Guerber, Helene A. *Classical Mythology*. New York: Fall River, 2016.
Hagee, John. *The Three Heavens: Angels, Demons, and What Lies Ahead*. Brentwood, TN: Worthy, 2015.
Harnack, Adolf von. *The Mission and Expansion of Christianity*. Translated by James Moffatt. New York: Putnam's, 1908.
Hawk, L. Daniel. *Joshua in 3-D: A Commentary on Biblical Conquest and Manifest Destiny*. Eugene, OR: Cascade, 2010.
Healey, John F. "Mot." In *Dictionary of Deities and Demons in the Bible*, edited by Karel van der Troon et al., 598–603. 2nd ed. Grand Rapids: 1999.
Heider, George C. "Tannin." In *Dictionary of Deities and Demons in the Bible*, edited by Karel van der Toorn et al., 834–36. 2nd ed. Grand Rapids: Eerdmans, 1999.
Heiser, Michael. *Angels: What the Bible Really Says about God's Heavenly Host*. Bellingham: Lexham, 2018.
———. "Deuteronomy 32:8 and the Sons of God." *Bibliotheca Sacra* 158.629 (Jan–Mar 2001) 52–74.
———. *The Façade*. The Façade Saga 1. Bellingham: Kirkdale, 2014.
———. *The Portent*. The Façade Saga 2. Crane, MO: Defender, 2017.
———. *Reversing Hermon: Enoch, the Watchers, & the Forgotten Mission of Jesus Christ*. Crane, MO: Defender, 2017.
———. *Supernatural: What the Bible Teaches about the Unseen World—and Why It Matters*. Bellingham, Lexham, 2015.

———. *The Unseen Realm: Recovering the Supernatural Worldview of the Bible.* Bellingham: Lexham, 2015.

———. "Where Do Demons Come From?" *LogosTalk* (blog), October 28, 2015. https://blog.logos.com/2015/10/where-do-demons-come-from/.

Herrmann, Wolfgang. "Baal Zebub." In *Dictionary of Deities and Demons in the Bible*, edited by Karel van der Toorn et al., 154–56. 2nd ed. Grand Rapids: Eerdmans, 1999.

———. "El." In *Dictionary of Deities and Demons in the Bible*, edited by Karel van der Toorn et al., 274–80. 2nd ed. Grand Rapids: Eerdmans, 1999.

"How Did Nephilim Reappear after the Flood?" https://hermeneutics.stackexchange.com/questions/34181/how-did-nephilim-reappear-after-the-flood.

Institute of Physics. "How Many Planets Are There like Earth?" http://www.physics.org/article-questions.asp?id=128.

Janowski, Bernd. "Azazel." In *Dictionary of Deities and Demons in the Bible*, edited by Karel van der Toorn et al., 128–31. 2nd ed. Grand Rapids: Eerdmans, 1999.

Jeremias, Joachim. *The Parables of Jesus.* New York: Scribner's, 1963.

Josephus, Flavius. *Antiquities of the Jews, Book V: From the Death of Moses to the Death of Eli.* Translated by William Whiston. Christian Classics Ethereal Library. http://www.ccel.org/j/josephus/works/ant-5.htm.

Just, Felix. "Virtue and Vice Lists in the Bible." http://catholic-resources.org/Bible/Epistles-VirtuesVices.htm.

Keel, Othmar, and Christopher Uehlinger. *Gods, Goddesses, and Images of God in Ancient Israel.* Translated by Thomas Trapp. 1998. Minneapolis: Fortress, 1998.

Keener, Craig. *Miracles: The Credibility of the New Testament Accounts*, Vol. 1. Grand Rapids: Baker Academic, 2011.

Kelser, K. W. *Demonology 201: The Book of Banishment.* Reynoldsburg, OH: New Occult Reviews, 2012.

Kimutai, Kenneth. "Religious Beliefs in Guatemala." *WorldAtlas*, February 02, 2017. https://www.worldatlas.com/articles/religious-beliefs-in-guatemala.html.

Knuth, Kevin. "Are We Alone? The Question Is Worthy of Serious Scientific Study." *The Conversation*, June 28, 2018. https://theconversation.com/are-we-alone-the-question-is-worthy-of-serious-scientific-study-98843.

Kosior, Wojciech. "The Underworld or Its Ruler?" *The Polish Journal of Biblical Research* 13.12 (February 2014) 29–39.

Kraft, Charles. *Confronting Powerless Christianity: Evangelicals and the Mission Dimension.* Bloomington, MN: Chosen, 2002.

———. *Defeating Dark Angels, Breaking Demonic Oppression in the Believer's Life.* Bloomington, MN: Chosen, 2016.

———. *The Evangelical's Guide to Spiritual Warfare: Scriptural Insights and Practical Instruction on Facing the Enemy.* Minneapolis: Chosen, 2015.

———. *I Give You Authority: Practicing the Authority Jesus Gave Us.* Minneapolis: Chosen, 2012.

———. *Power Encounter in Spiritual Warfare.* Eugene, OR: Wipf & Stock, 2017.

Ladd, George Eldon. *The Gospel of the Kingdom: Scriptural Studies in the Kingdom of God.* Milton Keynes: Paternoster, 1959.

Larson, Bob. *Larson's Book of Spiritual Warfare.* Nashville: Nelson, 1999.

Lewis, C. S. *That Hideous Strength.* New York: Macmillan, 1975.

Lewis, Philip. "Do Aliens Exist? Here's What Scientists Say About Life on Other Planets." *Mic*, April 07, 2016. https://mic.com/articles/139828/do-aliens-exist-here-s-what-scientists-say-about-life-on-other-planets#.D6oQiYT5D.
Lipka, Michael. "18% of Americans Say They've Seen a Ghost." http://www.pewresearch.org/fact-tank/2015/10/30/18-of-americans-say-theyve-seen-a-ghost/.
Loeks, Mary Foxwell. *The Glorious Names of God: Devotions for Church Groups.* Grand Rapids: Baker, 1986.
Long, Jeffery, and Paul Perry. *God and the Afterlife: The Groundbreaking New Evidence for God and Near-Death Experience.* New York: HarperCollins, 2017.
Lumpkin, Joseph. *The Book of Giants: The Watchers, Nephilim, and the Book of Enoch.* Blountsville, AL: Fifth Estate, 2014.
Luther, Martin. "A Mighty Fortress Is Our God." In *The United Methodist Hymnal*, translated by Frederick H. Hedge, 110. Nashville: United Methodist, 1989.
"Majority of Americans Believe in Ghosts (57%) and UFOs (52%)." *Ipsos*, October 31, 2008. https://www.ipsos.com/en-us/news-polls/majority-americans-believe-ghosts-57-and-ufos-52.
Mandryk, Jason. *Operation World: The Definitive Prayer Guide to Every Nation.* 7th ed. Colorado Springs: Biblica, 2010.
Metzger, Bruce Manning. *A Textual Commentary on the Greek New Testament: A Companion Volume to the United Bible Societies Greek New Testament.* 3rd ed. Stuttgart: United Bible Societies, 1971.
Molina, Brett. "Lasers Could Help Us Attract Aliens, MIT Study Suggests." *USA Today*, November 07, 2018. https://www.usatoday.com/story/news/nation-now/2018/11/07/lasers-could-attract-aliens-earth-mit-study-suggests/1917389002/.
Moore, David W. "Three in Four Americans Believe in Paranormal." *Gallup*, June 16, 2005. https://news.gallup.com/poll/16915/three-four-americans-believe-paranormal.aspx.
Moreau, A. Scott. "Demon." In *Evangelical Dictionary of Biblical Theology*, edited by Walter A. Elwell, 163–65. Grand Rapids: Baker, 1996.
"Most American Christians Do Not Believe that Satan or the Holy Spirit Exist." https://www.barna.com/research/most-american-christians-do-not-believe-that-satan-or-the-holy-spirit-exist/.
Mullen, Bradford A. "Heaven, Heavens, Heavenlies." In *Evangelical Dictionary of Biblical Theology*, edited by Walter A. Elwell, 332–35. Grand Rapids: Baker, 2001.
Mullen, E. Theodore. *The Assembly of the Gods: The Divine Council in Canaanite and Early Hebrew Literature.* Harvard Semitic Monographs 24. Chico, CA: Scholars, 1980.
Murphy, Edward F. *The Handbook for Spiritual Warfare.* Nashville: Nelson, 2003.
Newport, Frank. "Americans More Likely to Believe in God Than the Devil, Heaven More Than Hell." *Gallup*, June 13, 2007. http://www.gallup.com/poll/27877/americans-more-likely-believe-god-than-devil-heaven-more-than-hell.aspx.
———. "Most Americans Still Believe in God." *Gallup*, June 29, 2016. http://www.gallup.com/poll/193271/americans-believe-god.aspx.
Nickelsburg, George W. E. *1 Enoch: A Commentary on the Book of 1 Enoch.* Edited by Klaus Baltzer. Hermeneia—A Critical and Historical Commentary on the Bible. Minneapolis: Fortress, 2001.
Niehr, Herbert. "Baal Zaphon." In *Dictionary of Deities and Demons in the Bible*, edited by Karel van der Toorn et al., 152–54. 2nd ed. Grand Rapids: Eerdmans, 1999.

Otis, George. *The Twilight Labyrinth: Why Does Spiritual Darkness Linger Where It Does?* Grand Rapids: Chosen, 1997.

Payne, Karl I. *Spiritual Warfare: Christians, Demonization, and Deliverance.* Washington, DC: WND, 2011.

Payne, William P. *Adventures in Spiritual Warfare: Defeating Satan and Living a Victorious Life.* Eugene, OR: Resource, 2018.

———. "Discerning an Integral Latino Pentecostal Theology of Liberation." *Ashland Theological Journal* 45 (Fall 2013) 87–106.

———. "Folk Religion and the Pentecostal Surge in Latin America." *The Asbury Journal* 71.1 (Spring 2016) 145–74. doi:10.7252/Journal.01.2016S.11.

Philo of Alexandria. "On the Giants." http://www.earlychristianwritings.com/yonge/book9.html.

"Poll: Nearly 8 in 10 Americans Believe in Angels." *CBS News*, December 23, 2011. https://www.cbsnews.com/news/poll-nearly-8-in-10-americans-believe-in-angels/.

"Poll Results: Exorcism." http://cdn.yougov.com/cumulus_uploads/document/vhyn6fdnkp/tabs_exorcism_09121320 13%20%281%29.pdf.

Price, Paula. *The Prophet's Dictionary: The Ultimate Guide to Supernatural Wisdom.* New Kensington, PA: Whitaker, 2006.

Pugh, Ben. *Atonement Theories: A Way Forward.* Eugene, OR: Cascade, 2014.

Riley, Greg J. "Demon." In *Dictionary of Deities and Demons in the Bible*, edited by Karel van der Toorn et al., 234–40. 2nd ed. Grand Rapids: Eerdmans, 1999.

Roth, Sid, and Lonnie Lane. *Heaven Is Beyond Your Wildest Expectations: Ten True Stories of Experiencing Heaven.* Shippensburg, PA: Destiny Image, 2012.

Routledge, Clay. "Don't Believe in God? Maybe You'll Try U.F.O.s." *The New York Times*, July 21, 2017. https://www.nytimes.com/2017/07/21/opinion/sunday/dont-believe-in-god-maybe-youll-try-ufos.html?mcubz=0.

Russell, Jeffrey Burton. *Satan: The Early Christian Tradition.* Ithaca: Cornell University Press, 1994.

Segal, Alan F. *Two Powers in Heaven: Early Rabbinic Reports about Christianity and Gnosticism.* Waco: Baylor University Press, 2012.

Silvoso, Ed. *Prayer Evangelism: How to Change the Spiritual Climate over Your Home, Neighborhood and City.* Bloomington, MN: Chosen, 2018.

Skiba, Rob. "Moses Tells Us Exactly How the Nephilim Returned after the Flood." *YouTube*, January 5, 2016. https://www.youtube.com/watch?v=pby2Vh6AM48.

Sling and Stone. "Alien Abductions Are a Demonic Phenomenon, How to Stop Them and Testimonial Evidence." *YouTube*, January 23, 2017. https://www.youtube.com/watch?v=ysHayfxA0Bg.

Smith, Ed, and Michael Hennen. *Strategic Prayer: Applying the Power of Targeted Prayer.* Litchfield, IL: Revival Waves of Glory, 2013.

Snelling, Andrew. "The Flood." https://answersingenesis.org/the-flood/.

Snodgrass, Elizabeth. "Archaeologists Find a Classic Entrance to Hell." *National Geographic*, April 16, 2013. https://news.nationalgeographic.com/news/2013/04/130414-hell-underworld-archaeology-mount-olympus--greece/.

Sorensen, Eric. *Possession and Exorcism in the New Testament and Early Christianity.* Tübingen: Mohr Siebeck, 2002.

"South Korea's Park in Trouble over Choi Soon-sil Links." *Al Jazeera*, October 31, 2016. https://www.aljazeera.com/news/2016/10/south-korea-park-trouble-choi-sil-links-161031054423100.html.

Spangenberg, Izak J. J. "A Brief History of Belief in the Devil (950 BCE—70 CE)." *Studia Historiae Ecclesiasticae* 39.1 (March 2013) 213–45. http://www.scielo.org.za/scielo.php?script=sci_arttext&pid=S1017-04992013000300013.

Steiner, Mark Allan. "Looking Along the Line between Good and Evil: *Crash* and Evangelical Approaches to Popular Film." In *Evangelical Christians and Popular Christians: Pop Goes the Gospel*, edited by Robert H. Woods Jr., 1:71–85. Santa Barbara: Praeger, 2013.

Stolz, Fritz. "Seraphim." In *Dictionary of Deities and Demons in the Bible*, edited by Karel van der Toorn et al., 742–44. 2nd ed. Grand Rapids: Eerdmans, 1999.

Stuckenbruck, Loren T. *Angel Veneration and Christology: A Study in Early Judaism and in the Christology of the Apocalypse of John*. Waco: Baylor University Press, 2017.

———. *The Book of Giants from Qumran: Texts, Translation, and Commentary*. Tübingen: Mohr Siebeck, 1997.

Syed, Akramulla. "Asma al-Husna: 99 Beautiful Names of Allah (SWT)." http://www.ezsoftech.com/islamic/iqlas5.asp.

Toorn, Karel van der, et al., eds. *Dictionary of Deities and Demons in the Bible*. 2nd ed. Grand Rapids: Eerdmans, 1999.

———. "God." In *Dictionary of Deities and Demons in the Bible*, edited by Karel van der Toorn et al., 352–65. 2nd ed. Grand Rapids: Eerdmans, 1999.

Torre, Miguel de la. *Reading the Bible from the Margins*. Maryknoll: Orbis, 2002.

UAMN TV. "New Alien Abduction Documentary 2019 So Real, They Will Make You Question Everything!" *YouTube*, February 20, 2019. https://www.youtube.com/watch?v=sMBNuEXvw7Q.

van Henten, Jan Willem. "Mastemah." In *Dictionary of Deities and Demons in the Bible*, edited by Karel van der Toorn et al., 553–54. 2nd ed. Grand Rapids: Eerdmans, 1999.

———. "Typhon." In *Dictionary of Deities and Demons in the Bible*, edited by Karel van der Toorn et al., 879–81. 2nd ed. Grand Rapids: Eerdmans, 1999.

Van Rheenen, Gailyn. *Communicating Christ in Animistic Contexts*. Pasadena: William Carey Library, 1993.

The Vatican. *Catechism of the Catholic Church*. http://www.vatican.va/archive/ENG0015/_INDEX.HTM.

Velarde, Robert. "Did Eve Have Sex with Satan? The Serpent Seed View of Genesis 3:15." *Christian Research Institute*, August 4, 2017. https://www.equip.org/article/eve-sex-satan-serpent-seed-view-genesis-315/.

Wagner, C., and Rebecca Greenwood. "The Strategic-Level Deliverance Model." In *Understanding Spiritual Warfare: Four Views*, edited by James K. Beilby and Paul Rhodes Eddy, 173–98. Grand Rapids: Baker Academic, 2012.

Wall, Mike. "Stephen Hawking Is Still Afraid of Aliens." *Space.com*, September 24, 2016. https://www.space.com/34184-stephen-hawking-afraid-alien-civilizations.html.

Walton, John. "Demons in Mesopotamia and Israel: Exploring the Category of Non-Divine but Supernatural Entities." In *Windows to the Ancient World of the Hebrew Bible: Essays in Honor of Samuel Greengus*, edited by Bill T. Arnold et al., 229–46. Winona Lake: Eisenbrauns, 2014.

———. *The Lost World of Adam and Eve: Genesis 2–3 and the Human Origins Debate.* Downers Grove: InterVarsity, 2015.

Wenham, Gordon. *Genesis 1–15.* Word Biblical Commentary 1. Waco: Word, 1987.

Wink, Walter. "Facing the Myth of Redemptive Violence." *Ekklesia,* Nov 15, 2014. http://www.ekklesia.co.uk/content/cpt/article_060823wink.shtml.

———. *The Powers That Be: Theology for a New Millennium.* New York: Galilee, 1998.

———. "The World System Model." In *Understanding Spiritual Warfare: Four Views,* edited by Gareth Higgins, 47–71. Grand Rapids: Baker Academic, 2012.

Wise, Michael, et al., eds. *The Dead Sea Scrolls: A New Translation.* Translated by Michael Wise. New York: Harper, 2005.

Witzel, E. J. Michael. *The Origins of the World's Mythologies.* New York: Oxford University Press, 2012.

Wormald, Benjamin. "America's Changing Religious Landscape." http://www.pewforum.org/2015/05/12/americas-changing-religious-landscape/.

Subject Index

"A Mighty Fortress Is Our God"
    (Luther), ix–x
Abaddon, 4–5, 27, 29, 48, 50
Abraham's bosom, 37, 52
abyss, the, 38, 48, 50, 61
Accuser of the Brethren, 27, 29
Adam and Eve
    dominion over the earth, 113–115
    God's testing of, 129–130
    moral awareness of, 126–128
    temptation of, by Satan, 115–116, 124, 126–128
Adversary, 27, 28, 29
alien abduction, 103–104
Allah, 26, 27
American church, response to demons, 2–3
Ancient Aliens effect, 11–13
Angel of Light, 27, 29
angel of light, 23, 163
Angel of the Bottomless Pit, 28, 29, 31
Angel of the Lord, 68–69, 74, 172n11
angels. *See also* cherubim; fallen angels; seraphim
    American belief in, 8, 24
    assisting Christians, 7
    dwelling place of, 44
    as elohim, 114
    in evangelical literature, 90
    and giant origin theories, 77n10
    in the heavenly council, 50n4
    helpers of God, 65, 120, 158
    judgment by Christians, 114
    ministering to Jesus in the wilderness, 141
    relationship to humans, 114, 120
    role in spiritual warfare, 174
    visitations by, 8, 102
    worship of, 57–58
animals speaking, 119–120
Apollyon, 5, 27, 29, 34, 48, 50
Asphodel, 36, 37, 52
atonement for sin, Christ's, 6, 53, 136, 137, 149–150
Averbeck, Richard, 108
Azazel, 28, 140, 146–147

Baal, 32n17, 51n5
baptism of Jesus, 142n6
baptismal renunciation, 91
Beelzebub. *See also* Beelzebul
    Jesus accused of being, 98
    as Lord of Gehenna, Satan, 35, 51–52, 104
    names of Satan, 28, 29, 31–32
Beelzebul, 28, 31–32, 154. *See also* Beelzebub
Behemoth, 4
Belial, 28
biblical theology of liberation, 173–175
blessings and cursings, 160
Block, Daniel, 72n3
book of life, 53
Boyd, Greg, 4–6
Bright Morning Star, 67–68

SUBJECT INDEX

Caballeros, Harold, 84
Cain, 29, 67, 95n19, 102n34, 132
Campbell, Charles, 168n3
Campbell, Joseph, 110
Canaan and Canaanites, 74–78
casting out demons, 2, 22, 46, 108n4
Cerberus, 46
charismatic movement and the supernatural, 10
chasm, great. *See* great chasm
cherubim, 56–58, 65n3, 121–122, 131
Christians
    and belief in ghosts, 23
    and belief in Satan, 24–26
    instructions for regarding spiritual warfare, 161–165
    judging of angels, 114
    power and authority over Satan, 69–70, 150
church growth and persecution, 157–158, 159
Collins, Robin, 148
communication with the dead, 17–18, 22
cosmic-level spiritual warfare, 101
Crick, Dr. Robert, 17, 106
Crown of Life, 42
C.S. Lewis, 105, 119, 167
cursings and blessings, 160

Dagon, 26
darkness vs. light. *See* light vs. darkness
Day of Atonement, 28, 140, 146–147
Day of Judgment, 34–35, 38n8, 52–53, 54, 116n19
Dead Sea Scrolls, 22, 78n12, 89, 96, 146
death, 3n2, 48–50, 96n22. *See also* Thanatos
Death and Hades, 46, 49, 50. *See also* Hades
deeds of darkness, 6
deliverance ministry, 2, 85–86, 101
demonic hierarchy, 3, 104–105
demonization, 91, 94, 98, 117
demons
    in American culture and literature, 89–90
    appearing as humans, 102
    defined, 92–93
    demonic strongholds, 51, 91, 170
    fallen angels, 99–102
    fate of, 100–101, 108
    in Jewish literature, 87–89
    misconceptions regarding, 90–91
    in the New Testament, 97–99
    physical manifestations of, 154
    prevalence of, 101–105
    and rape of humans, 102–103
    references to in the Old Testament, 87–89, 93
    use of term in the Bible, 93–94
demythologizing the Bible, 108n4
devil, the. *See also* Satan; *individual names and titles of*
    as Beelzebub (Lord of Gehenna), 35
    belief in, 24–26
    and demons, 93
    fate of, 52, 61
    Jesus' authority over, 154
    Martin Luther and, ix–x
    names and titles of, 5, 28–31, 136
    persecution of the church, 42
    ransom theory of atonement, role in, 148
    rebellion against God, 130–132
    sons of, 51n5, 160
    spiritual warfare, role in, 3–4, 7, 161–165
    temptation of Christians, 130
    temptation of Jesus, 31, 142–145
devils, ix, 92n12, 93
dominion of darkness, 6
"Don't Believe in God? Maybe You'll Try U.F.O.s (Routledge), 12
Dragon, the Great Red, 28, 99
Dragon, the (Satan), 28, 29, 61, 100, 122, 132
Driver, John, 148

El, 56n3
elohim. *See also* heavenly council, the
    church's battle against, 156
    defined, 65–67
    interaction with Adam and Eve, 120
    Mormon error regarding, 68
    rebellion against God, 83–84

and reclaiming of the nations by
    God, 156
  relationship to humans, 114
  setting over the nations, 155
Elysian Fields, 36, 37
enemies of God, 3, 4, 54, 162
Enemy, the, 28, 29
Esau and Jacob, 128–129
eternal life, 41–43, 168. *See also* zoe
evangelistic mandate, 90n7
Evil One, the. *See also* devil, the; Satan;
    individual names and titles of
  God's plan, role in, 75
  heavenly council, the, 67n6
  Jesus' victory over, 152
  names and titles of, 27–31, 60
  power and authority of, 90n7, 136
  rebellion against God, 95, 111–113
  spiritual warfare, role in, 3, 5
  temptation of Jesus, 140
evolution of religion theory, 71n1, 87
exorcism, 91, 96n24, 154
extraterrestrials, belief in, 11–12

fall, the
  Adam and Eve, 116–117, 126–128
  ancient myths paralleling, 124–125
  parallel to Esau and Jacob, 128–129
  reality of, 108–111
  Satan's rebellion and, 111–113
fallen angels, 99–101, 104–105, 131
false teaching and prophets, 163
fasting of Jesus in the wilderness,
    140–142
Father of Lies, 28, 29
Fields of Punishment, 36, 37
first and second death, 52
folk religion
  and belief in ghosts and spirits,
    9–10, 19–22, 105
  and demons, 88–89, 102n34
  development of, 71
  Jesus' attitude about, 23
  and Satan, 29
  types of, 97n25
free will of man, xi–xii, 116–117, 130
fruit, forbidden, 124–125, 126

Gagarin, Yuri, 45
Gaia, 46
garden of Eden, the, 7, 56, 67, 95, 107,
    115n16
Gate of Heaven, 44
gates of Hades (Sheol), 41–47
Gehenna
  defined, 34–35
  Jesus' references to, 44
  origin of, 32
  as part of Hades, 38
  Satan as lord of, 35, 51–54
genocide, as byproduct of liberation,
    172
Geun-Hye, President Park, 17
ghosts and spirits
  American belief in, 8
  Christian belief in, 8, 9–10
  Christianity and, 23
  communication with the dead,
    17–18
  cultural influence toward beliefs
    about, 9–13
  as dead humans, 104–106
  Dead Sea Scrolls references to, 22
  demons and, 104–105
  disciples' belief in, 19–21
  folk religion and, 9–11
  ghost stories, 14–18, 106
  Jesus's belief about, 23
  Jewish beliefs about, 21–22
  Latin American beliefs, 9
  New Testament references to, 19–21
  Old Testament law and, 21–22
giants, 77–78. *See also* Nephilim
goat-demons, 147
God
  calling of Israel, 76–78, 155
  compared to national gods, 79–82
  heavenly council of, 63–65
  names and titles of, x, 26–27, 56n3,
    79, 115n18
  plan of salvation, 130, 136, 139
  testing Adam and Eve, 129–130
  as warrior God, 57–58, 167, 172n11
  worship of, vs. other gods, 81–82,
    83, 88

God at War: The Bible & Spiritual Conflict (Boyd), 151
god of this world, the, 4, 5, 28, 29, 31, 136, 151
gods, pagan
    culture and belief in, 85
    existence of, in the Bible, 81–82
    as gods of the nations, 83–84
    in Hebrew literature, 87–88
    names and titles of, 26, 48, 84
great chasm, 37, 38, 48
Great Commission, the, 85, 155–156
Great Dragon, the, 28, 29, 122
Great White Throne Judgment, 52, 53
Green, Michael, 35, 83n17, 113
grim reaper, 50
ground-level spiritual warfare, 101–102
guardian cherub (Satan), 28, 55–59
Guatemala, deliverance of, 85–86

Hades. *See also* Death and Hades
    and Gehenna, 51–52
    and hell, 53
    Jesus' descension into, 6, 40, 45, 46, 47, 54, 149, 175
    Jesus' triumph over, 46–47
    in letters of Paul, 48–49
    merging with Sheol, 37–40
    reality of, 45–46
    in Revelation, 49–50, 54
    as translation of Sheol, 5, 36
Hades (Pluto), 45
Hawking, Stephen, 12
heaven, 29n12, 36, 48–49, 51–52
heaven of heavens, 52
heavenly armies, the, x, 69
heavenly council, the
    Christians as members of, 107n1
    defined, 63–65
    elohim as members of, 65–66
    as emotional beings, 139
    interaction with Adam and Eve, 120
    Jesus as chief of, 67–70
    paralleled by gods of the underworld, 49n2
    Satan as leading member of, 28
    Satan as member of, 56, 121, 123
    as sons of God, 155

watchers, 50n4
Heiser, Michael
    on fallen angels, 99n28
    on the Garden of Eden, 110n8, 115n16
    on the heavenly council, 63
    on the identity of the serpent, 121–123
    on Mount Hermon and the Watchers, 45n7
    on the Nephilim, 94n17, 95n20
    on prophecies regarding Satan, 55–56
    on Satan's fall, 112
    on the scapegoat, 146n8
    on the Sons of God, 50n4
    on the two Yahweh theory, 68n7
    on UFOs, 13n13
hell, 34, 35, 44–45, 50, 53. *See also* Hades; Sheol (place)
henotheism, 80
high god myths, 71–73
highest heaven, 39–40, 52
Hungry Souls (van den Aardweg), 105

inclusivism, 52–53
incubi spirits, 102–103
inner healing, 154
Integrated Model of Liberation, 174–175
Isles of the Bliss, 36

Jacob and Esau, 128–129
Jesus
    as advocate of Christians, 30
    atonement for sin, 137
    authority over demons, 97–99, 116, 133
    casting out demons, 98–99, 154
    as chief of the heavenly council, 67–68, 97
    as Commander of the Lord's army, x–xi, 69, 101
    fasting in the wilderness, 140–142
    ghosts and spirits, belief about, 23
    as God, 68–69
    as kinsman redeemer, 138–139
    liberation, example of, 174–175

as Light of the World, 7
names and titles of, 27, 67–68, 97, 115n18, 137
ransoming of sinners, 137–138, 148–150
return of, 58, 143
speaking to the dead, 18
temptation of, by Satan, 115–116, 140–145
triumph over death and hell, 46, 149
victory over Satan, 46, 47, 54, 133, 148–149, 175
Jewish beliefs about ghosts, 21–22
Jews as God's chosen people, 76–78, 155
Jezebel, 162
judging of angels by Christians, 114
judgment, final, 34, 52–53

Kali, 170
kingdom conflict, 5–7
kingdom of God, 5, 44, 154
kinsman redeemer, 137–139
knowing good and evil, 118
Knuth, Kevin, 12
Kraft, Charles
    on demythologizing the Bible, 108n4
    on fallen angels, 99
    on Frank Peretti, 90
    on power encounter, 159n4
    on Satan's fall, 112
    on spiritual warfare, 102
krino, 34

Lake of Fire, 3n2, 4, 50–51, 52, 53, 101
lares, 21
Latino worldview regarding the supernatural, 9–10
Leviathan, 4, 26
liberation theology, 89–90, 170–175
light of the world (Jesus), 7, 31
light vs. darkness, ix, 6–7, 31, 35, 41, 60
Lilith, 102n34
Lion, the Witch, and the Wardrobe, The (Lewis), 119
Long, Jeffrey, 39
Lord of Armies, x–xi, 69, 97

Lord of Gehenna, 32, 35, 51–54, 104. *See also* Beelzebub
Lord of Hosts, x, 26, 69
Lord Sabaoth, x
Lucifer, 28, 29, 49n2, 60, 61
Luther, Martin, and spiritual warfare, ix–x

martyrs, 42, 43
material approach to liberation, 170–173
missional hermeneutic, 76
Mithra, 26, 29
Molek, 32
monotheism, 71, 80, 82, 87–88
Mormon errors about Jesus, 68
Morning Star, 29, 60–61
Moses, Egyptian gods and, 73–74
Mot, 4–5, 48–49, 146n8
Mount Hermon, 144n7
Mount Zaphon, 134–135
Mount Zion, 134–135
Murderer, the, 28, 29
myth of redemptive violence, 5n6, 166
myths, ancient, parallel to the Bible, 66n5, 109, 122n11, 124–125, 134–135

nachash, 122, 123
near-death experiences (NDE), 33, 38–39, 44, 104, 111
necromancy, 22
Nephilim
    alien abduction and, 104
    becoming demons, 94–97, 102
    in the demonic hierarchy, 102, 105
    as giants, 77–78
    judgment of, 115n18
    origin of, 66, 94–97
    relationship to Satan, 30, 67
    theories about, 91–92
New Testament references to demons, 97–99
New Testament references to ghosts, 19–21, 23
nonviolent resistance, 168

Odin, 26

original monotheism, 71, 87. *See also* monotheism

Paradise, 37, 38–40, 52
Paul and spiritual warfare, 158–159
Paul's instructions to believers, 69, 81, 82, 161–165
Payne, Karl, 164n6
Payne, William, 9n5, 73n5, 103n35, 114n15, 142n6, 164n7, 170n7
Pentecost, Day of, 156, 170
people returning from the dead, 104–105. *See also* ghosts and spirits
Peretti, Frank, 90
Pergamum, 51
persecution and church growth, 157–158, 159
persecution of the church, 42–43
physical maladies from demons, 98, 154
pit, the, 32, 36, 37, 38, 48
pneumographic, 165
political interventionism vs. spiritual warfare, 166–170
polytheism, 64, 71, 87–88
power encounters, 159–161
Prince of Darkness, ix–x
Prince of the Power of the Air, 27n8, 28, 29, 31, 136
Prince of this World, 7, 28, 90n7
Purgatory, 37

Quetzacoatl, 84–85

Rahab, 4
ransom theory of atonement, 137–138, 146n8, 148–150
rebellion of man, xi–xii
redemption, God's plan of, 74, 75, 137–138
Resheph, 4
Roaring Lion, 28, 29

Sabaoth, x
Samael, 28–29, 102n34
Satan
    as accuser of the saints, 27, 29–30
    American belief in, 24–26
    appearance as a serpent, 119–124
    children of, 34–35
    fall of, 55–56, 59–60
    fate of, 53–54
    guardian cherub, 55–59
    Jesus' victory over, 46, 47, 54, 133, 148–149, 175
    kingdom of, 43–44
    as Lord of Gehenna, 32, 51
    names and titles of, 27–32, 51, 56. *See also specific names and titles*
    origins of, 55–62
    plan to tempt God, 133–136
    power and authority of, 30–31, 44, 51–52, 67, 90n7, 133, 144, 155
    prophesies about, 61–62
    rebellion against God, 4–5, 95, 111–113
    and reign in the second heaven, 29n12
    spiritual warfare, role in, 161–165
    temptation of Jesus, 140–145
    throne, location of, 51
    timing of rebellion, 130–133
    usurpation of Adam's authority, 136
scapegoat, 93, 139, 140, 145–150
Schmidt, Wilhelm, 71
Screwtape Letters (Lewis), 105
second heaven, 29n12, 39, 51–52
sedim, 93
Segal, Alan, 68n7
Septuagint, 36, 48, 50n4
seraphim, 65, 121–122
serpent, the
    ability to speak, 119–120
    identity of, 121–123
Sethite view, 95n19
Sheol (being), 4–5
Sheol (place), 36, 37, 38, 45, 48–49
Shining One, 28, 49n2, 59–61, 134, 135n3
sin, 6, 116–117, 136–137
skotia, 6
social justice vs. spiritual warfare, 166–175
soldiers, Christians as, 6, 7
Son of the Dawn, 28, 29
son of the devil, 51n5, 160
sons of God. *See also* Watchers

believers as, 50n4, 107n1
creation of the Nephilim, 95
defined, 50n4
meeting place with God, 135
as members of the heavenly council, 64–65
Mormon error regarding, 68
as nation gods, 72n3, 83, 85, 101
rebellion against God, 66–67, 144n7
as rulers over the nations, 155
vs. the Son of God, 141
soul sleep, 18
spirits and ghosts. *See* ghosts and spirits
spiritual forces of evil, 42, 54
spiritual gifts, 164n7
spiritual warfare
and afflictions of Paul, 158–159
Christians and the elohim, 156
defined, 151
Jesus' conflict with Satan, 151–153
and liberation theology, 170–173
magicians in Acts, 159–160
Paul's instruction to the saints about, 161–165
and persecution of the church, 157–158
vs. physical warfare, 168
vs. political interventionism, 166–170
power encounters, 159–161
power to curse and bless, 160
and spiritual gifts, 164n7
strategic-level spiritual warfare, 101
Strong Man/strong man, 28, 31, 46, 47
substitutionary theory of atonement, 137
succubae spirits, 102

table of nations, 83n16
Tartarus, 4, 36, 37, 38, 46, 48, 50
temptation, 115–116, 126–128, 129–130, 140–145
Tempter, 27n8, 28, 29

territorial spirits, 84–86, 101
Thanatos, 3, 5, 47, 48, 50, 54. *See also* death
That Hideous Strength (Lewis), 167
Thief, 28, 29
third heaven, 29n12, 38, 39, 51–52
Thor, 26
throne of Satan, 51
Tippett, Alan, 72n4
Tree of the Knowledge of Good and Evil, 119, 125
Trump effect, 25
Two Yahweh theory, 68

UFOs, belief in, 11–13
underworld, 45, 48, 49n2

Van Rheenen, Gailyn, 9n5

Wagner, Peter, 101
watchers. *See also* sons of God
and Bashan, 45
Christians' superiority to, 69
creation of the Nephilim, 95–96
decision to rebel against God, 144n7
and fallen angels, 100n29
final punishment, 97, 108, 147
as holy ones, 115n18
as members of the heavenly council, 50n4, 64
rebellion against God, 66–67
and Tartarus, 38
wilderness, Jesus' temptations in, 140
Wink, Walter, 166n1
Witch of Endor, 19, 23
wolves in sheep's clothing, 163

Yahweh, 26–27
Yamm, 4

Zeus, 26, 51n5, 135
zoe, 42–43. *See also* Crown of Life

Scripture Index

OLD TESTAMENT

Genesis

Ref	Pages
1	120
1–2	94
1–15	118n1, 121n3
1:17	29n12
1:26	67, 113, 114, 120
1:26–28	112
1:30	119
2:5–7	113
2:7	113, 119
2:15	113
2:18–19	113
2:19–20	113, 126
2:23	113
2:24	113
2:25	107
3	56, 95, 96, 108, 111, 111n10, 121n3, 123, 125, 132n21
3:1	28, 120
3:1–5	118
3:6	124
3:7	136
3:8	120
3:14	59n12
3:15	67, 77, 95, 132
3:21	136
3:22–24	115
3:24	58, 125
4:26	95n19
6	38, 45, 95, 95n19, 96, 99n28, 100n29, 102, 120, 155
6:1–6	95
6:1–7	66
6:2	64
6:2–4	50
6:4	64, 94n17
6:17	119
7:15	119
7:22	119
8:17	114
9:1	114
9:4–5	114
9:7	114
9:21–25	77
9:22–28	75
10	83n
10:21–30	156
11:3–4	83
11:7	83
12:3	155
17:2	113
19–21	108
22:2	129
22:8	129
24:3	78
25:25	128
25–27	128
27	128

193

Genesis (continued)

28:12	52
28:17	44
32:22–31	128n18
63–64	118n1
72–73	121n3

Exodus

2:1–10	73
3	73
3:1	73
3:5	x
3:14	26, 68
6:6	138
7:8–12	122
7:11	73
7:22	73
8:7	73
12:12	81
12:23	50
12:40	138
13:13–14	138
14:13–14	74, 172n11
15:3	74, 172n11
15:11	81
15:13–15	138
18:10–11	81
19, x, 57	76
19–20	58
20:2–3	79
20:3	88
20:4	57
20:22	72
21:30	137
22:18	22
22:29	32n17
23:13	80, 81
23:20–26	74
23:23–26	74
23:33	81
24:29–35	60
25:18–20	121
34:15–16	79n

Leviticus

1–7	100
1:9	100
4	116n19
16	140
16:7–10	146
16:8–10	28
16:21–22	147
17	93
17:7	79n, 93, 140, 146n8
20:5–6	79n
25:23–28	137
25:47–53	146
25:47–55	137
25:49	137
25:54	138

Numbers

4:28	81
7:89	58
13:23–33	77
15:39	79n
16	50
17:9	74n7
21:6	122
21:8	122
21:9	123
22:21–39	120
28:36	81
28:64	81

Deuteronomy

3	77n10
4:19	83
5:8	57
7:8	138
9:26	138
10:14	52
10:17	82
15:15	138
17:17	83
18:9–12	22
23:9	77
24:18	138
26:15	29n12
28:12	29n12
31:16	79n
32	83n

SCRIPTURE INDEX   195

32:8	50n4, 64, 83n
32:8–9	83, 101, 155
32:9	155
32:17	93
33:2–3	64

Joshua

5:13–15	x, 6
6:6–7	58
23:7	80

Judges

2:17	79
6:21	74n7
8:27	79n
8:33	79n
9:23	93
16:23–30	26

Ruth,

2:20	137

1 Samuel

4:3–8	58
16:14–23	93
28	19
28:5–19	94n16

2 Samuel

21:15–22	78
22:6	36, 49
22:8–15	57
22:8–16	57

1 Kings

6	56
7:29	121
7:30	29n12
8:13	29n12
8:27	52
21	75n8
22	65
22:22	93

2 Kings

1:2	28, 31
2:8	74n7
2:14	74n7
4:31	74n7
5:1–19	79
23:10	32n17

1 Chronicles

5:25	79n
21:1	28

2 Chronicles

3:10–14	56n6
11:14–15	93
11:15	93
18:20–22	93
18:21	94n16
21:13	79n

Job

1–2	30, 67n6
1:6	50n4, 64, 141
1:8–2:8	129
2:1	50n4, 64
5:1	64
15:8	64
19:25–27	36
26:6	49
29:3	7
38:7	50n4, 60, 67, 83
38:10	41n2

Psalms

7–8	114
8	114
8:4–6	114
8:5	114
9:13	41n2
16:10	45
18:10	57
18:28	7
29:1	50n4, 63, 64
42:9	29n12
43:3	7

Psalms (continued)

45:7	67
46:7	6
47	80
48:2	135n2
58:1	63
58:1–2	4
66	80
73:27	79n
78:23	29n12
82	4, 4n4, 63, 155
82:1	63, 64
82:6	63, 64
86:8	63
86–87	80
88:4–6	36
88:6	36, 38
89:5–8	64
89:6	50n4, 64
89:7	64
89:8	64
89:27	69
91:3	7
95:3	63
96	80
96:5	80
97:7	64
97:9	64
98	80
100	80
102	80
104:3–4	58n8
104:24	26
106:37	93
106:39	79n
107:18	41n2
116:3	36
119:105	7
124:7	7
135:5	64
138:1	64
139:7–10	80
139:8	36

Proverbs

5:5	49
6:23	7
15:11	49
16:8	94n16
27:20	49
28:15	171

Ecclesiastes

9:10	36

Isaiah

2	80
5:14	50
6:1–10	65
6:3	26
7:14	62
8:19	22
10:26	74n7
13:21	93
14	55, 59, 60, 61n14, 100n29, 132, 132n21
14:4–20	59
14:9	36, 135
14:12	28, 49n2, 60, 132
14:13	4, 64, 135n2
14:13–14	134
14:29	122
24:23	65
27:1	122, 135n2
34:13	93
38:10	41n2
38:18	48
40:3–5	58
40:22	29n12
51:9	122
53:12	147
61:1–2	153
61:3	94n16
63:15	29n12
65:4	22

Jeremiah

16	80
23:18	64
23:22	64
32:35	32n17

Ezekiel

1	58, 121
1:11	121
6:9	79n
10	58, 121
23:30	79n
28	55, 56, 59, 61n14, 132n21
28:1–19	55
28:2	4
28:12	59
28:12–16	121
28:13	56n4
28:14–16	28
31:14	36

Daniel

4:13	50n4
4:17	50n4, 64
4:23	50n4
7:9–10	64
8:10	4, 100
10:6	123

Hosea

3:1	79
4:12	79n
5:4	94n16
9:1	79n
13:14	49

Amos

8:14	64

Jonah

1:4–9	57
1:9	80
1:16	80
2:2	36

Habakkuk

2	80

Zephaniah

2:11	80
3	80

Zechariah

3:1	29
8	80
12:8	68–69
12:10	143
14:1–5	143

Malachi

1	80

Apocrypha

Tobit

6:6–16	88

Sirach

17:28–30	113

PSEUDEPIGRAPHA

Apocalypse of Abraham

23:12	147

Jubilees

3:4	67
3:15	67, 120
3:19	124n15
3:28–29	119n2
3:90	67
4:15	66
5:2	96n23
5:3	96n23
7:7–17	75
7:8–9	30
10:7	30
10:8	96
10:11	96
10:27–34	75
10:32	75
11:5–6	30

Jubilees (continued)

17:15–16	30, 30n13
17:15–18	129n20
48	30

Life of Adam and Eve

33:1–3	124n15

1 Enoch

1:3–4	115n18
1:4–5	97
1:9	61, 97n26
4:15	66
6:6	66, 144n7
7:1	120
7:8	120
7–10	66
9:3–4	57
9:6	120, 146
10:7	120
10:8	146–147
13	147
14	65n3
14:23	65n3
15	94n17
15:8–10	96
15:8–12	94
19:7	58n9
21	38n8
22:8–13	38n7
54	147
65:11	120
69:6–7	121n3
85–89	60n13
86:1	61
86:3	61
86–88	60
88:3	61

2 Enoch

19–21	121
29:3–4	61

3 Enoch

14:2	29

NEW TESTAMENT

Matthew

1:23	62
2:2	60
2:9–11	60
2:16	5
3:2	5
3:3	58
3:7	34
3:9	141
3:10	34
3:12	34
3:22	98
4:1	140n4
4:1–11	5, 151
4:2–4	140k–
4:4	142
4:5–7	142
4:7	69
4:8–9	44n4, 90n, 155
4:8–10	144
4:10	69
4:11	98, 141
4:17	5, 152
4:24	93
5:16	7n10
5:29–30	34
5:37	28, 67
5:44	160
6:10	3, 7
6:13	3, 30, 167
7:13	34
7:15	34, 163
7:18	117
7:20	34
7:21	98
7:22	98
7:23	34
8:12	34, 67
8:16	93, 98
8:23–27	19
8:28	93
8:29	97, 116
8:33	93
9:32	93
9:34	31, 98
9:35	152

10:8	98	**Mark**	
10:25	31	1:2–3	58
10:28	34, 42	1:12	140, 140n4
10:33	43, 129	1:12–13	129, 151
12:22	93, 98	1:14	152
12:24	98	1:14–15	6
12:27	98	1:22–27	116
13:30	34	1:24	97
13:38	51n5, 67	1:26	98
13:38–39	28, 34	1:27	98
13:42	34, 35	3:22	31
13:48	34	3:26–27	28
13:50	34	3:27	46
14:22–33	19	4:35–41	5
15:22	98	4:37–41	99
16	45, 47	5:15	98
16:13–19	145	6:6	98
16:16	41	6:12	6
16:18	7, 43, 46	6:13	98
16:18a	41	8:35	130
16:18b	41	9:17–27	94n16
16:23	44, 145	9:25	94
17:1–13	18	9:28	98
17:2	60	9:32	98
17:18	98	9:38	98
17:19	98	10:18	116
21:32	6	10:45	137
22:13	34	11:12–21	160n5
23:13	34	11:14	35
23:33	34	11:20	35
24	163	12:22	98
24:4	34	16:15–16	155
24:30	143	19:26	98
24:38–39	34		
24:41–42	34	**Luke**	
24:42–43	34	2:41–52	142n6
24:51	34	2:52	126
25:10	34	3:4–6	58
25:13	34	4:1	140n4
25:30	34	4:1–13	151
25:34	139	4:5–7	31
25:41	34	4:6–7	144
26:38	145	4:8–19	153
26:39	145	4:13	151
26:41	34	4:34	115
26:53	x, 101	4:36	98
28:18–20	6, 155	4:39	98

Luke (continued)

4:43	152
6:18	98
6:28	160
6:35	160
8:2	98
8:22	154
8:32–33	99
8:36	98
9:1	98
9:35	115n18
9:42	98
10:17	98
10:17–18	60
10:18	132, 135n2
11:14	98
11:14–20	154
11:14–23	31
11:15	28, 98
11:18–19	31
11:21–22	46
13:1–5	6
13:7	35
13:11–12	98
13:11–13	94n16
13:15	6
13:32	98
16:19–31	37
20:35	35
22:31	3, 30
22:44	145
22:53	6
23:3	145
23:43	40
23:44	6
24:36–43	20
24:46–48	155
24:47	6
40:15	31

John

1:4–5	6
1:5	ix, 19, 31, 60
1:29	136, 137
3:16	27, 127
3:19	6
5:24	137
6:35	68n8
6:41	68n8
6:51	68n8
6:69	115n18
6:70	51n5
7:20	98
8:12	7n10, 31, 68n8
8:24	68n8
8:28	68n8
8:31–35	160
8:36	160
8:42–52	98
8:44	28, 34, 51n5, 67, 132, 160
8:58	68n8
10:7	68n8
10:9	68n8
10:9–10	28
10:10	171
10:11	68n8
10:14	68n8
10:20–21	98
10:28–30	42n3
10:34	64
11:17–34	41
11:25	68n8
11:43	18
12:31	7, 28, 90n
12:34	5n8, 43
13:19	68n8
13:27	145
14:3	40
14:9	68
14:10–11	68
14:16	68n8
14:30	28, 90n
15	35
15:1	68n8
15:16	68n8
16:11	28
17:15	30
18:4–6	68
20:11–18	20
20:21–23	155

20:27, 20

Acts

1:6–8	155
1:11	143
2:24	47, 148
2:27	45
2:28	6
2:47	157n3
3:19	6
4:4	157n3
4:17–18	157
5:12–16	157
5:14	157n3
5:16	98
5:33	157
6:1	157n3
6:7	157
7	43
7–8	157
8	51n5
8:3	98
8:4–26	159
8:7	98
8:7–8	159
8:22	6
8:31	98
9	160
9:31	157n3
10:38	51n5, 154
11:21	157n3
11:24	157n3
12:24	157n3
13	51n5
13:4–12	160
13:10	51n5, 67
13:13–14	26
13:35	45
14:1	157n3
14:1–7	159
14:8–20	159
14:19–20	38
16:5	157n3
16:16	120, 123, 164n7
16:16–18	94n16
16:18	159
17:12	157n3
17:18	92
17:22	92
17:30	6
19	160
19:1–20	98
19:4	6
19:11–12	98
19:12	98
19:13	161
19:20	157n3, 161
20:21	6
20:24	6
25:19	92
26:17–18	31, 158
26:18	7n10

Romans

3:23	117
4:18–22	129
5:12	96n22
8	107
8:14	50n4
8:15	94n16
8:37–39	42
8:38	3
12:1–2	162
12:5	6
12:14	160
13:12	6
16:12	161

1 Corinthians

2:7–8	139
2:9	39
4:5	116n19
4:12	160
5:5	163
5:6–7	163
6:2–3	50n4
6:3	114
6:18	6
8:5–6	81
9:7	6
9:24	6
9:29	6
10:9	139

1 Corinthians (continued)

10:19–20	82
10:20	84, 93
10:25–27	82
12:3	164
12:12–27	6
15:15	49n3
15:20	82
15:24	54
15:24–26	3, 54
15:35–57	53
15:45	115
15:54–55	49
15:55	49n3
16:26	80
21:25	82

2 Corinthians

2:11	161, 171
4:3–4	28
4:4	5
4:6	ix
5:1	40
5:8	52
5:21	127, 147
6:15	28
10:4	6
11:3	28, 127
11:13–14	163
11:14	23, 27, 60
11:23–27	158
12	39
12:2	38
12:2–4	29n12
12:4	38, 111

Galatians

1:7–9	163
1:8	60
1:8–9	160n5
1:18	57n7
2:2	6
2:4	163
3:26	50n4
4:8	81
4:14	57n7

5:7	6
5:16–21	168
5:22–23	130

Ephesians

1:20	49
2:2	28, 39
2:5–6	69
2:6	49, 165
3:6	6
4:8–10	47
5:5	168
5:11	6
5:25	127
6:10–13	164
6:10–17	6
6:11–13	42
6:12	ix, 3, 54, 69
6:16	30

Philippians

2:6–8	142
2:9–11	70
2:10	51
2:25	6
3:20	49

Colossians

1:5	49
1:13	6, 28, 31
1:15–17	69
1:16	3
1:18	6
1:24	6
2:15	7, 46
2:18	57
3:1	165
3:1–17	162

1 Thessalonians

2:18	161
3:5	28
5:15	160

2 Thessalonians

2:9	161
3:3	30

1 Timothy

1:18	6
1:20	163
2:5–6	137
2:14	116, 127
6:11	6
6:16	39, 60

2 Timothy

1:7	94n16
1:9–10	139
2:3–4	6
2:22	6
2:26	7, 161
4:1	94n16
4:7	6
4:18	49

Philemon

1:2	6

Hebrews

1:5–6	111n11
1:5–14	57n7
1:6	112n11
1:9	67
2:5–18	57n7
2:10	6
2:14	7
2:14–15	94n16
12:1	6, 43
12:15	94n16
13:2	102
13:20	47

James

1:13	129
1:13–15	94n16
1:17	60
3:9	160
4:7	6, 130, 171

1 Peter

1:18–19	137
1:19–20	xii, 138
2:1–3	163
2:9	7n10
2:24	147n9
3:9	160
3:19	47
3:22	3
4:7	161
5:8	3, 27, 28, 101, 161, 171

2 Peter

1:19	7
2	163
2:4	4, 38, 50, 66, 97

1 John

1:5	60
1:7	7n10
1:8–10	117
2:2	136
3:1–3	69
3:7–8	131
3:8	7
3:8–10	51n5, 67
3:12	95n19
4	163
4:1–6	164n6
4:3	94n16
4:6	94n16
4:8	27
5:18	30
5:19	31, 90n

Jude

1:6	50
1:9	18
6	97
14	61
14–15	97n26

Revelation

1:7	143
1:18	46
2:5	6
2:9–10	162
2:10	42
2:13	42, 51, 51n5, 162
2:16	162
2:16–22	6
2:20–24	162
3:3	162
3:9–10	162
4	65
4:4	65
4:7	121
4:38	29
5	57n7, 59
5:3	51
5:5–14	65
5:8	100
5:9	137
5:13	51
6:8	49
6:9	49
6–16	100n29
7:11–13	65
9:1	38
9:2	50
9:11	27, 28, 50
9:20	93
11:16	65
12	100, 122, 132
12:3	28
12:4	99, 100
12:7–9	28, 132
12:7–12	174
12:9	99
12:10	27, 29
12:12	53
12:14	70
13:8	138
14:3	65
17:8	139
19:4	65
19:10	x
19:11–16	6
19–21	56n4
20:1	50
20:1–3	50, 61
20:3	135n2
20:4	65
20:6	53
20:7	50
20:10–14	4
20:11–15	52
20:12–13	53
20:13–14	50
20:14	3n2
21:11	56n4
21:21	44
22	111
22:1–5	110
22:3–4	57n7
22:16	67
22:19	x

Dead Sea Scrolls

4Q510–11	22n4
4Q506	22n4
4Q560	96n24
11Q11	96n24

www.ingramcontent.com/pod-product-compliance
Lightning Source LLC
Chambersburg PA
CBHW060606230426
43670CB00011B/1998